GREECE AND SPAIN IN EUROPEAN FOREIGN POLICY

To Mika, my wonderful wife

Greece and Spain in European Foreign Policy

The influence of southern member states in common foreign and security policy

DIMITRIOS KAVAKAS
CEDEFOP

Routledge
Taylor & Francis Group

LONDON AND NEW YORK

First published 2001 by Ashgate Publishing

Reissued 2018 by Routledge
2 Park Square, Milton Park, Abingdon, Oxon OX14 4RN
711 Third Avenue, New York, NY 10017, USA

Routledge is an imprint of the Taylor & Francis Group, an informa business

Publisher's Note
The publisher has gone to great lengths to ensure the quality of this reprint
but points out that some imperfections in the original copies may be
apparent.

Disclaimer
The publisher has made every effort to trace copyright holders and welcomes
correspondence from those they have been unable to contact.

A Library of Congress record exists under LC control number: 2001093278

ISBN 13: 978-1-138-70129-8 (hbk)
ISBN 13: 978-0-415-79293-6 (pbk)
ISBN 13: 978-1-315-21007-0 (ebk)

Contents

Acknowledgements

This book is the work that resulted out of three years of research for my doctorate degree in the University of Leeds. It is almost impossible with only a few words to express my thankfulness to all those who assisted me during those years of my PhD research, which seems to me like a lifetime. Perhaps, the mention of their names here and a very warm thank you, is the least I can do from what they deserve. Perhaps you can allow me first of all to thank God, for he has been the source of life, strength, inspiration and guidance on a daily basis. Every success I have had, has been a gift from him and every failure, a lesson that I had to learn. Through his mercy and his love, not only he gave me a reason in life but also he is guiding my steps according to his will.

I would like to thank my wife Mika for she has been patient and very supportive to me during the times that it seemed that I was dedicating more time to my thesis than to her, particularly during my many research trips. Mika gave me the psychological support that I needed to see this work through to the end, and I wish to thank her for believing in me! I also would like to thank my parents for their support, whether it was through demonstrated love, a kind phone-call of support, or even a helpful cheque!

I would like to take this opportunity to thank from all of my heart Professor Juliet Lodge. I am grateful because she believed in me and gave me the support and the resources that I needed to complete this work. I wish to thank her not only for supporting my research but also for giving me the opportunity to develop my skills in several academic activities that have enhanced my future prospects. I would also like to thanks Dr Neil Winn for his time and effort, for giving me his comments on time, knowing that he must have worked long hours to do this. I would also like to thank Roger and Dot Carswell for they have been like parents to me and gave me the support when I needed it. Also, thanks to Joanna Barchet for the time and effort she took to correct my English. Thanks goes as well to Professor Kevin Featherstone and Dr Hugh Dyer, who were my PhD examiners and awarded me the degree.

List of Abbreviations

CFSP: Common Foreign and Security Policy
CiU: Convergencia i Unió (Catalan coalition party)
COREPER: Council of Permanent Representatives (acronym in French)
COREU: European Correspondence (acronym in French)
CSCE: Conference on Security and Cooperation in Europe
CSCM: Conference on Security and Cooperation in the Mediterranean
DASR: Democratic Arab Saharan Republic
DG: Directorate General
EC: European Community
ECJ: European Court of Justice
ECSC: European Coal and Steel Community
EDC: European Defence Community
EEC: European Economic Community
EMS: European Monetary System
EMU: Economic and Monetary Union
EP: European Parliament
EPC (1): European Political Community
EPC (2): European Political Cooperation
ETA: Basque Liberation Army (acronym in Eusquerra)
EU: European Union
FYROM: Former Yugoslav Republic of Macedonia
GS: General Secretary
IGC: Intergovernmental Conference
KAL: Korean AirLines
LA: Latin America
MEPs: Members of the European Parliament
MFA: Ministry of Foreign Affairs
MFO: Multilateral Force and Observers
MLF: Multilateral Forces
MPs: Members of Parliament
NATO: North Atlantic Treaty Association
ND: New Democracy (Greek political party)
OSCE: Organisation for Security and Cooperation in Europe
PASOK: Pan-Hellenic Socialist Movement (acronym in Greek)

ix

PLO: Palestinian Liberation Organisation
PP: Popular Party (Spanish political party)
PoCo: Political Committee
PSOE: Spanish Socialist Workers Party (acronym in Spanish)
QMV: Qualified Majority Voting
RMP: Renovated Mediterranean Policy
SALT: Strategic Arms Limitation Talks
SEA: Single European Act
TEU: Treaty on European Union
UN: United Nations
VMRO: Macedonian Liberation Organisation (acronym in Macedonian)
WEU: Western European Union

1 Introduction

Foreign policy cooperation in the European Union (EU) has taken the form of concentration of national foreign policies. From the early development of European Political Cooperation (EPC) to the formation of the Common Foreign and Security Policy (CFSP), national foreign policies have followed a process of adaptation to a structure of common approaches that allowed for enhanced cooperation. The common approach was the willingness of the founding Six of the European Community to achieve peace and stability in Europe during the Cold War. The structure constituted a method of producing a common position for negotiations for the Conference on Security and Cooperation in Europe (CSCE). This was a method of cooperation in foreign policy through ministerial meetings so that the EC would be represented as one negotiator rather than six.[1] Although EU Member States largely retained their sovereignty in foreign policy-making, the changing nature of the EU policy-making meant that decisions and developments in any EU state increasingly became part of the domestic policy arena. Just as domestic politics directly influence the foreign policy of a Member State, similarly, developments in the EU institutions or any of the Member States have the same effect. The development of a European foreign policy can be described as a two-way relationship. On the one hand, the progress of integration has developed a European domestic environment, which is a factor that influences the national foreign policies of Member States. On the other hand, to a varying extent from one state to another, the different national foreign policy priorities influence the European environment and the efforts to develop an EU common foreign policy. Taking into account this complex relation, this book looks at how national foreign policies influence the Common Foreign and Security Policy in the EU. The argument of this book is that national foreign policy behaviour affects the influence of the State in CFSP. This book studies whether and how the geopolitical situation of the state, its domestic political environment, and its political orientation and participation in Europe condition the State's foreign policy behaviour in CFSP. It can be argued that this forms a circle of influence where the above factors affect national foreign policy behaviour, the latter conditions State influence in CFSP, which in turn, has an impact on the initial factors. The European political environment has an impact on these factors and results in changes in the national foreign policy. This book studies the levels of interaction between national and European foreign policy. Its objective is to determine the level of influence that a Member State can have, and the extent to which changes in the factors mentioned above could alter this level of influence. In defining influence, it can be argued that it is the relationship between two actors that modifies the behaviour of one actor because of the position of the other. Essentially, this book tests whether endogenous and exogenous factors can alter the variables mentioned above and thus affect foreign policy behaviour.

Case Studies

This book deals with two Member States of the EU, Greece and Spain. There are several reasons why these two Mediterranean Member States have been chosen as the case studies of this book. As southern Member States, they are characterised by limited structural power. This means that the capability and scope of their foreign policy is limited compared to Member States such as the UK, France and Germany who have long-standing extensive networks of foreign policy. The term 'southern' is not taken in the strict geographical sense but in a more political sense, referring to states with limited resources and structural power. However, despite this, they are states that have strong priorities and perceptions of national interest in foreign policy compared with other Member States, such as Ireland, Belgium and Denmark. Greece and Spain entered the European Community in the 1980s after a period of transition to democracy which followed the end of dictatorial regimes in both countries. During the accession negotiations and also since their eventual membership, foreign policy and security have been prime concerns of both states in the European development.

Apart from obvious similarities between the two states and their common differences with other Member States, Greece and Spain have a number of differences which make them interesting for comparison. The first difference is size, both in terms of geography and population. By comparing a large with a small state, this book examines the possible relevance of size in determining the degree of influence of the national foreign policy in CFSP. However, one argument is that size is not the prime determinant of influence in the cases of Greece and Spain. Instead, the geopolitical situation of Greece and Spain and their surrounding environments have an important impact upon their influential activity, regardless of their size. The two case study countries have been selected in order to test this assumption, since in geographical terms Spain is a large state and Greece a small one. For this reason this book focuses on these two states and does not include Portugal, another small state which otherwise meets the criteria as a southern Member State. The second difference has to do with domestic politics.[2] As argued, the domestic political environment has an important impact upon foreign policy behaviour.[3] This book tests whether factors in domestic politics have a direct impact upon influence in the European foreign policy structure, to the extent that behaviour patterns affect the influence of the state in CFSP. Upon entry into the European Community, the Greek and Spanish domestic political forces each reacted in a different way. In Greece, the political parties were divided into pro-EC and anti-EC, while in Spain there was a consensus between all political forces in favour of Spain's accession. The differences in the shaping of domestic factors in the two Southern Member States affected the domestic political debate on Europe and might have an impact upon the country's behaviour and political orientation. This book looks at whether this has been one of the reasons why Greece and Spain have followed different policy strategies in participating in the EC/EU and particularly in European Political Cooperation (EPC). However, the distinct political orientations of the two governments is a difference in itself. In the early 1980s, both Greece and Spain experienced a change of government. Socialist governments took control of the two traditionally right-wing countries. Both the Greek and the Spanish socialist parties wanted to bring about a change from the past, which had been dominated by a lack of democracy, social injustice and foreign policy dependence. However, to achieve their aims, the two political leaders, Andreas Papandreou in Greece and Felipe Gonzalez in Spain, followed very different routes. Papandreou endeavoured to achieve democracy and independence through keeping a distance from his European partners and promoting a different policy for Greece, while Gonzalez saw the same values as achievable through the total integration of Spain in the European framework. That is why this book looks at personalities as factors which might influence the political orientation and the participation patterns of the Member State in European foreign policy.

This book tries to test whether there are three different sets of contradictions between the two states. The first being nationalist versus

Europeanist behaviour, the second, cooperation versus a confrontational attitude, and the third, compromise versus national victory pursuit.

Structure of the Book

This book is divided into two parts. The first part gives an extensive historical account of the development of European foreign policy and the participation of Greece and Spain in its shape and function. This is important because it provides the background and lays the foundation on which it builds on in the second part.

Part I

Chapter 2 The second chapter provides the context to European foreign policy development. The cases of Greek and Spanish foreign policies are both examined within the framework of European Political Cooperation and with the purpose of evaluating state attitudes towards the development of political integration and towards European foreign policy action in different cases. The priorities and behaviour of the two states compared with the outcome lead to conclusions about the degree of influence which they have exercised.

This chapter follows the origins and development of European foreign policy from EPC to CFSP. It looks at the integration process in foreign policy between the Member States and outlines the events, but also analyses the reasons and driving forces behind these developments. It can be noted from the chapter that in the cases where there was a collective action, it was for the benefit of all Member States. However, in cases where such collective action was not possible, it was because of the dominant position and interest of one or more Member States that contradicted the anticipated common position. In a collective action, Member States that are not in a position to exercise a high profile foreign policy on the international stage can find themselves influencing the collective outcome through the EC's institutional arrangements. The two southern Member States that are the subject of this book are as such. In the absence of a consensus, these Member States can find themselves marginalised or isolated if they disagree with the dominant position. If the objection to the collective action comes from a state like Greece or Spain, these states can become further marginalised, something that does not happen in the case of the powerful states. Therefore, it may be the case that Member States such as France and the UK can go alone in foreign policy with fewer consequences than states such as Greece and Spain.

The discussion of the structural characteristics of European foreign policy in this chapter tests the argument that, from the development of an institutionalised and integrated European foreign policy, Greece and Spain benefit in their degree of influence and in their priorities. This chapter ends with a discussion on the input the two states have had into the institutional reform of EPC and CFSP, as well as their priorities and preoccupations for a supranational development at the time of accession and during the institutional reforms.

Chapter 3 The third chapter continues setting the historical background that is necessary to analyse the foreign policies of Greece and Spain. However, it is focused directly on the two states. Having set the general picture of European foreign policy cooperation in the second chapter, the third looks at the participation of Greece and Spain in political cooperation since their accession to the European Community. The purpose of this chapter is to look at the major issues of foreign policy, both in the European framework and in the individual relations of Greece and Spain, and to analyse their policies, priorities and attitudes in these cases. The aim is to provide an evaluation of the degree of influence that Greece and Spain have exercised in each of the cases or periods of time. This chapter also makes an assessment of the reasons behind the difference in the degree of influence at different periods of time and between the two countries.

This chapter looks at a number of major issues of foreign policy in three periods of time. The first runs from the beginning of the 1980s and the accession of Greece to the EC, to the Single European Act and the accession of Spain in 1986. In this period it examines the first years of Greek interaction in the EPC, its ideological differences and the peculiarities of its attitude. It also looks beneath the surface of the expressed or enacted policies to look for the mainly domestic factors that shaped this attitude and policies. The second period goes from 1986 to the signing of the Maastricht Treaty in 1992. This period is characterised by the institutionalised EPC and the changes in Eastern Europe. The Greek stance changed during this period from anti-European to Euro-sceptic, while Spain made an impact in its first years in European political cooperation with its euro-enthusiasm. The chapter analyses the behaviour of both countries, examines the reasons for the different attitudes and evaluates their impact.

The final period follows the Maastricht Treaty to its revision in Amsterdam in 1997. This period sees the development of CFSP and the disintegration of Yugoslavia together with other changes in Central and Eastern Europe. During that period since the Treaty on European Union there has been a process of Europeanisation of national foreign policies. This chapter looks at different cases in that period to evaluate the level of convergence of the national foreign policies of Greece and Spain to a common European approach.

These two chapters set the historical background of the argument. The assessment of the participation of Greece and Spain in the formation and expression of European foreign policy is necessary to test the validity of the argument. The third chapter in particular tests whether Greece and Spain, through the European institutions, can increase their influence in the construction of common policies and also their role as actors in international relations, since CFSP gives them the opportunity to influence world politics.

Part II

Chapter 4 After the historical setting, the fourth chapter looks at the domestic political environment of the two Member States. It focuses on the adaptation process of national foreign policy to the European Union. The objective is to see how foreign policy is formed and executed and to identify the factors that influence its formation. This chapter intends to develop the foundations of the argument by looking at the domestic origins of foreign policy formation. It studies the way in which membership of the EU has affected the domestic factors that shape foreign policy. This has taken place in different degrees and varies according to the area. The main three areas under consideration are: (1) the administration of foreign policy; (2) the policy formation; and (3) the execution of policy action. The purpose of this chapter is to test whether the domestic political environment to a certain degree shapes foreign policy behaviour. In order to do that, this chapter examines the relationship between domestic factors and foreign policy action. This is a two-way relationship since there is interdependence between them as the one influences the other. The domestic environment helps shape foreign policy and the latter affects domestic developments.

From the existence of an adaptation process to its influence upon foreign policy behaviour, the Europeanisation of foreign policy is a major concern of the fourth chapter. If domestic factors are important for shaping foreign policy behaviour and these factors change due to the adaptation process, then according to the degree of adaptation achieved, the foreign policies of Greece and Spain follow a process of convergence to the European Union. This chapter aims to study this process of convergence and identify the areas where this has not taken place or took place to a lesser extent. It examines the factors that hindered the adaptation process and discusses the areas in which differentiation between national foreign policy and European common policy still exists. The objective is to test the proposition that this differentiation is more likely to occur when there is a low degree of adaptation, and also that a continuing differentiation from the common European position causes the isolation of the Member State and feeds the nationalist elements in its national foreign policy-making.

Chapter 5 The fifth chapter moves from the domestic sphere and policy formation to focus directly on foreign policy action and particularly its development in the framework of European foreign policy. This chapter is a continuation of the argument that was given in the first two chapters on a historical basis. It tests the argument that constructive participation, which is participation that attempts to construct consensus in CFSP decision-making through the institutions of CFSP, can result in an increase in the role and degree of influence of Greece and Spain, both in the EU and in their regional or international bilateral relations. This is done by weighing the evidence from the cases of foreign policy involvement. Since the attitude of constructive participation requires an integrationist political orientation, this chapter studies governmental policies towards further integration in foreign policy. These policies can change according to the political party in power and so this chapter pays particular attention to the ideology of the government and important personal figures that have influenced the political orientation of the Member State.

Additionally this chapter looks at different forms of participation in European foreign policy. It covers the involvement of Greece and Spain in Intergovernmental Conferences which shape the structure and instruments of CFSP. It also looks at their occupation of the office of the Presidency of the European Council. It examines the foreign policy initiatives that Greece and Spain have taken and the ability that they show to come up with such initiatives. Foreign policy initiatives can take different forms. They can either be part of the institutional responsibilities of the Presidency or they can arise from the priority that the Member State gives to a particular foreign policy issue. Also, these initiatives can be taken within the framework of CFSP, trying to generate a European response, bilaterally or unilaterally outside its scope. The argument of this chapter is that constructive participation is related to the ability to take successful initiatives in CFSP in the sense that participation patterns generate a reputation for the Member State. This in turn has an impact on its ability to succeed in taking initiatives.

Finally this chapter aims to test whether a developed reputation of constructive participation increases the chances and the opportunities of successful initiatives. It also addresses whether such a reputation makes consensus possible because of the process of convergence of national foreign policy implemented by constructive participation. To the extent that the above arguments are valid, the likelihood of success in foreign policy initiatives is influenced by two factors. The first is the reputation that the Member State builds up through its participation patterns in developing a consistent and coherent policy to gain the respect and support of other Member States. The second is convergence in foreign policy positions between Member States that develop a constructive attitude.

Chapter 6 The sixth chapter moves from the changing factors that influence foreign policy behaviour, such as the domestic environment and participation in CFSP due to the political orientation of the government, to a factor that is unchangeable, that of the geopolitical situation of Greece and Spain. The purpose of this chapter is to ascertain whether geopolitics is an important factor that influences foreign policy behaviour. It tests the validity of the argument that geopolitics may condition perceptions of policy makers. In turn, these perceptions can condition behaviour and determine policy priorities. In order to do that, this chapter examines the geopolitical characteristics of the two states under consideration and tries to establish the links between these characteristics and other factors which influence the formation of foreign policy. This chapter expands on the idea of two different responses from a given geopolitical situation. These are two logics that affect the State's response to a particular geopolitical problem. The first is the geopolitics logic, which is concerned with territorial integrity and with threats from neighbouring countries or even with irredentist thinking. The second is the geoeconomic logic. This logic sees the geopolitical situation not as a threat but as an opportunity. It is concerned with the economic development of the whole region which the State is in and contrasts the conventional concept of military security, dominated by an arms race, with a concept of security, which arises from the process of economic interdependence. This chapter explores the policies of Greece and Spain, in relation to the two logics, in different areas of foreign policy activity.

An important aspect of the geopolitics logic is the 'securitisation' of a foreign policy issue. Securitisation is a process that moves an issue outside public debate and transforms it into an issue of 'vital national interest'. This chapter examines the frequency and the intensity of the 'securitisation' process, as well as the issues to which it is applied. These are measured according to economic and political criteria, such as the level of adaptation, the degree of openness to international institutions and the degree of adaptation to international norms and procedures. Finally, it studies the implications which this process has on the formation of foreign policy and the manner of its implementation. Although the geopolitical situation of a Member State is not changeable, this chapter tests the argument that by the application of the geoeconomic logic, the State can overcome a number of disadvantages that its geopolitical situation might have.

Notes

---

[1] EC and EU are used to refer to the European Communities and European Union before and after the enaction of the Maastricht Treaty on 1 November 1993 respectively. EC/EU is used when reference is made to an overlapping period.

[2] J. Rosenau, 1967.

[3] W.F. Hanrieder and G.P. Auton, 1980, p.xvii.

PART I

2 Origins and Development of European Foreign Policy

Although states maintain a legal dimension of sovereignty, globalisation has resulted in the erosion of political and economic sovereignty.[1] States are no longer the only actors in international politics and are suffering from a progressive loss of real authority.[2] Erosion of sovereignty and loss of national control over economic and political developments are characterised by the notion of complex interdependence.[3] The process by which states and societies have become interconnected and dependant upon each other through various links and channels gave rise to the need for a collective notion of sovereignty. Arguably, the degree to which erosion of sovereignty takes place depends on the structural power of the state. Powerful states experience erosion to a lesser degree than less powerful states.[4] This is why some authors argue that integration is more beneficial for states with limited structural power. Integration is the institutionalisation of interdependence.[5] This is due to the fact that integration develops a collective sovereignty which counter-balances the loss of national sovereignty in the area in which integration takes place. The increased number of international organisations dealing with these specific areas suggest that collective sovereignty can help to solve those problems which national policy-making is not able to tackle. The European Union has likely experienced the deepest form of integration, compared with other international organisations. It has developed strong supranational institutions and decision-making powers in order to promote integration. The argument is that integrated foreign policy develops a collective sovereignty, something which is of prime importance for Greece and Spain. Collective sovereignty enhances the international role of Greece and Spain through CFSP by giving them the opportunity to be significantly involved in world affairs, most notably during the period in which they hold the Presidency, a capacity that they would not otherwise have.[6]

European and International Context

At the beginning of the 1960s and after the change in the British position regarding EEC membership, the political environment in Europe could be characterised as one of confusion and political tension. The UK wanted to purchase the most modern nuclear missile launch of the day, Polaris, from the Americans. This would have upgraded British nuclear power, making it superior to the French.[7] The UK's change of position on membership was perceived by the French as suspicious. At the same time, France's attitude towards the UK could also be described as one of jealousy towards the special Anglo-US relationship. The Fouchet plan designed by France, to strengthen French political and military power, given that France would have been the dominant partner in the intergovernmental framework of cooperation, as outlined in the plan.[8] Confusion arose when the Netherlands and Belgium opposed the Fouchet plan on the grounds that it was extremely intergovernmental and ignored the role of the European Commission, a supranational institution. However, the condition required by those two states in order that they would consent to the plan was the accession and participation in it by the UK. This contradiction was where the confusion lay, since the UK had been the main opponent of supranationalism. The failure of the Fouchet plan was one of the reasons for that France first used the veto against UK accession on January 1963.[9]

An Optimistic Atmosphere

The close of the 1960s was characterised by a change of atmosphere surrounding European integration. The end of the de Gaulle era in France brought the termination of the French veto of the UK accession and consequently led to optimism for the first enlargement of the Community.[10] The principles of economic and monetary unification and the evolution of the Community's own financial resources, set up during the Hague Summit of December 1969, also gave the impression that the Community was moving forward.[11] This atmosphere, together with a need for developing a common European position before the Conference for Security and Cooperation in Europe (CSCE) and the Middle East crisis, led the founding Six to think about acting more as a coherent political force in international relations. This took the form of a framework through which they could coordinate their foreign policies and work as a unitary actor in international affairs.[12] The choice of a collective approach, instead of loose coordination, was a product of two factors. Firstly, the end of the transitional period of the EEC in 1972 meant that the Community had to develop a common policy on external trade relations. The second factor was Germany, who was anxious to avoid any suspicion of renewed ties with the countries of Eastern Europe.[13] The CSCE was one of the reasons which led to the need for developing the EPC. It was also the first case of a European common action,[14] in the sense that it was the first time that the EC acted on a foreign policy issue as a unitary force and not as several actors with a coordinated position. The beginning of the 1970s, when the USA was more preoccupied with the closing stages of the Vietnam War than with multilateral diplomacy, EPC now had the chance to take the lead in multi-lateral talks with the Soviet Union and make good use of the opportunities arising from CSCE.[15] The close cooperation of member states in EPC resulted in the signing of the Helsinki Final Act in 1975 after five years of work, and the setting of the agenda for the successful development of CSCE.[16] The second issue which formed part of the EPC agenda during the first half of the 1970s was the Middle East. This was actually the first item on the agenda of the first EPC ministerial meeting in Munich in 1970. From the outset, the goal of EPC has been to achieve the development of a common approach to the Middle East conflict by the Member States. Considering that during the 1960s Member States were divided in two camps, with Germany and the Netherlands being pro-Israeli and France on the pro-Arab side, the common position described in the Schumann Document produced six months after the Munich Summit was a success. This marked the difference in the European approach to the two wars. In June 1967, the European Community was unable to agree upon a uniform approach to the Arab-Israeli conflict because of isolated responses of the Member States and the lack of a mechanism for the development of a common position. In contrast, during the October 1973 war, the now Nine Member States were more successful in developing a common position and tackling some of the problems created by the discrimination of the oil embargo imposed by the Arabs on different Member States.[17]

The mid-1970s saw a period of turmoil and change in Southern Europe. The start of the democratisation process in three southern European states, together with the crisis in Cyprus provided the political environment within which the Nine had to respond. In regards to the developments in the south of Europe, the Community started to develop a strategy that led to the eventual accession of Greece, Spain and Portugal in the 1980s. The fact that EPC encouraged and supported the democratic transition in Southern Europe led to increased dynamics in those countries in favour of accession and also helped in stabilising and developing democratic institutions. In the case of Cyprus, EPC issued three common positions during 1974-75, asking for a cease-fire and a resolution of conflict under the auspices of the UN.[18] The intervention in the Cypriot crisis demonstrated the possibilities of the Nine, to act collectively in a rapid and efficient way, under certain circumstances.[19]

Revival of East-West Tensions

By the end of the 1970s a new political environment had been created. The Soviet invasion of Afghanistan in 1979 marked the renewal of East-West tensions that characterised the first years of the 1980s. The tensions in East-West relations dominated the EPC agenda during the first half of the 1980s. The number of incidents such as the Polish crisis in 1981, the shooting down of the Korean Jumbo jet by the Soviet air force in 1983 and the invasion of Grenada by the USA the same year confirmed that impression.[20] The inability of the existing structure of cooperation in EPC to deal with such complex international crises is demonstrated by several proposals for its revision issued during this period. However, in a period characterised by intense bi-polarity, EPC failed to deliver a common voice. Its structure was inadequate and Member States were unable to either change the structure or agree on a common position under the current one. During this time, Greece had become the tenth member of the Community and contributed to the confusion and inability of EPC by demonstrating its particular ideological differences.

The second half of the decade saw Mikhael Gorbachev as leader of the Soviet Union and the start of the reform period that was going to change history in the twentieth century. This period was marked by the signing of the SEA, the institutionalisation of EPC and the third expansion of the Community to include Spain and Portugal. The changing environment signified a degree of optimism that was noted in political cooperation between Member States. Spain and Portugal entered into EPC with positive dynamics while Greece moderated its negative attitude. The positive environment that was linked to the easing of East-West tensions and the development of the single market in Europe created, the need for further political integration. This was enhanced by the Yugoslav crisis and the failure of the EC's political cooperation to express a uniform and coherent strategy.[21] However, possibly the most important event that led to the development of the Common Foreign and Security Policy (CFSP) in Maastricht was the reunification of Germany. With the fall of Communism in Eastern Europe, a unified Germany brought back fears of the past. These fears could only be accommodated with the inclusion of German foreign policy within a common structure. For this reason, it was both in the interests of Germany and its partners, particularly France, to develop the CFSP.

The Post-Cold War Period

The decision to hold an Intergovernmental Conference (IGC) on political union was an after-thought of the decision to have an IGC for EMU and was made at a time when radical changes occurred in Central and Eastern Europe. In April 1990, the proposals for an IGC on political union appeared at a time when the European Council was obliged to discuss developments in Eastern Europe and to develop a strategic plan for the Community's relations with Central and Eastern Europe, as well as to discuss the implications of German reunification. All these developments in the political environment created a need for the now Twelve to deepen European integration. The end of the Cold War and the disappearance of the long-established enemy also signified a change in the security structures in Europe, something which had to be addressed. During the second half of 1990 the Iraqi invasion of Kuwait in August had an impact on the Italian proposals for the IGC. This event highlighted the military role that Europe might be called upon to play in the post-Cold War era.[22] The Iraqi conflict provided renewed arguments to those in favour of a closer political union.

As the IGC negotiations were conducted, the developments in the Balkans, with the start of the Yugoslav disintegration, found the Twelve unable to respond to the events. The new situations in Eastern Europe together with the lack of a common European voice in foreign policy gave rise to national approaches and responses without former consultation among the Twelve.[23] Even after the signing of Maastricht, the EC was preoccupied with the ratification politics and in particular with the Danish problem rather than concentrating its efforts on developing a common policy towards the Yugoslav crisis. It can be argued that when the EU finally developed a joint action in the Balkans after November 1993, and the TEU came into effect, it was too late for an effective management of the conflict.[24] The imposition of the Greek embargo on Macedonia in 1994 further complicated the Union's situation, since one of its members was perceived to have pursued nationalistic policies in a nationalist dominated regional conflict.[25] It was at this time that the EU chose to start the proceedings for the revision of the Maastricht Treaty. Because of its failure in the Yugoslav crisis, it was arguably the best time to consider the weaknesses of CFSP as established by the TEU. Two years afterwards, at the start of the 1996, IGC discussions were dominated by the prospect of enlargement. Three new Member States had already entered the Union and the number of applicants from Central and Eastern European States was high. The prospect of enlargement developed institutional reform issues as well as questions on effectiveness and voting methods.

The political environment in Europe in the 1990s has been one of confusion, as far as the definition of European security is concerned, which has generated the debate between Atlanticists and Europeanists. The end of the Cold War and the traditional separation of the opposing camps developed the need for a new definition of security. In this environment, the development of the European Union tried, among other things, to address the question of European security. Although the SEA introduced security issues in EPC, it was the Maastricht Treaty which included all questions of security and the eventual outline of a common defence policy in CFSP.[26] The Western European Union (WEU) became almost a defence arm of the EU, although not formally incorporated in CFSP. In the political environment of the 1990s, the main concern for a common security policy in CFSP was the peacekeeping and humanitarian operations, the so-called Petersberg tasks. These tasks were to be performed by the WEU, under the instruction of CFSP.[27] In addition, the EU was involved in security issues through a multilateral framework, the Organisation for Security and Cooperation in Europe (OSCE), and on issues involving the non-proliferation Treaty and the use of economic sanctions for security purposes. The problems of effectiveness of CFSP, particularly during the Yugoslav crisis, developed the need for a revision of CFSP provisions during the 1996 IGC. Due to the lack of consensus over the extension of qualified majority voting, this issue was not successfully addressed in the Amsterdam Treaty. However, the development of an analysis and planning unit was designed to analyse and ultimately to help prevent similar conflicts in the future and to avoid any further embarrassment of CFSP as in the Yugoslav crisis.[28] The role of the High Representative of CFSP (Mr or Mrs CFSP), as a high political figure, can help to improve the external image and representation of the EU's foreign policy.[29] This came as a response to the confusion created, as the office of the Presidency was difficult to be distinguished by the Member State that holds it.

From the European Defence Community to the Common Foreign and Security Policy

The willingness of the six founding members of the European Economic Community (EEC) to develop political integration goes back to the 1950s, even before the creation of the EEC. The attempt to develop a European Defence Community (EDC), which included the blueprint for a 'political community' was drafted and signed in May 1952 by the six members of the European Coal and Steel Community (ECSC).[30] However, this attempt failed when the French National Assembly voted against it in 1954 during its ratification process. The EDC was a premature attempt at a supranational framework. Its failure was a failure of the federal approach and that gave way to the neo-functional approach and the development of the EEC. The need for the development of greater political cooperation was to be pursued through intergovernmentalism. The first attempt at such cooperation that was made by the French President de Gaulle, failed when the Fouchet Plan was rejected in 1962 by the other five members because of disputes over the UK's accession and intergovernmentalism. It was not until 1969 that action was taken on the need for political cooperation.

At the Hague summit of December 1969, after the decision for the first enlargement of the Community, the six heads of state or government gave a mandate to their foreign ministers to study the best way of progressing in the sphere of political unification.[31] This study led to the proposal for the development of a system of European Political Cooperation that resulted in the signing of the Luxembourg Report on 27 October 1970. This report is considered as the 'birth certificate' of political cooperation in the Community. The Luxembourg or Davignon Report[32] set the following as the two main objectives of cooperation in the field of foreign policy,

'to ensure greater mutual understanding with respect to the major issues of international politics, by exchanging information and consulting regularly;' (Part II, I a)
and 'to increase their solidarity by working for a harmonisation of views, concertation of attitudes and joint action when it appears feasible and desirable.' (Part II, I b)[33]

The Davignon report created the Political Committee (PoCo), which was to comprise of the heads of the political departments of the Member States' foreign ministries. The PoCo was to meet at least four times a year with the purpose of developing the groundwork for the ministerial meetings, which were to take place at least twice a year. The report also included provision of a conference of the heads of state or government, instead of foreign ministers, if the issue was of importance and justified such a development. The first meeting of EPC took place in November 1970 in Munich and the issues on the agenda were the Middle East and the Conference on the Security and Cooperation in Europe (CSCE). The launch of EPC was perceived as very successful and in light of the enlargement to include the UK, Ireland and Denmark, the Six expressed their will, in the Paris Summit of October 1972, to advance the Community to a European Union before the end of the decade.[34] This was not to be achieved though, since the political environment during the second half of the 1970s was different than anticipated and the integration process froze.

However, after the Davignon report there were further developments of the EPC framework. In November 1973, the Copenhagen report proposed certain innovations in the structure of EPC.[35] The ministerial meetings were increased to at least four a year, with the PoCo to meet whenever necessary and at least once a month. Copenhagen also created a number of working groups on EPC, notably the group of 'European Correspondents', comprising of diplomats. However, arguably the most important development proposed by the report for the future of European Political Cooperation was the development of a system of European Correspondence in foreign policy information known as 'COREU'. This telex system connected the Nine ministries of foreign affairs, providing rapid confidential information to the foreign policy-makers and assisted in the understanding and coordination of national positions. The next piece in the puzzle of EPC, which was slowly building, was the creation of the European Council by the decision of the Paris Summit of 9-10 December 1974. The European Council was to assemble the heads of state or government at least three times a year. The communiqué of the Paris Summit gave a special importance to the Permanent Representations of the Member States as the ones to assist the development of the agenda of the European Council.

> Greater latitude will be given to the Permanent Representatives so that only the most important political problems need be discussed in the Council. To this end, each member state will take the measures it considers necessary to strengthen the role of the Permanent Representatives and involve them in preparing the national positions on European affairs.[36]

The Paris Summit asked the Belgian Prime Minister Leo Tindemans to prepare a report on the nature of European Union to be pursued. The Tindemans report of 29 December 1975 included certain proposals for the development of a common foreign and defence policy.[37] These proposals failed to be accepted as they touched the very sensitive issue of national sovereignty, which even today continues to be the reason for the lack of a genuine CFSP. The Tindemans report proposed the incorporation of EPC in the Community decision-making process, the introduction of majority voting on foreign policy issues and the consideration of defence issues in

EPC, including the production of arms. The proposals were considered as too radical, and even today, the problems that led to the failure of the report still exist.

After a period of six years of stalemate, an initiative was taken by Lord Carrington, the British foreign minister, in the form of the production of the London Report in October 1981.[38] The London Report was a product of the disappointment which followed the failure of EPC to promote a common voice on the international stage during the second half of the 1970s and particularly during the Soviet invasion of Afghanistan in December 1979. The London Report was different from the Tindemans Report in that it did not mention the development of a common foreign policy. The objective of the report was to develop a system in which the national positions and initiatives in all the important issues of foreign policy could not take place unless there was previous consultation with the rest of the EC partners. The London Report resulted in the development of the 'troika' system of contact of the Presidency with third countries, as well as the procedure which allows for the call of a meeting at ministerial level or of the PoCo in cases of crisis within forty-eight hours, and at the demand of three Member States. The last development of EPC before the Single European Act was the Solemn Declaration of Stuttgart.[39] This was the result of a German-Italian initiative that Colombo and Genscher, Italian and German foreign ministers respectively presented in November 1981. It was a project for a European Act which consisted of three aspects. Its purpose was to develop a political objective for the European construction; to offer a global vision for the cooperation of the Ten by making European foreign policy cooperation coherent and incorporating in it issues of security; and finally, to develop its organic structures within the existing institutions. In this spirit, it was proposed that the Community's decision-making structures would be integrated with those of EPC and an EPC Secretariat would be created. However, as a result, the Solemn Declaration of Stuttgart in June 1983, lost most of the initial ambitions of the Genscher-Colombo initiative and there was hardly any progress made from the London Report. The failure of the Genscher-Colombo initiative was mainly due to the Danish and Irish reservations to accept the inclusion of security problems, the UK opposition towards supranational frameworks and to the Greek declaration of their right to determine their own foreign policy according to their national interest.[40]

The Institutionalisation of EPC

As soon as the budgetary dispute between the UK and the Community was solved at the European Summit of Fontainebleau on June 1984, and after the agreement for the third enlargement of the EC to include Spain and Portugal, the way was opened for the first reform of the Treaty of Rome. The Intergovernmental Conference that produced the Single European Act ended with the Twelve signing the Act in February 1986. During the negotiations for the Single European Act, proposals for the development of a genuine common foreign and security policy entered the agenda. These proposals were based on the Genscher-Colombo plan, the Tindemans Report and on the European Parliament's 1984 draft treaty establishing the European Union.[41] However, the same disagreements between Member States which caused the failure of the Genscher-Colombo initiative also limited changes to the Treaty. Despite this, the SEA marked the institutionalisation of EPC and provided the basis from which the framework of the common foreign and security policy was to be developed in Maastricht. The EPC framework, which included the ministerial meetings, the European Council and the Political Committee, was thus incorporated into the Community.[42] In addition, the SEA created the EPC Secretariat in the Council of Ministers with the function of assisting the work of the Council on EPC matters. The EPC Secretariat was the only innovation that the SEA introduced apart from the institutionalisation of the process. The next major change in European political cooperation was about to happen at Maastricht in 1991 with the Treaty on European Union.

Common Foreign and Security Policy

At the beginning of the 1990s, European Political Cooperation was transformed into the second pillar of the European Union.[43] Although EPC had been institutionalised since the Single European Act, a number of factors created the need for the development of a common foreign policy. The main factors were the radical changes in Eastern Europe and the new political environment, the failure of the Twelve in developing a common voice during the Gulf War and the reunification of Germany. It was agreed to hold an Intergovernmental Conference on European Union and consequently the new Treaty of Maastricht emerged, which created a Common Foreign and Security Policy as the second pillar of the European Union (EU).

During the first months of 1990, several reports and memoranda from different Member States and institutions were launched proposing a new Intergovernmental Conference on Economic and Monetary Unification and on Political Union. On 14 March 1990 the European Parliament presented an important report which outlined its main objectives for the upcoming IGC.[44] On 21 March 1990, the Belgian government issued a memorandum asking for the convening of an IGC on political union.[45] The memorandum covered issues of institutional reform, and although foreign policy was not the primary subject, it was an important part of the Belgian proposals. The primary focus of its reference on foreign policy was the creation of a genuine common foreign and security policy that could successfully confront the developments in Central and Eastern Europe. The Belgian proposal stressed that the characteristics of such a policy should be its incorporation into the Community structure and its inclusion of security and defence issues. Almost a month later, on 19 April, a joint Franco-German letter (signed by President Mitterrand and Chancellor Kohl) was addressed to the Irish Presidency. It complemented the Belgian memorandum by proposing the development of a political union with the implementation of a common foreign and security policy. Both documents became subjects of discussion in the extraordinary European Council in Dublin on 28 April 1990 that was scheduled to discuss the issue of German reunification. The decision to call an intergovernmental conference on political union was postponed until the next Dublin Summit because of reservations of one Member State, the UK. At the Dublin Summit of 25-26 June 1990, the decision was made and the date for the start of the Conference on political union was fixed for the 14 December 1990 together with the conference on EMU.[46]

During the second half of 1990 and during the Italian Presidency, many reports and memoranda were published by Member States despite the fact that the IGC negotiations did not start before December 1990. Several contributions suggested that a common foreign and security policy should be created. The Italian Presidency, with its proposal on 18 September 1990, moved a step forward to suggest that the competencies of the Union should be extended to all aspects of security without limitation.[47] This proposal was opposed by the 'Atlantisists', the UK and the Netherlands, who did not want the development of a common defence policy. On 12 April 1991, the Luxembourg Presidency submitted a "non-paper" of a draft treaty that proposed the eventual 'pillarisation' of the European Union.[48] The "non-paper" was criticised widely. Integrationists and particularly small states such as Belgium, who feared the domination of large states in an intergovernmental union, opposed the proposed new structure of the Community. On the other side, the 'Atlantisists' opposed to mentioning the prospect of a common defence that has been included in the "non-paper". The European Commission was also critical of the proposal on the grounds that it affected not only its institutional role but also the unity of the European integration process.[49] The Presidency considered the criticism, making certain modifications to the original document. A draft treaty was presented on 18 June 1991. Most of the modifications were made to please the integrationists and therefore the draft treaty was immediately rejected by the UK and Denmark. Although it retained the pillar structure, the proposal stressed the single institutional framework of the Union. Apart from mentioning the long term development of a defence policy, the main obstacle for Denmark and the UK was the reference in the draft Treaty that characterised it as a step towards a Union with a federal character. At the European Summit of 28-29 June 1991, it was agreed that the document should form the basis for further negotiations and a decision was postponed until the end of 1991 to be taken during the Dutch Presidency.[50] After an unsuccessful attempt on behalf of the Dutch Presidency to present a completely new draft treaty, which was rejected by ten Member States on 30 September, the Presidency produced a revised version of the Luxembourg text on the 4 October. The final meeting in Maastricht on 10-11 December 1991 resulted in the development of a common foreign and security policy as the second pillar of the European Union. The treaty included the confirmation that defence policy could, in time, lead to a common defence and that the WEU is an integral part of the EU development.[51]

The Treaty on European Union signed in Maastricht on 7 February 1992 included the provision of its revision in 1996. It was in Corfu on 24-25 June 1994 that the European Council set up the Reflection Group on the 1996 IGC headed by the Spanish Secretary of State for European Affairs, Carlos Westendorp. The report of the group that was published on 5 December 1995 included an assessment of CFSP and made certain proposals for its improvement, of which the most important was the creation of a planning and analysis unit and the role of the High Representative of CFSP.[52] The Westendorp report formed the basis for the proposals of the Italian Presidency during the first half of 1996. By December 1996 and the Dublin European Council, a new draft treaty was on the table that seemed to enjoy the wide support of the Member States.[53] For this reason there have been few substantial changes to the draft treaty when it was eventually agreed in Amsterdam in the European Council of 16-17 June 1997.

Structural Developments

The start of EPC was marked by the development of the ministerial meetings and the Political Committee. The meetings of foreign ministers at least four times a year in the capital of the Member State holding the Presidency had been the main decision-making body in political cooperation. The meetings enabled the ministers to produce reports on different issues of concern in foreign policy, to understand the different position of the Member States and to seek to address the differences. Although EPC operated outside the boundaries of the European Community until the SEA, a common practice was for the foreign ministers to take advantage of their monthly meetings in the Community to discuss an urgent issue of EPC. This practice was introduced for the first time in July 1974 when the foreign ministers used the European Council meeting to make a declaration on Cyprus.[54] Another practice that was introduced after 1974 was that of the informal meetings. Foreign ministers started to meet twice a year in an informal way without any assistants, collaborators or diplomats. The objective of these meetings was informal discussion between the ministers on important issues of foreign affairs. These informal meetings were named as 'Gymnich meetings' after the Gymnich castle near Bonn where the first meeting was held in 1974.

The Political Committee brought together the political directors of Member States' foreign ministries once a month. Before the SEA, the PoCo used to meet at the capital of the Presidency. After the SEA and the creation of the EPC Secretariat in Brussels, meetings took place at the Secretariat's headquarters. The frequency of the meetings of the PoCo created an intimate atmosphere between the members that allowed for the in depth examination of the problems and the possibility for members to change their points of view and adapt more easily to a common approach. In the event of a crisis, and after the London Report the PoCo, like the ministerial meetings, could be called within 48 hours on the demand of three Member States.[55] The PoCo was assisted by a number of working groups which were set up by the Committee for a specific mandate and under its control. The groups consisted of the chiefs of service of a particular sector in the foreign ministries of Member States, according to the subject-area of the working group. The Davignon report developed the system of 'European Correspondence', known by its French acronym, COREU, to assist the work of the Committee and the working groups. COREU is a system of information transfer, through telex, that connects the foreign ministries of the Member States. This system facilitates the distribution of confidential documents between the ministries and the setting of the dates and meeting agendas, exchanging suggestions and proposals. The number of COREUs was calculated at about 5000 a year during the 1980s.[56]

The development of the European Council in Paris in 1974 gave EPC the high political status necessary to achieve common positions and actions in future issues of foreign policy, particularly during a crisis. EPC was not the only subject of the European Council agenda since the latter was also created to deal with institutional changes and Treaty reforms. However, the majority of the issues on its agenda have been issues of EPC. After the Stuttgart Solemn Declaration, the European Council started to design the strategic framework of the general policy of the European Community and of political cooperation. It has been the body to introduce cooperation in new sectors of activity for both the Community and external relations in EPC. In the European Council, as well as in the ministerial meetings, PoCo, and working groups, the State that holds the Presidency of the Council of Ministers plays an important role in chairing the EPC meetings and also in representing the Member States in relations with third countries through the system of the 'troika'. The 'troika' system was formalised by the London Report and aimed at ensuring continuity in EPC external relations.

The two characteristics of EPC before the Single European Act were the absence of a legal basis and an institutional basis. EPC had developed as a series of meetings between ministers or between diplomats without being regulated by any legal Treaty. The absence of a legal basis meant that political cooperation between Member States was an activity of making some common declarations which were not binding and were very fragile. Any country could, at least in theory, back off from its agreement because EPC declarations and common positions had no legal substance in international law. An example of such a development was the EPC declaration of January 1992 on the imposition of martial law in Poland. After Greece's foreign minister made the initial agreement to the condemnation of the Soviet Union, it retreated and withdrew its agreement after a personal intervention of the Prime Minister Andreas Papandreou.[57] The second characteristic was the absence of an institutional basis. The participation patterns in EPC were set out by a series of reports, therefore making the whole system very fragile since there was no institution to govern the structure and function of EPC. The EPC meetings at all levels had been meetings of representatives of states with no institutional basis in the European Community. The General Secretariat, who played an important role for the preparation of the work of the Council of Ministers in the Community framework, was left outside EPC where all the work was prepared by the foreign ministries and particularly the one of the Presiding State. The only exception was the presence of the Commission in some of the meetings but even then it was without any powers of initiative or proposal. However, the SEA rectified the absence of a legal and an institutional basis with the institutionalisation of EPC into the Treaty of the European Communities.

There are two characteristics of EPC that have remained intact despite its institutionalisation, these being its confidential and intergovernmental character. All meetings of EPC, from the PoCo to the ministerial and European Council meetings were confidential. Information on national positions, tactics and negotiation procedures were kept from the press and the public awareness. The only thing which has been made public is any declaration that was reached unanimously, and in such a case it has been presented by the Presidency after the meeting in a press conference. The minutes of the meetings, together with the huge amount of correspondence between the ministries through the COREU system are still kept classified even to this date. EPC has also been characterised by intergovernmentalism. Member States have been most reluctant to give up any degree of sovereignty on issues of foreign policy, so, from the creation of EPC through to its institutionalisation, it has maintained its intergovernmental character with limited participation of supranational institutions.

Despite some problems and a lack of effectiveness that resulted from a reluctance to give up national sovereignty, EPC was successful in developing a common European response to a number of issues of foreign policy.[58] The debut of EPC was very successful with its involvement in the CSCE multilateral negotiations. During the negotiations leading up to Helsinki, the Nine acted as a united body with a common voice, negotiating not as individual Member States but as a single actor.[59] This common action gave EPC a leading role in the CSCE negotiations and great influence in the successful result. The common EPC approach was demonstrated in 1975 when in Helsinki, Aldo Moro, the Italian Prime Minister and President of the Council signed the final act on behalf of the Community. In the second issue, which showed the priority of the Member States, the dialogue with the Arab states and the Middle East peace process, EPC had to find a way to strike a balance. On the one hand EPC had to find a happy medium to develop good relations with both Israel and the Arab states and on the other hand, to start an effective dialogue with the Arabs without damaging its relations with the USA, its most important partner.

Despite a series of misunderstandings, particularly with the USA, the final outcome of EPC diplomacy can be described as successful. The Middle East was a subject on the EPC agenda since its first meeting in Munich. However, it was the Yom Kippur War of 1973 that created the need for an EC-Arab dialogue. By then, EPC had managed to accommodate the pro-Israeli and pro-Arab national positions into a neutral common perspective. However, the selective imposition of an oil-embargo by the Arabs on some European states, namely the Netherlands and Germany, who were regarded as pro-Israeli, required immediate reaction. The fact that the main target of the embargo was the USA, any attempt of the Nine to develop an EC-Arab dialogue was perceived, especially by the foreign secretary of USA, Henry Kissinger, as undermining the Americans. By mid-1974, EPC had succeeded in improving relations with the US and also in responding, at least in part, to the Arab request for a new relationship.[60]

Achievements of EPC

During the two decades of EPC, several cases of foreign policy were included in its agenda. Over the years 1974-75, several developments in Southern Europe developed a particular Mediterranean orientation with the creation of a Southern European working group. The Portuguese revolution of April 1974, the Sampson coup in Cyprus in July 1974 and the partition of the island following the Turkish intervention, the execution in Spain of five Basques in September 1975 and the eventual death and succession of Franco, as well as the fall of the military regime in Greece, attracted the attention of EPC to southern Europe. In the case of Cyprus, as mentioned earlier, EPC issued a series of declarations condemning both the coup and the Turkish intervention and asked for the peaceful resolution of the conflict through the UN.[61] However, without the existence of any instrument of operation in EPC European responses were left in crisis management at the declaration level. In the rest of the cases, EPC supported the democratic transition in Greece and Portugal in 1974. Spain, however, became another issue of crisis management in EPC. The death sentence of five Basques separatists, who were prosecuted by Franco under a military anti-terrorist law, provoked a response from EPC.[62] The European response, however, was not consistent. Some states were harsher in criticising the Franco regime, particularly Italy, while others preferred a more moderate response on a humanitarian basis. The lack of a coherent position led to the failure of the EPC intention to avoid the executions that were realised on the 27 September 1975.

EPC developed a custom of coordination of Member States' positions in the UN general assembly. In several cases, the EC managed to present a uniform and coherent position after a process of pre-consultation among its members. The percentage of common positions at the UN, however, decreased rapidly after the incorporation of Greece in the EC in 1981. The reason was the regular differentiation of Greece in the UN assembly from the position of its fellow members in the EC. One of the successful cases of EPC has been South Africa. The first need for a common action was the need to form an EPC position in the light of the UN Conference on Apartheid in Lagos in August 1977. Although there were difficulties due to the fact that three out of nine member states had significant economic interests in South Africa and were unable to agree on an embargo, EPC managed to agree on a Code of Conduct for European firms operating in South Africa.[63] After a state of emergency was declared by the South African government in July 1985, the twelve[64] reacted in a way that had a significant impact on the further developments in South Africa. The European reaction consisted of a series of restricted measures, in the form of economic sanctions, and a series of positive measures, in the form of assistance to the victims of apartheid.[65] This common EPC action provided an example for other states and added to the international community's condemnation, which ultimately led to the end of the apartheid regime. The coordination of Member States' positions in the UN has not always been successful. As mentioned above, the Greek accession contributed to that development. An example of such a case was the Falklands/Malvinas War. The invasion of the Falklands/Malvinas islands in April 1982 by Argentina was followed by a swift statement of the Ten condemning the intervention and asking for the Argentine withdrawal.[66] Under Article 113, the Community also decided on the adoption of economic sanctions against Argentina. However, the solidarity that the Community offered the UK was not asked for by Britain and neither was it appreciated. The UK failed to inform and consult its fellow members on the development of the conflict and this resulted in the breakage of Community solidarity.[67] Soon after the British military action and particularly after the sinking of the Argentine battle cruiser General Belgrano, which caused the death of 368 Argentine soldiers, many Member States withdrew their imposed sanctions. Community solidarity was also absent during the UN assembly's discussion of the crisis in 1982 in which EC Member States were divided into pro-UK and pro-Argentine camps.

The Structures Developed by the TEU

The Treaty on European Union which was signed on 7 February 1992, states in its preamble that the Heads of State of the twelve Member States are 'resolved to implement a common foreign and security policy including the eventual framing of a common defence policy, which might in time lead to a common defence, thereby reinforcing the European identity and its independence in order to promote peace, security and progress in Europe and in the world'.[68]

The Treaty outlines CFSP as an objective of the Union in Article B, where it also opens the way for a future incorporation of WEU in the Treaty and a common defence of the EU. CFSP has since been established as the second pillar of the EU, which can be described as an intergovernmental framework within a supranational institution. That is because all powers for the development of a common position or a joint action lie with the Council. However, the European Commission and the European Parliament have since been introduced into the Treaty, though with minimal contribution. Article J.9[69] states that 'the Commission shall be fully associated with the work carried out in the common foreign and security policy field'. That actually gives the Commission two rights. First, it has the right to request a meeting of the Council in order to discuss an issue that has arisen (Article J.8.4),[70] and second, the right to carry out foreign policy agreed by the Council through its Delegations in third countries (Article J.6).[71] The European Parliament is also involved in CFSP, though only with consultative powers. The EP has the right to be kept informed by the Presidency and the Commission of the developments of common foreign policy, and may also ask questions and make recommendations to the Council, as well as hold an annual debate on progress in implementing the CFSP (Article J.7).[72]

An important aspect of the second pillar of the TEU is the issue of security. Although the European Union is not a security organisation, it was the first time that a clause referring to the security of the Member States was introduced.[73] Although it is still to be proved in practice, it is a considerable change that has been introduced and at least strengthens the psychological sense of security of Member States.[74]

The TEU gives the responsibility of the preparation of CFSP meetings to the COREPER. This task, which has been a responsibility of the PoCo, created a conflict of competence, since the exclusive task of the Political Directors was now shared with the Permanent Representatives. The conflict of competence was solved with a formula that kept the PoCo in its key role on the establishment of the CFSP agenda and the implementation of CFSP policies, while the COREPER was given the responsibility of technical preparation of the Council meetings.[75] The TEU allotted CFSP two new instruments for the implementation and expression of foreign policy. Until then, EPC was characterised by a series of joint declarations whereas CFSP is equipped with common positions and joint actions. The common position existed in the SEA institutionalisation of EPC but had a different legal basis. For the first time, common positions became binding for Member States. There is no obligation for the Member States to a reach common position, yet, if they do, they are bound by them. According to the TEU, common positions are defined by the Council and constitute guidelines for the Member States, which 'shall ensure that their national policies conform to the common positions'.[76] The joint action is a completely new instrument of foreign policy introduced by the TEU.[77] Joint actions can only be considered in the priority areas already identified and set out by the European Council. The inclusion of a priority area as well as the decision on a joint action is subject to unanimous voting. However, decisions on the implementation procedures of an already decided joint action can be made on qualified majority voting. Despite its limitations, this was the first introduction of QMV in foreign policy cooperation between Member States.

The successes and failures of CFSP during its first five years can be assessed under the light of the institutional arrangements. Particularly with the prospect of enlargement to include Central and Eastern European states, the problems of effectiveness, rapid response to crises, and resources for actions to back up common positions are more relevant than ever. The problem of effectiveness depends on the decision-making procedures. Qualified Majority Voting was introduced in a very limited way and does not have any impact on the primary decisions on common policies. All declarations, common positions and joint actions are subject to unanimous voting. This means that decisions with fifteen partners are kept to the lowest common denominator. In an enlarged EU of more than twenty, this denominator will be shifted to an even lower level. Unanimity decreases the level of effectiveness in two ways: it limits the number of common policies and delays their implementation. The consensus rule was not addressed during the Amsterdam revision of the Treaty.

Member States are reluctant to make the decision and introduce majority voting in CFSP, even if that means that the effectiveness of decision-making is harmed. However, there has been an attempt to address the delay of implementation by trying to tackle the question of finance for CFSP. Although the result still leaves gaps open, it can be characterised as a step forward. The second problem, that of the rapid response to crises, was addressed with the development of a crisis management team, the Analysis and Planning Unit. Despite the promising title, the unit can only be assessed in practice. The Amsterdam Treaty states that this unit will draw personnel from the Secretariat of the Council, the Member States, the Commission and the WEU.[78] The last one looks problematic since it is yet to be agreed for the incorporation of WEU in CFSP. It would therefore be interesting to see and assess how this link will develop in practice. The case of the WEU is linked to the third problem, that of resources. CFSP does not have its own military resources to implement decisions and actions of foreign policy, thus leaving a gap between stated policy and actual policy. Unless the WEU becomes the defence wing of CFSP and unless a political will is developed to create a genuine and effective CFSP, foreign policy in the EU will remain ineffective.

Although the Amsterdam Treaty does not take CFSP as far as some Member States would have liked, it does introduce some changes. The General Secretariat of the Council introduced by SEA has been upgraded. Since the ratification of the Treaty, the Secretary-General exercises the function of High Representative for the common foreign and security policy. S/he is a political figure, currently the former NATO General Secretary, Javier Solana, and form part of the new 'troika' system. According to Article J.8 of the Amsterdam Treaty[79] the 'troika' consists of the Presidency, the High Representative and the President of the Commission. Also, to ensure continuity, when necessary, the next state to hold the Presidency can participate. The Amsterdam Treaty developed a new unit entitled Policy Planning and Early Warning Unit.[80] The unit is established in the General Secretariat of the Council and will be responsible for monitoring and analysing development in foreign policy, as well as providing assessments of foreign policy interests and early warning of events that can have important implications on the EU. Another change brought on by Amsterdam is the financing of CFSP. The Treaty on European Union makes a separation between administrative and operational expenditure.[81] While the first was charged to the Community budget, the second was left in ambiguity, leaving the Council to decide in each case if financing will come from the Community's budget or from the Member States. The Treaty of Amsterdam incorporates the operational expenditure into the Community budget except for 'such expenditure arising from operations having military or defence implication'.[82] It is only in these cases that the Council has to decide where to charge the expenditure.

Achievements of CFSP

One of the most important developments of the 1990s has been the war in ex-Yugoslavia in which the involvement of CFSP has been extensively discussed. Just a few days after the Maastricht Treaty entered into effect, CFSP adopted its first joint action supporting the convoy of international aid to the former Yugoslavia.[83] This was also the first example of the complications that Treaty provisions could create for the effectiveness of CFSP. The issue of financing the operation resulted in a four month delay in implementing the joint action. After that period, humanitarian aid was no longer needed and the funds were distributed to the administration of the city of Mostar.[84] On 16 May 1994, the Council decided to carry out a joint action to support the administration of Mostar. The conflict in former Yugoslavia became the primary issue for a large number of common positions and joint actions, including that of the 27 July 1994 when, for the first time the EU requested the WEU to assist in the implementation of a joint action in the form of the creation of a police force with the support of 182 WEU police officers. The general impression from the EU's involvement in former Yugoslavia is that of failure. There are many reasons which explain and analyse this argument and it is widely explored in literature, therefore it is not within the scope of this chapter to expand on it. However, it can be argued that CFSP lacked the leadership and the resources required for the effectiveness of such a peacekeeping operation.

On 20 December 1993, the Council decided on a joint action concerning the French initiative to create a Stability Pact for Europe.[85] The purpose of the Pact was to develop a process by which to solve ethnic and border disputes between countries of Central and Eastern Europe, to guarantee minority rights and to promote regional stability. The inaugural conference took place in May 1994 in Paris and brought together a large number of states. The stability Pact initiative has been one of the successes of CFSP since it demonstrated its ability for crisis prevention rather than crisis management. Other joint actions of CFSP include the participation of EU observers during the Russian parliamentary elections in December 1993, the support of South Africa's democratic transition by sending a special electoral unit to assist the preparation and monitoring of the first all-racial elections, and the dispatch of a special envoy of the EU to the region of the Grand Lakes. In addition, there were other joint actions concerning the nuclear non-proliferation treaty, the restrictions on anti-personnel mines, the control of exports of dual-use goods and the support for the Middle East peace process.

The main barrier to the further development of an integrated CFSP is the confrontation between the minimalist-intergovernmentalists and the maximalists-integrationists. However, the division between the two groups is not as clear in CFSP as it is in other policy areas and for this reason, foreign policy integrationist states such as France seem very reluctant to introduce majority voting, or the Commission as policy initiator. The picture here is not black and white but is composed of many shades of grey. Different countries to varying degrees are in support of integration or support intergovernmentalism to a greater or lesser extent. This is the subject of the next section which looks at Greece and Spain, as examples of Member States' attitude towards further integration in the area of foreign and security policy.

The Position and National Preoccupations of Greece and Spain

Themes

This section of the chapter looks at the priorities of the two states in the area of integration in foreign policy, their characteristics, and the level of success which they had. A theme that is evident in the Greek as well as in the Spanish case, is that integration in Europe was sought as making them more independent of the US.

Spain During the time of its accession and the negotiation of the SEA, Spain solved the question of NATO membership through the referendum of 1983, when the Spanish public decided to remain in the Atlantic Alliance. The prospect of integration in a supranational policy framework made the threat of US domination less likely. However, the traditional sense of anti-Americanism in the Spanish society made the development of a European orientation and an attitude of defence cooperation easier. Its long isolation in foreign policy resulted in the development of an active and enthusiastic participation in the Community's political cooperation. The radical changes in Europe by the end of the Cold War developed an interest in furthering integration in foreign policy and the main priority of the socialist government in Spain was to influence the agenda of this new structure. This could be done by supporting its development and by being part of the mainstream states during the design of a post-cold war common foreign and security policy. During the Amsterdam negotiations, the Spanish position was influenced by a wider reluctance in Europe towards more integration in foreign policy.[86] In this environment the new Spanish government lost the prominent role in political integration that it had enjoyed during Maastricht and shifted its priorities to other areas. Spanish public opinion was not that of the overwhelming euro-enthusiast it used to be during the first five years of its membership. This new degree of scepticism was translated into an interest of the government to strengthen areas which directly affect people, for example citizenship and European identity, issues of finance and the structural funds.

Greece In Greece the main preoccupation of the government was security. Whenever there was a discussion on common foreign and security policy in Europe, the issue of Greek security from its neighbours took priority. That is because, despite the fact that integration in Europe decreased US domination, Greece's independent action in respect of Turkey must be maintained at all costs because it takes precedence in the Greek perception. During the SEA negotiations, the socialist government of Andreas Papandreou wanted to make a stance to demonstrate an independent foreign policy for Greece. He was reluctant to accept a system of foreign policy coordination in which Greece would be forced, in a way, to compromise its own idea of what independent foreign policy means.[87] This Greek position came about after a series of confrontations on foreign policy issues by Papandreou with his fellow partners during the first half of the 1980s. The change of government in 1989 brought back to power the party that had negotiated and signed Greece's accession to the Community. The new government was committed to change the image and the European orientation of Greece in the Community. During Maastricht the change of position was clear. However, it was also clear that national interests and security preoccupations were part of the Greek priorities regardless of the government in charge.[88] Following the Yugoslav crisis and the failure of the Greek policies towards Macedonia in the beginning of the 1990s, Amsterdam found a new Greek government with a new leader committed to the European ideals.[89] However, as mentioned previously, the changes in the Greek attitude did not change the priorities regarding security. This created the contradiction that a country which desperately wanted the development of a common foreign policy, including a common defence, objected to the abolition of the intergovernmental character of CFSP because it feared it would lose its veto power.

National Positions

Greece The first time that Greece had to present its opinion about furthering integration in foreign policy was during the negotiations for the Single European Act.[90] The Greek position was opposed to the development of a common foreign and security policy. It opposed the institutionalisation of EPC into the Treaty even though the proposal had a purely intergovernmental nature. For that purpose, Greece found allies in the UK and Denmark in order to pursue its objective. The creation of a General Secretariat was another issue that Greece tried to avoid. However, for economic reasons and particularly in order to secure the Integrated Mediterranean Programs that were bringing a large number of funds into the Greek economy, Greece finally agreed to sign the Treaty. A few years later during the negotiations for the Maastricht Treaty, a different Greek government altered the orientation of the Greek attitude towards integration by supporting the development of the CFSP.[91] Its position was now with those states that supported the pillar system while retaining the intergovernmental character of political cooperation. The main Greek priority, which turned out to be an unsuccessful one, was to develop a CFSP that could guarantee the territorial integrity of its members.[92] Greece wanted to guarantee CFSP involvement in the event of a future dispute with Turkey, something that was always a Greek concern and an objective ever since its application for accession in the EC. However, the proposal failed because Greek behaviour during the negotiations suggested that they wanted to safeguard national interests by exposing and tying the other members into compromises against their own interests. However, Greece gained the entry to the WEU, a long awaited development. Although this was agreed before the signing of Maastricht, Greek accession to the WEU was finally ratified in February 1995. In the revision of the Maastricht Treaty that was to follow, Greece defended its demand for the Treaty to guarantee the Union's external borders.[93] The Greek priorities in Amsterdam were the incorporation of the WEU as the defence wing of CFSP and the eventual development of common defence policy. However, it objected to any introduction of further majority voting since it wanted to retain its right to veto in order to preserve its interests, as they are perceived in the area of its national issues.

Spain Spain entered the European Community with an enthusiasm for European foreign policy. During the SEA negotiations, although Spain was not yet a full member, it expressed its enthusiasm for the institutionalisation of EPC and the development of European integration to areas of foreign and security policy. The Spanish priority was to become an active partner in an integrated common foreign and security policy. During the Maastricht negotiations, Spain was one of the mainstreamers and part of the federalist group of countries.[94] Spain supported a common foreign policy as the basis for the political union, which was seen as essential for the development of further integration, along with the creation of new diplomatic and military mechanisms. In the area of defence, Spain supported the development of a European defence identity with the incorporation of the WEU in CFSP while retaining strong links with NATO. On this issue, Spain was in line with the mainstreamers, France and Germany. During the last IGC, Spain followed along the same lines regarding foreign and defence policy.[95] However, the Conservative government that had just taken power followed a different, more defensive attitude on the second pillar than the previous socialist government had taken. During Amsterdam, CFSP was no longer a priority for Spain, as it had been before. While Spain concentrated its reform priorities on the first and third pillar, its position, regarding the second, was that of continuity and maintenance of the status quo.

Greece and Spain compared There are certain similarities and differences in the characteristics of the priorities of Greece and Spain regarding the integration process in foreign policy. Looking at the European integration model in foreign policy, it can be argued that although the two states have followed different paths, they have now arrived at the same place. Although the dilemma in European integration arises dues to differences between integrationists and intergovernmentalists, in the second pillar of the EU the separation is between three groups. On one side there is the intergovernmentalists who want a system of coordination of foreign policies based purely on an intergovernmental level outside any Community competence. On the other side there is the federalist group that is in favour of a total integration of foreign policy in the Community framework. However, there is also a middle group, which supports the Communitarisation of CFSP while maintaining unanimous voting. During the SEA, Greece was not even part of the intergovernmental group, instead, Greece's position can be characterised as isolationist in character because of its refusal to participate in any foreign policy coordination. After the end of the 1980s, Greece moved to the limited integrationist camp. Spain, on the other hand, started on the basis of an active federalism supporting full integration and majority voting, yet in Amsterdam, Spanish policy shifted towards the middle group when the conservative government became reluctant to accept the extension of majority voting in CFSP.

Two similarities between Greece and Spain can be found, first in their priorities for the European defence model and second in their geographical position. Both countries are characterised as Europeanists. This term is used to separate the countries in favour of a European defence framework from the Atlantisists, who support a strong NATO framework. Greece and Spain also belong to the South, as opposed to the North, which has an impact on foreign policy priorities.

The two main differences are the size of the states and their foreign policy orientation. Although the North-South difference has an impact on the position of states during institutional reforms, the small-large difference breaks down the former and complicates the procedure. Greece can be associated with Spain and Portugal as states of the South, but also with Belgium and Netherlands as small states. In both groups, Greece can find common interests. The same applies to Spain, though in the small-large separation, Spain belongs to the latter group. As far as the foreign policy orientation is concerned, Greece has always had a nationalist orientation. From the isolationist years of the 1980s to the integrationist of 1990s, Greece's main concerns have been its national issues. On the contrary, Spain has had an internationalist orientation. Its foreign policy concerns were to develop an international voice for Spain and to increase its influence. So, while the Greek approach was inward, Spain displayed an outward looking behaviour.

The assessment of any achievements of a State during the negotiations for the development or the revision of CFSP relates to the nature of its proposals. Greece in the SEA was against the institutionalisation of EPC despite the fact that it demanded the guarantee of the Community's external borders. Greece failed to succeed in any of these priorities and was forced to agree on the final Treaty text. In Maastricht, the external borders were back on the Greek demands together with the demand of accession in the WEU. Although the overall position of Greece was supportive of the CFSP development, it failed to influence the inclusion of the clause on external borders. Its second objective was successful only to the extent that Greece became a full member of WEU. However, Greece's concerns were not fulfilled since Turkey became an observer and the Article 5 of the Brussels Pact that guaranteed the territorial integrity of its members, was amended to exclude any Greek-Turkish conflict.[96] At Amsterdam, Greece for the first time managed to include the clause on external borders, and although vague, it was a pleasing development for the Greek government. Article J.1, paragraph 1 was amended to state one of the objectives of CFSP as:

to preserve peace and strengthen international security, in accordance with the principles of the United Nations Charter, as well as the principles of the

Helsinki Final Act and the objectives of the Paris Charter, *including those on external borders.*[97]

The Spanish objective during the Maastricht negotiations was the development of a Common Foreign and Security Policy. Although Spain formed part of the Franco-German group meaning the common perspective shared between France and Germany for the development of the EU, the Spanish objectives, as pursued by Felipe Gonzelez, were to develop an integrated CFSP into the Community framework, introducing majority voting in the decision-making process.[98] In that sense, the final agreement was a compromise for Spain, since its objectives were to take integration further. The Spanish priorities went further to support an eminent function for the European Council in defining CFSP and the strengthening of the defence role of the Union. In Amsterdam, the new government of Jose Maria Aznar supported the maintenance of the second pillar as it was. The only exception was the Spanish support for the analysis and planning unit that was to be created in the General Secretariat of the Council. Although Spain recognised the importance of majority voting for the effectiveness of CFSP, it refused to allow the subordination of highly important national issues to majority voting. In general terms, Spain has been in line with the majority of the Member States, however, it did unsuccessfully object to the development of the High Representative of CFSP (Mr or Mrs CFSP), arguing that this role could be played better by the Presidency with the assistance of the Commission.[99]

Notes

[1]   See G.L. Goodwin, 1974, F.H. Hinsley, 1969 and G. Ionescu, 1974.
[2]   See S. Strange, 1996.
[3]   See R. Keohane and J. S. Nye, 1977 (2nd ed. 1989).
[4]   See P.C. Ioakimidis, 1980, p.25.
[5]   K. Deutsch, 1974.
[6]   See C. O'Nuallain and M. Hoscheit, 1985, S. Bulmer and W. Wessels, 1987, and E. Kirchner, 1992.
[7]   Panos Tsakalogiannis, 1996b, pp.64-65.
[8]   Paul-Henri Spaak, 1971, pp.438-40.
[9]   Charles de Gaulle, 1970, pp.66-70.
[10] See general literature on EC development, U. Kitzinger, 1963, R. Mayne, 1962, 1970 and 1983, J. Pinder, 1991, D.W. Urwin, 1991.
[11] Bulletin of the EC, 1970, no.1, pp.11-16.

12   Davignon Report, Part I, art. 8, Bulletin of the EC, 1970, no.11, pp.9-12.
13   Simon Nuttall, 1997, p.24.
14   This should not be confused with 'joint action' that was developed later after the Maastricht Treaty. However, although not institutionalised as 'joint actions' it followed similar procedures of acting together as one voice.
15   Ibid., p.23.
16   Declaration of Mr Moro after the signature of the Helsinki Final Act, Helsinki, 30/7/1975.
17   EPC Declaration of Foreign Ministers, Brussels, 6/11/1973.
18   Communiqués of the Nine on Cyprus, Paris 16/7/1974 and Brussels 22/7/1974.
19   Philippe de Schoutheete, 1986, p.97.
20   See chapter 3 for in depth discussion of these cases, pp.49-56.
21   A. Kintis, 1997, p.148.
22   Philippe de Schoutheete de Tervarent, 1997, p.48.
23   G. Edwards, 1997, p.174.
24   Decision of the Council 93/603/CFSP on 8.11.93, Official Journal L 286 of 20.11.93.
25   Decision of the government of Greece on measures against 'FYROM', 16 February 1994.
26   Article J 4.1 of the TEU.
27   Article J 4.1 of the TEU.
28   Declaration to the Final Act on the establishment of a policy planning and early warning unit, Revised Title V of the TEU.
29   Revised Article J.8 of the TEU.
30   The Luxembourg Resolution, 10 September 1952, in D. Folliot, 1955, pp.214-16.
31   Bulletin of the EC, 1970, no.1, pp.11-16.
32   The ad hoc committee that produced the report took its name from its chairman, Etienne Davignon, Belgian diplomat and future commissioner.
33   The Davignon Report Document, in A.G. Harryvan and J. van der Harst, 1997, pp.173-75.
34   Paris Summit, in Texts Relating to EPC, Bonn: Press Information Office, 1974.
35   Document on the European Identity, Copenhagen 14/12/1973.
36   Communique of the meeting of heads of state or government, Paris, 9-10 December 1974, clause 7.
37   Bulletin of the EC, 1976, Supplement no. 1, pp.14-22.
38   London Report, UK Presidency 13/10/1981.
39   Bulletin of the EC, 1983, no. 6.
40   S. Nuttall, 1992, p.188.
41   J. Lodge, 1994, p.14.
42   SEA, Bulletin of the EC, 1986, Supplement no.2.
43   Title V of the TEU.
44   EP Report (Martin report) on the IGC on Political Union, 14/3/1990, A3-270/90.
45   Agence Europe: Europe Documents no. 1608, 29 March 1990.
46   Agence Europe, 27 June 1990.
47   Marit Sjovaag, 1998, p.28.
48   See European Summit conclusions, Luxembourg 28-29 June 1991, European Foreign Policy 91/193.
49   Philippe de Schoutheete de Tervarent, 1997, p.55.
50   European Summit conclusions, Luxembourg 28-29 June 1991, European Foreign Policy 91/193.
51   Article J 4.2 of the TEU.

[52] 1996 IGC Reflection Group Report, General Secretariat of the Council of the EU, Brussels, December 1995.

[53] Irish Presidency, *A general outline for a draft revision of the Treaties*, Council of the EU, Brussels, February, 1997.

[54] Communiqué of the ministerial meeting, Brussels, 22/7/1974.

[55] London Report, UK Presidency 13/10/1981.

[56] Philippe de Schoutheete, 1986, p.42.

[57] S. Nuttall, 1992, p.202.

[58] See S. Nuttall, 1997.

[59] Gotz von Goll, 1982.

[60] David Allen, 1982, p.72.

[61] Declaration of the 18th EPC ministerial meeting, Dublin, 13/2/1975.

[62] N. Van Praag, 1982.

[63] S. Nuttall, 1997, p.35 and M. Holland, 1995.

[64] It took more than a year for the final agreement on measures in EPC and by that time Spain and Portugal had become members.

[65] S. Nuttall, 1997, p.36.

[66] Ibid., p.34.

[67] P. de Schoutheete, 1986, pp.117-18.

[68] Treaty on European Union, preamble.

[69] Amended to Article J.17 in Amsterdam.

[70] Amended to Article J.12 in Amsterdam.

[71] Amended to Article J.10 in Amsterdam.

[72] Amended to Article J.11 in Amsterdam.

[73] Article J.2 states as an objective of CFSP 'to strengthen the security of the Union and its member states in all ways'. This has been amended in Amsterdam by dropping 'and its member states'.

[74] Greece and Spain in particular have been trying to upgrade this clause in order to safeguard the external borders of the Union. Amsterdam added the mention on external borders to the objectives of CFSP on the amended Article J.1.1.

[75] E. Regelsberger, 1997, p.76.

[76] Article J.2 of the TEU.

[77] Article J.3 of the TEU.

[78] Declaration to the Final Act, art. 3, Revised TEU.

[79] Former J.5.

[80] Declaration to the Final Act of the Treaty of Amsterdam.

[81] Article J.11.

[82] Article J.18 (former J.11).

[83] Joint action 93/603/PESC of 8/11/93, official journal L. 286(20-11-1993).

[84] Arnhild and David Spence, 1998, p.52.

[85] Joint action 93/728/PESC of 20/12/93, official journal L. 339(31-12-1993).

[86] Memorandum of Spain, *Elements for a Spanish position in the 1996 IGC*.

[87] Y. Valinakis, 1987, pp.325-26.

[88] Memorandum of Greece on Political Union, MFA Athens, 15 May 1990, art. 7 on foreign and defence policy.

[89] The Socialist Party (PASOK) came to power with a new leader, K. Simitis, a committed pro-European.

[90] Memorandum on Greece's government views on the issues of the IGC, MFA Athens, 11 October 1985.

[91] Memorandum of Greece on Political Union, 15 May 1990.

[92] Ilias Kouskoubelis, 1995, p.313.

[93] Memorandum of Greece on the 1996 IGC.

[94] E. Barbe, 1998, p.148.

[95] Memorandum of Spain on the 1996 IGC.

[96] Revised Brussels Convention, originally signed on 23 October 1954 in Paris, revised on 19.02.92 with the Petersburg Declaration.

[97] Title V of the TEU, Article J.1 as amended by the Treaty of Amsterdam.

[98] Udo Diedrichts, 1996, p.244.

[99] Fernando Rodrigo, 1996, p.32.

3 Greek and Spanish Participation in European Foreign Policy

Following the analysis of the previous chapter of the development, functions and achievements of European foreign policy in the form of EPC and CFSP, this chapter looks at the way that Greece and Spain responded to different cases which have been subjects of the EPC/CFSP agenda during these years.

The aim of this chapter is to analyse the behavioural patterns of the two states in foreign policy in order to identify the reasons, strategy and outcome of their specific policy positions in some of the most important cases of European foreign policy cooperation during the years of Greek and Spanish membership. This chapter aims to develop the historical background against which the patterns of participation of Greece and Spain can be analysed in the next chapters. The main argument of this chapter is that active and positive participation in the structures of European foreign policy create an environment for improving the state's image and its increased influence on the agenda and common policy outcomes. The chapter examines whether and how (1) the fact that Spain entered the Community with an active attitude towards contribution to the development of a common foreign policy increased its potential for influencing the common policies and the agenda that set them, and (2) the hostile attitude of Greece in the 1980s developed a negative atmosphere for Greece to influence foreign policy-making in the Community. However, the late 1990s illustrated that the change in the Greek foreign policy attitude in the European Union, led to the improvement of Greece's image and with it, the degree of influence it had in European foreign policy-making. This was a determined attempt by the new administration in Greece, after 1996, to promote Greece as a pro-integrationist member and turn Greece into an adapted modern European Member State.

From Greek Accession to the Single European Act

Nine months after the official accession of Greece in the European Community, the Pan-Hellenic Socialist Movement (PASOK) was elected in October 1981 and formed the first ever left-wing government in the history of Greece. The new government altered the Greek attitude and approach to the concept of European political cooperation. The new approach was characterised by suspicion, reserve and differentiation from its partners. Greece associated EPC with the Cold War and so was suspicious that agreement within EPC could mean alignment with anti-Communism. This attitude introduced the practice of entering reservations, a practice of footnoting Greece's reservation in the agreed common position texts. This also developed Greece's differentiation in several cases where Greece not only reserved its agreement but blocked the consensus so no decision could be made. During its years in opposition, PASOK had been hostile to EC membership. The ratification of the accession Treaty of Greece in the Greek Parliament became the theatre in which PASOK demonstrated its opposition by ordering the withdrawal of its MPs from the chamber during discussion and voting. Just before their election to government, the socialists promised a referendum for Greece's membership of the EC as soon as they were in power. However, the referendum was not realised and the Greek government decided only to renegotiate with the Community certain aspects of the accession treaty. After this renegotiation, Andreas Papandreou openly accepted EC membership at the PASOK congress of 1984, which marks the change in perspective of the EC during the second socialist term in office (1985-1989). In foreign policy, Greece was actively engaged in a differentiated behaviour. That is to say that the Greek government, under Andreas Papandreou, promoted an independent foreign policy for Greece as a different policy from the West. The thinking behind this approach was that during the Cold War an independent foreign policy could only mean a policy that did not belong to any of the two camps. However, as the case studies later illustrate, in many cases, this attitude made Greek foreign policy sympathetic to the Soviet Union.

There are several reasons behind the awkward attitude of the Greek government during the first years of membership. One reason was the ambiguity that characterised the first term of the socialist government concerning the issue of Greece's position in the Community. The promise of a withdrawal from the EC was never realised, but neither was there a declaration of acceptance of membership. Papandreou used this ambiguity in order to achieve benefits for Greece at the renegotiations of the terms of membership. Perhaps the most important reason for the Greek position was the socialist ideology of PASOK for an autonomous international presence of Greece. Papandreou perceived EPC as an obstacle to the implementation of a different foreign policy.[1] The constant differentiation which characterised particularly the first few months of the Greek participation in EPC, arose from the implementation of two Greek objectives. The first was to inactivate EPC as a tool of imposition on Greece of the positions of the rest of the Member States (especially the large ones). The second was to repell any collective decision that could entail a political, economic or any other cost for Greece. The Greek differentiation is illustrated in that period in the failing of the common position of the Community in the case of the peace mission to Sinai, and the Polish case.

The Case of Sinai

On 3 August 1981, the protocol signed by Egypt and Israel gave the United States the responsibility of organising a multinational force to monitor the Sinai Peninsula for the withdrawal of Israeli forces as part of the Camp David process. The US was very keen to include the EC in the Multinational Force and Observers (MFO) since that would guarantee the status of the force as multinational and not as a United States operation. However, Alexander Haig, the US Secretary of State did not invite EPC to join the force but instead asked Britain, France, Italy and the Netherlands individually. This is significant because it demonstrated the perception of the Americans that EPC was ineffective and divided. Nonetheless, they wanted to capitalise on the usefulness of the multinational force by including individual European States. The Americans wanted to halt the process developed by the Venice Declaration and bring the Europeans in line with Camp David. In the Venice Declaration of the European Council of 13 June 1980, EPC declared its priorities for a peace process in the Middle East that should be based on the right of existence of all states, including Israel, but also expressed the legitimate rights of the Palestinians for self-determination. This Declaration was not acceptable to Israel or to the Americans. During the second half of 1981 and the British Presidency of the EC, Lord Carrington wanted to proceed with the Venice process and opposed European participation in the American plan for the MFO. However, the positions of France, Italy and Holland were not so opposed to the participation idea, particularly after Secretary Haig secured the support of Margaret Thatcher, Lord Carrington had no other option than to agree.[2] The issue was presented in front of the Ten in Luxembourg on the 26 October 1981. Agreement could not be reached because of Greek and Irish dissatisfaction, each for different reasons. Ireland was objecting on military grounds, particularly to the fact that the operation was not under the auspices of the UN. Greece, on the other hand, disagreed because the employment of the MFO was not acceptable to the Arabs. The Greek action can be attributed, to a large extent, to its long-standing amiable relationship with the Arab world. This action was in line with the Greek suspicion, reserve and differentiation mentioned earlier, since a pro-Arab stance was considered as anti-American. Greece was blocking a common action in EPC because of its disagreement with the political framework of the Camp David agreement,[3] whilst at the same time, the Camp David process was rejected by the Arab states. After a series of tense negotiations with the Arab Nations, Lord Carrington managed to secure an agreement on 4 November by clearly stating the Venice principles. It took also an intensive diplomatic process to secure the Greek agreement, which was achieved on 21 November 1981. However, Israel found the mention of the Venice Declaration unacceptable and was not willing to cooperate. The final result was that in order to secure the Israeli withdrawal from Sinai, the Europeans had to give way to the Israeli demands. It was the four states of Britain, France, Italy and Holland that issued a joint declaration on 3 December 1981 demonstrating their commitment to Camp David and disassociating any links with the Venice Declaration. The final result was a failure for the EPC. As far as the Greek participation in the case was concerned, Greece was not willing to compromise its pro-Arab position. The agreement of 21 November was reached because of the success of the British Presidency to achieve the agreement of the Arabs. The final text of 23 November included a mention of the Palestinian right of self-determination. Although the declaration of the four on 3 December was not brought to an EPC meeting, it was clear that it would have failed because of Greek opposition. This reveals the determination of the Greek policy-makers during that period to obstruct common European positions for ideological and domestic political reasons.

The Polish Case

At the beginning of the 1980s, the situation in Poland attracted the attention of the Community. The economic crisis together with the growing influence of the anti-regime Trade Union, Solidarity, in Polish society, created fears within the Nine that the Soviet Union would respond in a similar way to that of Prague in 1968. The European Council tried to offer economic aid in order to avoid an economic crisis that could justify Soviet interference. On several occasions in late 1980 and during 1981, the EC had offered food and financial aid to Poland, while the European Councils of December 1980 and March 1981 warned the Soviet Union not to interfere in the Polish situation. However, the worsening of the economic situation in the autumn of 1981 and the increased tensions between the Communist Party and Solidarity resulted in the proclamation of martial law by General Jaruzelski on 13 December 1981 and the arrest of several thousands of Solidarity activists. The imposition of martial law in Poland by General Jaruzelski put pressure on the Ten for a common response. At a scheduled EPC ministerial meeting on 15 December in London, the Ten expressed their sympathy with the Polish people. However, the lack of time for analysis of the situation led the Ministers to postpone any further declaration and decision on aid at the Brussels meeting in January. The US measures, as announced by President Ronald Reagan on 29 December, included suspension of export licenses, Aeroflot flights to the US and the review of all US-Soviet exchange agreements. These measures against the Soviet Union intensified the pressures on the Ten from the other side of the Atlantic to respond.

The next response took place at the Council of Ministers meeting on 4 January 1982. In a declaration, the Ten issued a warning against Soviet or Warsaw Pact intervention, and acknowledged the need to consider economic measures against the Soviet Union by the European Community. At the meeting, the Greek deputy foreign minister Asimakis Fotilas agreed and signed the common declaration, which was accepted unanimously. Despite this, the Greek government, with the initiative of Papandreou, withdrew its agreement almost immediately, and the deputy foreign minister found himself dismissed whilst on an aeroplane returning to Athens.[4] The official explanation given by the Greek government was that the deputy foreign minister disobeyed the orders that he had been given and agreed on the declaration. However, it is doubtful that there were any orders. The Socialist government had been to power for less than three months and, because of its negative approach to EPC, they did not pay attention to the significance of a common EPC declaration. The insignificance with which Papandreou regarded the EPC ministerial meetings can be seen by the fact that he sent the deputy and not the foreign minister. When the Prime Minister realised what had been achieved with the declaration, he then decided to act himself. This shows the lack of strategic vision for the potential of EPC that the Greek government had because of its extreme attitude. The next attempt of the Council to agree to a reduction of the Community's imports from the Soviet Union on the basis of Article 113 of the Treaty of Rome on 23 February was met with a persistently negative response on the part of Greece. In addition, Denmark, had reservations on the legal nature of the use of Article 113. Greece's refusal to cooperate in the Council was concentrated on two aspects. First, the Greek government was unwilling to condemn the inability of the totalitarian regimes of Eastern Europe to adapt themselves in a way which would reflect the interests of their population, as argued in the declaration. This was because of the ideological orientation of the PASOK's government. They did not consider the Soviet block as totalitarian regimes but as a political system of socialism that was reacting against the capitalist West. Second, Greece refused to participate in Community sanctions against the Soviet Union since if it did it could identify itself with the West ideology and the market economy, something that was opposed by PASOK. The agreed proposal of the Commission to reduce quotas on certain Soviet products was adopted by the Council regulation on 15 March limiting access to sixty products of the European market, covering 1.4 per cent of imports. In a second regulation, Greece was excluded from the application of the first. However, Greece had successfully blocked any EPC agreement on a common declaration and the only way that the Community could act was through the economic sanctions provision in the Treaty of Rome (Article 113). The main reason for the Greek behaviour extensively using its right to veto has been its domestic politics. There was no particular interest that Greece could gain with such an attitude. On the contrary it created a negative atmosphere against Greece in the Community. However, the Greek government opted for such behaviour in order to justify its pre-electoral claims for an independent foreign policy and its anti-Western rhetoric.[5] This attitude served as a proof of change to the domestic environment, despite the opposition to it from the conservative party.

The Korean Airliner

Another case, which can be studied together with the Polish crisis as a case of East-West confrontation, is the case of the South-Korean civilian airliner shot down by the Soviet air force in the early days of September 1983. The event had a direct impact on East-West relations and on the CSCE, which in those days was at the closing weeks of the Madrid meeting. The US strongly condemned the attack and it was expected that the Community would do the same. However, that was not possible because of the opposition from Greece. During the second half of 1983, Greece held its first presidency of the European Council. After the incident of shooting down the aeroplane by the Soviet Union, Greece successfully attempted to block any common condemnation of the Soviet Union by the Community. The Greek foreign minister, Giannis Haralambopoulos had been trying to make an ideological point on the differentiation of Greece on the East-West tension. During the first meeting of the Presidency, Mr Haralambopoulos put the question of disarmament on the EPC agenda. This was an ideological issue that dominated Greek public opinion at that time and justified the increased number of peace movement demonstrations. He tried to apply the new provisions of the Stuttgart Solemn Declaration that enabled EPC to discuss the 'political and economic aspects of security'. Before Stuttgart, issues of security were excluded from the EPC scope.

This development gave the Greek foreign minister the opportunity to make an ideological stance. It caused considerable embarrassment to Ireland and as a result no discussion took place.[6] Due to the neutral status of Ireland, issues of security relating to the Cold War were excluded from EPC discussion. However, the Greek attitude created fears between Greece's partners that were to be confirmed at the next meeting on 12 September, just after the KAL was shot down. As in the Polish case, Greece refused to accept any declaration that would condemn the Soviet Union. The result was a lukewarm declaration expressing the deep distress of the Ten for the destruction of the aircraft and the loss of human life. The Soviet Union was not even mentioned in the EPC declaration. The Greek behaviour generated anger from its partners, who instead had to rely on the traditional form of national declarations, with strong words of condemnation, since EPC failed to produce a result.

In these two cases, Greece used the consensus rule in EPC in order to avoid the development of a common position by the Community, and particularly in the second case, abused the institutional powers of the presidency to achieve that aim. The influence which Greece exercised can only be characterised as negative, as it had used the power of veto. Although the power of veto is an institutional power granted to Member-States, the actual effect of its abuse is an elimination of influence, rather than an increase in the power of the Member State. That is exactly what happened with Greece, especially during the period of the first socialist government, from 1981 to 1985. The displeasure of Greece's partners towards its attitude, placed Greece on the margins of decision-making in the European Community.[7] However, the policies of the Greek government enjoyed the support of the majority of the public and was easily re-elected in 1985.

The damage that was caused to Greece's power of influence by its early negative participation in the mechanisms of EPC, was illustrated by the angry responses of the 'Nine' to Greece's attitude. In the Polish case a tendency developed, which was supported by the large majority of the 'Ten', to overcome the consensus rule and to come to an agreement in order to impose economic sanctions on the Soviet Union under the article 113, by excluding Greece from applying the sanctions. This was what finally happened after the proposal of Lord Carrington. Greece and Denmark, for different reasons, were excluded from applying the sanctions. The most damaging case for Greece, however, was the South-Korean civilian airliner case. The issue that most annoyed Greece's partners, was not the simple fact that Greece refused to condemn the Soviet action, but the manner in which the presidency was used. The issue was not initially included in the agenda of the ministerial meeting on 12 September 1983 by the Greek foreign minister Giannis Haralampopoulos, so the condemnation, which had been proposed, could not be achieved. The displeasure of Greece's fellow members with its attitude was such that there had been proposals to overcome the presidency and to announce a declaration of the 'Nine', in which they would condemn the Soviet Union with strong language, and thus undermine the Greek practice in EPC.

Similar attitudes and practice on the part of the Greek government resulted in a lack of reliability and influence, and a poor reputation for Greece in the mechanisms of European Political Co-operation. This actually produced completely different results than those expected by the Greek policy-makers. That is because this attitude developed scepticism on behalf of its partners that jeopardised Greece's potential to present an influential position in the future. By developing an 'independent foreign policy', as was the famous slogan of the Papandreou government, the Greek attitude damaged its international voice. Greece had misunderstood and miscalculated the importance of EPC collective action, not only for its own benefit but also its importance for the other members. The result was that Greece's partners considered it had a problem-creating attitude.

The Falklands/Malvinas Islands Crisis

The principle that has been used and is still used in Greek rhetoric, in an attempt to obtain the support of fellow members in disputes with its neighbours, is the subject of the case of the Falklands/Malvinas crisis. The issue of solidarity in this case has been something that the British government took for granted. Community solidarity can not be a one-way relation. That is to say that, in the expectation of solidarity the UK should have offered the importance to the institutions and its partners in the Community that was necessary to maintain this solidarity. On the contrary, Britain ignored its partners after its initial demonstration of solidarity.

After the invasion of the Falklands/Malvinas islands by Argentina on the night of 1 April 1982, the 'Ten' were very quick to agree to a declaration demanding 'an immediate cessation of hostilities and an immediate withdrawal of all Argentine forces from the Falkland islands, and called on the two governments to seek a diplomatic solution'.[8] Argentinean forces occupied Port Stanley and deported its Governor and the British forces based on the islands to Uruguay. The Community felt, that it had, in a way, been attacked and the quick response demonstrated the solidarity between the Member States. However, the British government did not ask the EPC for support.[9] On the contrary, it started an intensive diplomatic campaign through other routes. The first result was the Security Council Resolution 502 of the UN, which was adopted on the 3 April 1982. Despite the UK's orientation towards the UN and Washington, EPC gave full support to the British cause. Indeed, on 10 April the Belgian Presidency issued the agreement of the Ten for a series of measures against Argentina, including an economic embargo on imports imposed for one month after a Community regulation adopted on the 16 April.[10] The embargo expired on 7 May and Britain's partners hoped that by that day a peaceful solution would have been achieved. This was not to be the case. On 25 April peaceful resolution was out of the question after the start of the British military campaign and the retake of South Georgia. However, it was the sinking of the General Belgrano battle cruiser and the loss of 368 Argentine soldiers on the 2 May that ultimately broke up the consensus within the Community. At a special meeting of the Political Directors on 4 May, Britain was asked to explain its actions while Ireland, followed by Italy and later, by Denmark, renounced the economic measures against Argentina.[11]

Although Greece was not responsible[12] for the abandonment of the consensus, a different Greek position could have led to a Greek initiative for the promotion of a Community solidarity principle. This may have had positive implications if Greece were to have need of that principle in the future. Instead, at the UN general assembly in 1982, Greece took a position in favour of Argentina condemning the British use of force and asking for a peaceful settlement of the dispute. The implications of this position for Greece were such that, in a similar hypothetical case where a Turkish invasion of a Greek island occurs, fellow Member States should ask Greece not to use force but to find a solution through peaceful negotiations. Thus, the application of Community solidarity can not be an exclusive right of Greece in times of need. Rather, Greece should offer to reciprocate the same solidarity for others. However this did not form part of the government's considerations for two reasons. First, Greek foreign policy at that time was dominated by ideological concerns and the conflict was perceived as a demonstration of the colonial West's power. Second, the lack of strategic planning in Greek foreign policy made it short-sighted, lacking the ability to analyse the consequences of events in a long-term perspective to determine the Greek interest.[13] This was a period of strong ideological confrontation where geopolitics was yet to be influential. That was about to change with the securitisation of the Turkish issue after 1985.

Grenada

During the second half of 1983, the Greek presidency of the European Council provided yet another case in which Greece was damaged by the negative attitude of the government, in particular the case of the Grenada crisis. On 3 October 1983, Bernard Coard, the deputy President of Grenada, a small island in the East Caribbean, took power by force and executed Maurice Bishop, the elected President. Coard consequently established a Marxist regime on the island. As concern within Europe was growing, particularly in UK, because of the number of British citizens on the island, the main question that dominated discussion was whether the US would invade Grenada. The Europeans had no specific interest and no financial resources to spare for an operation in the region.[14] On the European Council in Vouliagmeni, a suburb of Athens, on 22-24 October, the Greek foreign minister Yiannis Haralambopoulos prevented the issue from being placed on the meeting's agenda. Therefore no collective action could be taken on Grenada. According to the Socialist ideology of PASOK, the people of Grenada were revolting against the oppressive regime opposed by the US. However, as is mentioned later, the Greek position was influenced by feelings of retaliation because of Cyprus. With this stance Greece was trying to assert its independence from the Western sphere and by doing so wanted to develop its links and special relations with countries and leaders with similar ideologies, such as Muammar Quadaffi of Libya.[15]

It was only a few hours after the end of the Summit, on 25 October, that the US, together with the Member States of the Organisation of Eastern Caribbean States invaded Grenada to overthrow the Marxist regime. The following day, France and Germany strongly condemned the US invasion, but the UK refused to take similar action. Although disappointed because of the lack of information and consultation on behalf of the Americans, the UK supported the invasion. Four days later, on 30 October, the European Parliament came to the UK's assistance by justifying and applauding the US actions on the grounds of humanitarian intervention.[16] Once more, Greece manipulated its role in the presidency to prevent this issue from being placed on the agenda of the Athens Summit. The reasons for the Greek position in this case are different from that of the South-Korean airliner case. In the Grenada case, Greece acted as a vetoer by using negative influence because of retaliation. In other words, the Greek government used EPC mechanisms to 'punish' its fellow members for non-involvement in the discussion of the Cyprus problem. The Turkish invasion of Cyprus was considered by Greece as US sponsored and since EPC was perceived by Papandreou's government as nothing more than a tool of the Cold War, Greece wanted to use this case to demonstrate a discriminated policy of the Europeans. It was more than a year since Papandreou submitted a memorandum to his partners to inform them about Cyprus and to challenge them to act.[17] He must have been disappointed that no action had been taken. In the Korean airliner case, Greece wanted to demonstrate its ideological differences with the Western European perspective of foreign policy making.

An Evaluation of Greece's Behaviour between 1981-1985

During these first years as an EC member, Greece demonstrated a behaviour in foreign policy that had a significant impact on Greece's reputation for the years to come. In the three first cases of Sinai, Poland and the Korean airliner, Greece followed a policy of total differentiation from its partners to the point of not only blocking a consensus, but also of using the powers of the EC Presidency to avoid the discussion of an issue. The

Greek behaviour was not a product of a sensitive approach because of national interest, since there was no particular interest for Greece in these cases. Rather, it was a product of ideological differentiation that the Greek socialist government wanted to make both for external purposes to illustrate the difference from the previous government and for domestic and electoral purposes, since such behaviour was proclaimed during the electoral campaign and seemed desirable to the people.[18] It can be argued that in most cases, the behaviour of the Greek government can be explained according to four factors: ideology, domestic politics, perception of Europe, and lack of strategic planning. The socialist government wanted to demonstrate its ideological differences from the West, as its main argument was that it pursued a foreign policy independent of the sphere of influence of the two great powers. It objected to the American interference in the Arab world with the Camp David process (Sinai), it refused to condemn the Soviet block as totalitarian regimes (Poland), it objected to the Western exploitation of a 'mistake' (Korean airliner), and could not see a Marxist regime as a threat (Grenada). In the domestic sphere, the Greek government wanted to make clear the change that occurred in Greek foreign policy (Sinai), to transmit signals of socialist solidarity in order to invest in the anti-Americanism that brought it to power (Poland), and also to present its attitude as a punishment of the selective response of EPC (Grenada). At that period, Greece perceived the Community as a tool of the Cold War, and thus linked to US policy from which Greece wanted to become independent. The reaction to the Polish crisis and the Korean airliner demonstrate this perception. An EPC operation in Sinai would not have been anything else than a Western and US led intervention in Arab matters. In the Falklands/Malvinas case, Greece failed to foresee the benefits that the support and promotion of Community solidarity could bring for the Greek interests. The evidence of the behaviour of Greece suggests that there was no strategic design of Greek foreign policy during that period.[19] There was a lack of a long-term perspective on EC-Arab relations that the positive contribution of Greece could enhance. The good Greek-Arab relations could better be served by an influential Greece in EPC rather than by a marginalised actor. This lack of vision of the consequences of isolation is evident in all cases. The ideological campaign of the socialist party was implemented by transforming Greek foreign policy into a series of party slogans. The result was not only detrimental for Greek foreign policy in this period, but also had a serious impact on Greek reputation and affected the way that Greece was perceived by its partners for years to come. Considered as the worst period for the Greek foreign policy, it was this particular behaviour pattern that created the image of Greece as an awkward partner in Europe. A similar behaviour on issues of national security can at least be considered acceptable, although not always an advantage. However, examples such as the Greek foreign policy behaviour in this period which had no particular national interest, is regarded as an act against partnership. There have been many cases when Member States blocked common policies because of particular reasons of national importance. However, the Greek case, which blocked policies for ideological reasons, is unique and proved detrimental for Greek interests in the future.

From the SEA to the Maastricht Treaty

In January 1986, Spain officially became a full member of the European Community. Spanish foreign policy has traditionally been concentrated in three areas: Latin America, the Mediterranean, and the Middle East. Although Spain's foreign policy orientation differed noticeably from the 'old northern members', Spain adopted a pro-integrationist approach and 'joined' the Franco-German group favouring constitutional reforms towards further integration, immediately after its accession in the Community. The accession of Spain coincided with the signing of the Single European Act and in fact, the first time Spain took part in the institutions of the EC was in an EPC meeting at the European Council of Milan on 28-29 June 1985. Despite holding observer status, Spain made its stance in favour of further integration. It was in this meeting in Milan that the proposal of the Dooge committee was adopted, and opened the way for the signing of the Single European Act in February 1986. Spain not only began to actively participate in EPC, but also supported the proposed incorporation of it in the Treaty and the development of a common foreign policy.

Latin America

The first significant impact of Spain in EPC was the revival of EC relations with Latin-America. Just before Spain's official accession to the EC and still with observer status, Spain participated in the signing of the co-operation agreement between the European Community and the countries of Central America in November 1985.[20] Spain was a member of the San

José conferences even before its full membership of the European Community. The San José conferences brought the EC, the five Central American States and the Contadora group together in economic and political co-operation. In a very short period of time Spain managed to take advantage of its membership of the EC in order to strengthen its international position and also to draw the attention of the Community to the area of Latin-America, which had been long neglected. However, the start of the involvement of the Community in Latin America was before the Spanish accession.

EPC first developed an interest in the region after the coming to power of President Mitterrand in France in May 1981. In its suggestions to the Council in December 1981, with the initiative of the French Commissioner Claude Cheysson, the Commission proposed a program for economic development of Central America that could contribute to the stability of the region. The European idea behind this was that, unlike the Americans, they believed that conflict and political instability in Latin America was caused by the social and economic imbalances and was not a product of East-West tensions, which was the thrust of the statement issued by the European Council on 30 March 1982. In November of that year, the Council agreed to an increase in financial aid for Central America.

On January 1983, four Latin American states started the peace initiative of Contadora. The foreign ministers of Mexico, Colombia, Panama and Venezuela met in the Contadora island in the Gulf of Panama calling for a peaceful resolution of the Central American conflict through multilateral negotiations. The Contadora Group achieved the support of the Community when the European Council of Stuttgart on 17-19 June 1983 declared its support for the Contadora Group Initiative. As a result, the Community aid was increased and inter-ministerial meetings were arranged. Following an initiative of President Monge of Costa Rica in September 1984, an EC and Central American foreign ministers Conference was celebrated in San José, the capital of Costa Rica.

Participation in the San José Conference was extended to include non-Central American members of the Contadora Group and the two EC candidates Spain and Portugal. The San José Conference was developed into a process of dialogue with the aim of strengthening the political, economic and cultural relations between Europe and Central America. By doing that, the EC wanted to promote democracy and human rights in the region. On 11-12 November 1985 in Luxembourg, the San Jose II Conference approved the Cooperation Agreement, which was negotiated by the Commission according to the Council's directives. Political stability, social and economic conditions and human rights were the three main priority areas for cooperation between the EC and Central America referred to the Agreement.

The invitation to Spain to participate in the EC-Latin American dialogue even before its official accession in the Community signalled imminent upgrading of the relation that Spain could offer because of its special links with the region. It was done soon after the conclusions of accession negotiations and before the official accession date, in order to first contribute to Spain's familiarisation with EPC and second, to contribute to the EC goal which was the development of relations with Latin America. Indeed, Spain contributed to the improvement of EC relations with Latin America, not only through the Contadora and San José processes, but also by developing further links with groups of states in South America, such as the Rio Group, the Andean Pact and the Mercosur. The Spanish objective, however, was not to take the role of a 'bridge' between Europe and Latin America.[21] On the contrary, Spain's priority was its full integration in Europe and the transformation of the Spanish priorities into European ones. In other words, Spain's objective was to contribute to the development of an EC common objective towards Latin America and not to become a 'bridge' of influence in Europe on behalf of the Latin American countries. The success of Spain in this aspect, however, lies in the fact that Spain not only tried to Europeanise the Spanish objectives but also incorporated the European objectives into a part of their own.[22]

International Terrorism

During the 1980s, evidence that suggested the existence of 'state sponsored terrorism' developed the need for the issue to become part of the EPC agenda. The two suspect states were Libya and Syria. However, consensus on a common action on international terrorism was difficult to achieve since relations with the Arab world could be harmed if the Twelve were seen to be giving in to American pressure.[23] An event in April 1984 became the opportunity for the issue to be discussed in EPC. A policewoman was shot dead in London from a shot fired from the Libyan embassy in St James's Square. The event resulted in the break of diplomatic relations between the UK and Libya. The EPC response, though, was not according to the UK's expectations since the other Nine were reluctant to follow with similar actions. However, EPC set up an ad hoc Group on Terrorism and

Diplomatic Immunity. On 11 September 1984 in Dublin, the Ten adopted a declaration announcing a set of measures that began in 1975,[24] to strengthen existing cooperation, and to declare their willingness to a common action in the case of serious terrorist attacks.

Following two terrorist attacks at Rome and Vienna airports in December 1985, Italy demanded a discussion in EPC. In a meeting on 27 January 1986, the Twelve issued a statement condemning the attacks and announced their commitment to enhance cooperation in areas such as security at airports and control of persons entering and circulating in the Community. In the same meeting, EPC set up a Working Group on Cooperation to Combat International Terrorism. However, EPC did not go as far as to impose economic sanctions against Libya, as the American pressure insisted. The bombing of the La Belle discotheque in Berlin in which a number of US soldiers were killed, brought the American pressure to a climax. Spain and Italy took advantage of the new procedure for crisis management introduced by the London Report[25] to call for an urgent meeting of foreign ministers in The Hague on 14 April. This is an illustration that Spain used EPC as a tool of Spanish foreign policy. The success of its attempt is due to the fact that Spain did not try to impose its own interest but presented its policy as common interest. The declaration issued in The Hague did not meet the American requirements. It condemned any State which supported terrorism and asked Libya to renounce such activities. The Libyan staff in diplomatic missions in the EC Member States was reduced and visa requirements were made stricter. However, no decision was made on economic sanctions. On the contrary, the last paragraphs of the declaration dealt with the US threats on military attacks. It was stated that, in order to avoid further escalation of military tension in the region, there was a need for restraint on both sides, meaning Libya and the US.[26] On the same day that the foreign ministers were trying to avoid a US military operation against Libya, the US carried out a bombing raid on Tripoli. The Europeans were outraged and felt deceived by the Americans and also by the UK, which allowed the use of air bases in British soil for the attack, and thus knew about the operation even before the meeting at The Hague.

At the request of Greece and Spain, according to the procedures of the London Report, a meeting was convened in Paris on the 17 April. The EC countries were fearful of repercussions against European targets following the US raid, so the main priority of the meeting in Paris had been the maintaining of European solidarity, the reaffirmation of their support for a political solution and the avoidance of any escalation of the crisis. Despite the EPC refusal to impose sanctions against Libya, on 21 April, the Twelve decided to extend the diplomatic restrictions on Libya. On 10 November 1986 in London, the EC Member States, with the exception of Greece, agreed on the imposition of similar restrictions on Syria after several incidents which implied the direct involvement of Syrian authorities with terrorist activities. Greece dissociated itself, arguing that the Syrian authorities should not be held responsible, not wanting to disrupt its good relations with Syria or its regime and to please the domestic pro-Arab public. It is worth noticing that Greece, in all cases of international terrorism initially blocked the consensus in EPC. However, it joined soon after the publicity had died down, as illustrated by the Greek foreign minister's Theodore Pangalos statement in the Syrian case that Greece had already applied the measures in practice.[27] This is another example of Greek foreign policy being made for domestic purposes. This tactic was not directed to the substance of the policy but to the impressions that the initial attitude was to bring to the public.

The reasons behind the Greek attitude were based on both ideologies and domestic politics. The Greek Prime Minister Andreas Papandreou had special relations with Libya and Syria and felt ideologically close to the two leaders, Qadhafi and Asad. Greece had also traditionally been a pro-Arab country. On a domestic level, the Greek government wanted to use its disagreement in EPC to make an ideological stance as a socialist government. However, ideology had to be counterbalanced with realism. The Greek government knew that in the end it had to get in line with its partners on measures against terrorism, but it only did so after its initial disagreement in order to take advantage of its ideological stance while the issue attracted publicity. Another example of this has been the case of the extradition of a Palestinian terrorist in December 1988. Against the decision of the Greek High Court, the government refused to extradite the Palestinian terrorist Al-Zomar to Italy with the excuse that he was prosecuted for his political activity. However, when Greece set him free to leave for Egypt, the authorities of that country arrested him and handed him over to Italy.

The Middle East

The Middle East is an area in which Spanish foreign policy has been particularly active since its accession in 1986. Its joining the EC was followed by the diplomatic recognition of Israel on 17 January 1986. This decision to modify Spain's position was evidence of Spanish strategic planning. The Middle East has been an important area for Spanish policy and it would have been damaging for Spain to proceed to a unilateral recognition of Israel. Spain deliberately accepted the recognition as a requirement in the EC accession Treaty in order to move to an impartial position between Jews and Arabs.[28] Although Spain maintained a traditional friendship with the Arab world, the act of recognition particularly helped Spain in pursuing a constructive European policy towards the Middle East during its first Presidency of the European Council in 1989. This was also assisted by the decision not to recognise the proclamation of the Palestine State, which was made in 1988 by the Palestine National Council. However, Spain offered a diplomatic status to the Palestinian Liberation Organisation (PLO) office in Madrid, although it was not an embassy, and in 1989, Yasser Arafat was received in Spain as Head of state. The significance which was given by Spain to the Middle East peace process is demonstrated by the initial actions of the Spanish Presidency in January 1989. The first Spanish activities were the visit of its foreign minister to Israel, the meeting of the 'troika' with Arafat in Madrid and the 'troika' visit to Egypt, Syria and Jordan.[29]

The Spanish success of finding a balance, neither pro-Arab nor pro-Israeli, but to develop good relations in a moderate way with both sides was one of the reasons that Madrid became the appropriate place for the Middle East Peace Conference of 30 October to 3 November 1991. A second reason was the Declaration of Madrid of 27 June 1989, during the Spanish Presidency in which Spain took a leading role for the promotion of the peace process through an international conference. There was the element of Spain being rewarded by the US for its positive contribution to the allied forces during the Gulf War.[30] Finally, Spain strengthened its position in the Middle East peace process after its initiative was launched in Mallorca in September 1990 on the Conference for Security and Cooperation in the Mediterranean similar to the CSCE. The proposed CSCM wanted to start a process of gradual establishment of security and enhanced cooperation in the region. Although the initiative was not successful in 1990, it helped the Spanish reputation as a leader in the Mediterranean, both Western

(Maghreb) and Eastern (Middle East), and led to the Madrid Conference on the Middle East in 1991 and later to the Barcelona process in 1995.[31]

In this area, which includes not only the Middle East but also the whole of the Arab world, Spain took a leading role in EPC promoting the importance of the region for European security, something that was a strategic objective of Spanish foreign policy. The Spanish Presidency's initiative and interest in the region resulted in the establishment of dialogue between the EC and the Maghreb Arab Union as well as the talks between the EC and the Arab League.[32] Spain sustained its reputation by promoting a common EPC approach rather than a unilateral Spanish one. The Spanish government of Felipe González perceived the Middle East as part of the European security concerns, which could only be dealt by collective action.[33]

Unlike Spain, Greek foreign policy has always been actively pro-Arab. It can be argued that the one-sided approach has been the reason that Greece played an insignificant role in the Middle East peace process. In 1988, Greece was one of the few European states to recognise the Palestinian State. The PLO has had a diplomatic status in Athens since the beginning of the 1980s, since Athens was the first Western capital to accept a visit of Yasser Arafat, who was given the status of the head of state by Papandreou. The pro-Arab foreign policy of Greece was such that during the late 1980s Greece was associated with the states that supported terrorism, because of its special relations with Libya and Syria, and Athens airport was included in the 'black list' of the State Department as a high risk airport for terrorist activities. With such behaviour, Greece not only deprived itself from contributing in the Middle East peace process, which is of national interest because of its proximity in the region, but also created tensions and problems with its fellow Europeans, and thus worsened its reputation in EPC, as an uncooperative member.

Western Sahara

According to the United Nations (UN), Western Sahara is still a non-autonomous territory, which means that it is not yet decolonised. Since 1965 when the UN issued the first resolution on Western Sahara[34] asking for its decolonisation, Spain was looking for a way to resolve the problem, since it felt morally obliged to do so because of the responsibility of the Franco regime for the situation in the region. On the one hand Morocco was claiming the territory and on the other a nationalist movement of the

Western Saharan people developed. The Popular Front for the Liberation of Western Sahara and the Golden River (Polisario Front) was founded in 1973 and gained popular support to the point that when two years later, in 1975, the UN mission visited the region, it was concluded that there was a popular will in favour of independence. On 20 November 1975, Spain signed the Three-party agreements of Madrid with Morocco and Mauritania that signified the end of the Spanish colonial policy. After the Spanish evacuated Western Sahara, it was invaded in the south by Mauritania and in the north by Morocco. On 26 February 1976, Spain officially ended any colonial responsibility with the region. However, the Spanish government defended the right of the people of Western Sahara for auto-determination and in 1979 it was recognised as the only representative of the Saharan people, the Polisario Front. The Front represented the Democratic Arab Saharan Republic (DASR) that was established in 1978. After an agreement of DASR with Mauritania, the latter withdrew from the Saharan territory only to open the way for the total occupation of Western Sahara by Morocco. In 1984, for the first time Spain ended its abstentionist attitude and voted in the UN general assembly for the auto-determination of Western Sahara after a resolution presented by Algeria. This was a new development that was caused mainly by the fact that the socialist party which had come to power in 1982 had traditional links with the Polisario Front. In 1986 representatives of Morocco and the Polisario met for the first time in New York under the mediation of the UN general secretary. King Hassan II met with a Polisario delegation in Marrakech two years later. Despite this, the promised referendum for auto-determination still has not happened and according to the UN the territory is not yet decolonised.

In the 1970s, Spain was desperate to disassociate itself from colonialism due to strong international pressure. For this reason, even after the Moroccan invasion, Spain retained a neutral position. It was the socialist government that was supportive of the Polisario Front which changed the Spanish position. However, the relationship with Morocco was very important for Spanish foreign policy and each action on the case was carefully designed so as not to upset the Moroccan authorities. That was because the Spanish policy was driven by the geoeconomic logic of cooperation for security rather than confrontation.[35] Its accession in the EC gave a new orientation to the Saharan issue when Spain favoured a European response supportive to the UN peace plan. The Spanish attitude in favour of the Europeanisation of foreign policy, and particularly its priority for consensus building in EPC, is demonstrated in the Western

Sahara case. The first time that EPC discussed the issue of Western Sahara was during the Greek Presidency in 1988 and under Spanish pressure on 7 September, the first political declaration was produced. In that declaration, the Twelve announced that they would join in the UN peace plan for Western Sahara. The significance of that declaration is that the PSOE government, who traditionally supported the Polisario Front, actually adopted a moderate approach in EPC in order not to be confronted with France, who traditionally supported Morocco in the dispute. This Spanish position served three main causes. First, it supported the settlement of the dispute under the UN, second, it favoured a European approach supporting co-operation and common position in EPC, and finally it used its European commitment as an alibi before the Spanish public opinion, which was favourable to the Polisario Front.[36] This was profound evidence of the successful adaptation of Spanish policy in Europe.

The Persian Gulf War

Following the Iraqi invasion of Kuwait in August 1990, the Twelve were very quick not only to produce a common declaration condemning Iraq on 2 August, but also to announce their decision to impose an embargo on oil imports from Iraq and Kuwait two days later.[37] After a draft legislation proposed by the Commission on 6 August and the Security Council's Resolution 661 on the same day, the Council issued a regulation on 8 August with which the Community imposed sanctions on all products originating in Iraq and Kuwait. Greece and Spain formed part of the general consensus in EPC. After the imposition of the sanctions both of these two southern Member States had expressed their support for a peaceful resolution of the crisis, but they also made clear their willingness to participate in an international force against Iraq if the latter would not withdraw. Apart from supporting the UN plan and the Mitterrand initiative,[38] the Spanish diplomacy took a step forward and attempted mediation with the Arab States under the auspices of the PLO and Algeria.[39] However, since the hostilities began, both Greece and Spain participated with one and three warships respectively. In Greece, the new right-wing government was very keen to demonstrate its willingness to agree with its fellow-Europeans and point out its difference with the previous socialist government. In Spain, despite the fact that the Prime Minister had described the crisis as 'regional', by the time of the operation Spain participated in the international force. This participation caused immense opposition in both Greece and Spain. In Greece the opposition, and particularly the socialist party of Papandreou, attacked the government for getting in line with 'American imperialism'. In Spain, the opposition as well as the public opinion were particularly displeased because, unlike his earlier declarations, Felipe Gonzalez decided to send the warships to the Gulf, and without any consultation with the Spanish Parliament. However, the new international order that was developed at that time, which created a notion of international community, together with the participation of the Arabs in the multinational force, made the justification of Spain's participation easier for González. The inability of the EPC to take the lead in the implementation of a crisis management policy demonstrated the lack of a common foreign policy and crisis management capability, despite the timing of the declarations. This further developed the desire in the Community to create a common foreign and security policy, which became a subject during the Maastricht negotiations.

Evaluation of Greece's and Spain's Behaviour between 1986-1991

From the time of its accession, Spain demonstrated its willingness to actively participate in European foreign policy, to promote consensus and avoid being an awkward partner. This European orientation transformed Spain from an isolated outsider into a first runner and leader in European Political Cooperation.[40] The success with which Spain handled the issue of the Middle East throughout this period, from its recognition of Israel to the Madrid declaration, and its initiative during the Gulf crisis led to the hosting of the Middle East International Conference in Madrid. This success can also be attributed to the charismatic leadership of Felipe Gonzalez, who gave the most importance to foreign policy and the Spanish image. He was also committed to a European orientation of Spanish foreign policy.[41] This was clear during the Gulf War when Gonzalez made his choices according to his vision for the Spanish international reputation and not for domestic purposes, in spite of opposition and criticism. In contrast with Greece, Spain was more consistent in its policy against international terrorism. Spain took a leading role in bringing about the discussion in the EPC meetings, both on 27 January 1986 at Brussels, which led to a general statement condemning international terrorism, and on 14 April 1986 at The Hague, which took specific measures against Libya. Considering its geographical position, fearing retaliation, but also demonstrating its

European orientation, Spain favoured an EPC common approach to the crisis and peaceful settlement of the problem and grouped together with Belgium, Germany and Italy in opposing the US use of force.[42]

After realising the benefits of Community membership Greece slightly altered its total opposition which had characterised the first half of the 1980s. These benefits were mostly economic and Greece was determined to continue and increase these benefits, which were used by the government to increase its electoral support.[43] Its behaviour during the SEA negotiations was not against foreign policy cooperation, but against its institutionalisation. As a contradiction to this, Greece supported the development of a common European defence policy because it wanted EPC as a defence alliance against Turkey, since NATO could not provide that forum. The main reason for the change in the Greek attitude towards European security was the process of 'nationalisation' of Greek foreign policy which a product of the 'securitisation' of its policy towards Turkey.[44] In this context, this term means that during the first five years of the socialist government, the ideological difference with the West was the principal factor of foreign policy formation. After Mikhael Gorbachev came into power in Soviet Union and the prospects for the ease of East-West tension looked more promising, Greek foreign policy turned more nationalistic and focused on the conflict with Turkey. Greece began to perceive the Community as a security guarantor against Turkish aggression. It has to be noted that the perception of the guarantor was Greece's imaginary ideal because of its obsession for belonging to an international organisation with defence responsibilities that excluded Turkey. This was a policy that conveyed to the Greek public opinion an image of a government that is fighting for its vital national interests. This attitude gave the impression that Greece was trying to take advantage of the privileges of membership for its own benefit at the expense of its partners. The change of government in 1989 gave a glimpse of hope to Greece's partners that a more European and less nationalistic orientation in foreign policy was in sight. Indeed, the first years demonstrated signs of a change of attitude. Apart from the different policy during the Gulf War, Greece entered the Maastricht negotiations on the pro-integrationist side, breaking past alliances with the UK and Denmark. However, the Yugoslav crisis proved this change to be superficial.

The accession of Spain was followed by the realisation among the EC Member States that Spanish participation in European foreign policy would have no similarities to that of Greece.[45] In the domestic political debate,

Spain enjoyed a total consensus among the political forces in favour of membership, in contrast with the divided image of the respective Greek scene. During the second half of the 1980s, Spain followed an integrationist approach with an offensive participation, as illustrated in Table 2 below.[46] This type of participation counter-proposes alterations to the proposal in which the State disagrees, instead of blocking it, which is the characteristic of defensive participation. Spain realised that through the institutions of EPC, it could enhance its foreign policy potentials and its international role. It pursued the role of initiator in order to contribute to the construction of common policies. The notion of offensive participation is concentrated in the fact that Spain demonstrated a preference for common rather than national policies. That is why it avoided vetoing after disagreements, and tried to counter-propose with persistence to achieve common positions. On the contrary, Greece followed the defensive participation pattern of blocking common policies or abstaining from participating in the agreed positions. The participation patterns and the political orientation of the two states led them to associate themselves with different perspectives on European integration. From the beginning, Spain demonstrated its integrationist approach. On the other hand, after the initial years of marginalisation, Greece abandoned its isolation but not its defensive position. In the second half of the 1980s, Greece pursued an intergovernmental approach, receiving the economic benefits but avoided the conceding of national sovereignty, particularly on foreign policy.

From Maastricht to Amsterdam

The Treaty on European Union

During the negotiations for the Treaty on European Union, it is argued that Spain took a 'supranational intergovernmentalist' approach.[47] This term characterises the willingness of the Spanish diplomacy to promote the institutionalisation of EPC to Common Foreign and Security Policy integrated into the European Union with an increased role for the Commission and the Parliament, but focused on the political negotiation at the highest level. However, Spain was even ready to accept some qualified majority formulas on issues of foreign policy which suggests that it was ready to disregard any *realist* consideration in favour of a *liberal internationalist* approach.[48] A greater Spanish participation and interest in a common foreign policy of the European Union quickly increased the role and influence of Spain in the EPC mechanisms. An illustration of this is the adoption of the Spanish proposal by the Lisbon European Council in June 1992, to incorporate Maghreb and Middle East in the liable areas to Joint Actions. This meant that policy in these areas was to be made collectively at the European level instead of at the national level. Also, in the security field, Spain joined WEU in 1988 favouring its incorporation in the EU as its 'armed branch'. In 1993, Spain was integrated into Eurocorps with France, Germany and Belgium, and also established the Joint Naval Force with France and Italy.[49] Spanish priorities during the TEU negotiations can be placed into three groups. The first is economic and social cohesion; Spain stressed the importance of cohesion and the need for efficiency. The second is the issue of the democratic deficit; Spain campaigned in favour of more democratic and effective European institutions. Finally, the third is CFSP. The development of a CFSP was according to the Spanish perspective, the reinforcement of the capacity of the EU to take international initiatives which makes it a single actor in the international stage.[50]

Greece participated in the Maastricht negotiations with a newly elected government. After eight years of socialist governance, the Papandreou government gave way for the 'New Democracy' conservative party. The new Prime Minister, Constantine Mitsotakis, wanted to change the Greek image in Europe and to demonstrate the new pro-European and integrationist face of Greece. The Treaty on European Union was the perfect opportunity as negotiations started two months after the formation of the new government.[51] The priority of the new Greek government during Maastricht was to support further integration. With its memorandum, Greece supported the Franco-German initiatives. Its attitude towards common foreign policy was very positive, hoping that a common defence would be developed which could act as a security guarantee for Greece's problems. That was the main reason for Greece's desperate moves to become a full WEU member. This issue dominated the Greek negotiation strategy during Maastricht. Particularly because of the reasons for the Greek agreement with the development of CFSP, which was its own security, Greece was reluctant to accept the introduction of majority voting in foreign policy. That is why Greece, unlike Spain, was happy to accept the French design of the pillar system which introduced common foreign and security policy in the European Union structure while retaining its intergovernmental and unanimous nature.

The Mediterranean

The second Spanish Presidency of the EU in 1995 was characterised by the decisiveness of the Spanish government to turn the European attention to the Mediterranean region, which was neglected after the events in Eastern Europe and the interest that the EU had attached to the former Communist states. The Spanish proposal to hold a Conference on Security and Co-operation in the Mediterranean on the model of CSCE can be said to have been realised during the Spanish second Presidency of the European Council in November 1995 in Barcelona, in the form of the Euro-Mediterranean Partnership Initiative. It was a historic encounter where the 15 Member States of the EU met at ministerial level with the 11 non-EU Mediterranean states and the Palestinian National Authority with which they had signed agreements.[52]

In June 1994 and during the Corfu Summit, the European Council called for a new policy towards Eastern Europe and the Mediterranean. Following this call, the foreign affairs council asked the Commission on 18 July 1994 to submit guidelines for the development the EU Mediterranean policy. The European Commission produced a document in October 1994 which outlined the Community's vital interests in helping Mediterranean countries meet the challenges they face.[53] It expressed the objective to work towards a Euro-Mediterranean Partnership by the progressive establishment of free trade, supported by substantial financial aid. It also promoted a close association through closer political and economic cooperation. This document was used as the basis for the Essen Summit of December 1994 recommendations. The Spanish government's initiative during the second semester of 1995 brought the representatives of the 27 mentioned states together in Barcelona to launch the Euro-Mediterranean Partnership in November 1995. The success of the Spanish initiative was not only to counterbalance the Eastern European orientation of the Community by developing its Mediterranean relations but also to promote cooperation and security in the Mediterranean region. The fact that Barcelona brought together Syria, Lebanon, Israel and the Palestinian Authority, something that not even the American-inspired Conference of Madrid managed to do in 1991, illustrates the importance of the process and highlights the Spanish achievement.

The Balkans

As mentioned earlier, the overwhelming Europeanism of the Greek government in the beginning of the 1990s was soon confronted by the Yugoslavian crisis that took Greece by surprise. Apart from the obvious threat that it posed, a civil war in Greece's neighbourhood formed an excellent opportunity for Greece to exercise its influence and play its role as a member of the European union, within the stability of the Balkans. However, rather than being an important actor involved in the solution of the problem, Greece became part of the problem itself. The rise of nationalistic feelings which characterised the issue of Macedonia, and the actual policy deadlock that the Greek government put itself in, damaged attempts for Greece to regain its lost reliability and reputation and to play a constructive and influential role in Europe's Common Foreign and Security Policy.

The change of Prime Minister in 1996 after the resignation of Papandreou brought a change in Greek foreign policy attitude. In the spring of 1996, Turkey openly doubted Greek sovereignty over a group of small islands in the Aegean, and particularly the islets of Imia.[54] The deployment of Greek commandos to secure one of the Islets led to the Turkish reply of occupying another and resulted in a moment when the navies of the two States were face to face over the Imia islets. Engagement could have been an easy and popular option, but the Greek government chose gradual disengagement, which brought on furious opposition from other political parties who criticised the government for giving up the Greek rights to the Turks. However, in the end this resulted in the strengthening of the Greek reputation in Europe and had positive implications for the Greek role in the European Union as it proved the newly developed Greek determination to play a constructive role for peace and stability in the region.[55]

A second case that illustrates the change which had begun to take place and the potential influence that Greece could exercise, was the mediation of Greece in the signing of a peace treaty and exchange of diplomatic missions between Yugoslavia and Croatia. This took place in Athens in the summer of 1996 under the efforts of the Greek prime-minister Simitis. The Greek position during the Albanian crisis and its participation for the resolution of the problem, as well as Greece's new rapprochement with Turkey for a peaceful negotiation for the solution of their problems also strengthened Greece's position in Europe and started to radically change its negative reputation. With several efforts and initiatives Greece has been trying to improve its image in the Balkans and to promote stability and economic development. The most successful initiative was the Balkan Conference that was launched in Crete in November 1997. The Conference brought together the leaders of eight Balkan states, who expressed their willingness and determination to develop an environment of partnership and stability in the region. The process provided for annual Summits of the Balkan leaders and the second Summit took place in Antalya, Turkey, in October 1998.

The 1996 IGC and the Treaty of Amsterdam

The Greek proposals during the IGC were characterised by a high degree of institutional reforms towards a federal system. Greece supported the strengthening of the legislative and political role of the European Parliament, as well as the increased participation of the national Parliaments in the formation of European policies, the upgrade of the Committee of the Regions and of the role of the European ombudsman. In addition, the substantial and effective role of the European Commission, for which Greece proposed to be accountable to the Parliament and its President to be elected from it, are some of the most important Greek proposals. With regard to the CFSP, Greece proposed the incorporation of it in the Community pillar with the safeguarding of the vital interests of the Member States, the effective implementation of the solidarity principle and the protection of the EU's external borders.[56] The issue of the recognition of the Union's external borders which was finally achieved in Amsterdam has since been the main target of the Greek diplomacy. However, the demonstration of commitment to the development of a genuine CFSP was counterbalanced by the contradiction that Greece opposed the extension of majority voting in the second pillar. According to Greece, the Communitarisation of CFSP should not go to the point of abolishing the veto power for the Member States.

In 1996, Spain witnessed a change in government. The Popular Party of José Maria Aznar formed the first centre-right government since 1982. Aznar's position on Europe has not been an ideologically Europeanist as González's, but was still in support of the European orientation for Spain. By being conscious of the fact that only within Europe can Spain advance its national interests and unlike the British Eurosceptics, González believed that without the EU's commitment to solidarity and cohesion it would add up to little more than a single market.[57] Although Spain in its White Paper on the 1996 IGC was in favour of flexibility, it rejected the idea of a 'Europe à la carte'.[58] Flexibility for Aznar's government is necessary in the light of the future enlargement of the EU. Spain was presented as sceptical towards the increased powers of the European Parliament and the Commission. It argued that current attributes are satisfactory. In the CFSP pillar, the Spanish memorandum favoured a greater use of qualified majority voting as this could help to improve the efficiency of the second pillar. However, although the memorandum that was prepared by the socialist government was accepted by Aznar, in practice Spain favoured the recognition that a fundamental or vital interest of a state may prevent a common position or action, thus preserving the right of veto.[59] As an overall picture it can be said that the Spanish attitude towards Europe altered considerably with the change of government. The unquestionable supranationalism of Felipe González changed into the intergovernmental institutionalism of José Maria Aznar. The final text of the Treaty of Amsterdam can be described as a compromise between intergovernmentalists and supranationalists, but as regards to Greece and Spain, there seems to have been a radical change to their positions since the SEA IGC.

Evaluation of Greece's and Spain's Behaviour between 1992-1997

It can be argued that the positions of Greece and Spain on the level of integration to be pursued in foreign policy, shifted during the years of their membership to end up in a similar position during the Amsterdam negotiations. Greece started from an isolationist position before the SEA, moved to an intergovernmental approach during and after the SEA and slowly reached a moderate integrationist posture.[60] Spain reached the moderate integrationist position in Amsterdam but had moved from the opposite side which was the total integrationist approach of Felipe Gonzalez.

The adoption of the Barcelona declaration marks the beginning of a new stage in Euro-Mediterranean relations.[61] Perhaps this was the more important achievement of the Spanish diplomacy during that period. It is also important to note the personal effort of the Spanish foreign minister Javier Solana who contributed to the organisational success of the conference, a success that led him to the General-Secretariat of NATO. In less than fifteen years Spain moved from being an isolated state at the edge of Europe into an influential actor and integrated participant of the European Union. The policy developed by Spain during its membership shows its attempt to Europeanise its special interests.[62] This attempt was not only successful[63] but also increased the Spanish image and influence in foreign policy. The change of government in 1996 brought about a slightly different prioritisation of policies. Foreign policy has ceased to be the first priority for the Spanish government which is more concerned with domestic issues. As a reflection of this, the new government's priorities in Amsterdam were the first and the third pillar, which directly reflect on domestic issues.

Greece was confronted with a crisis in its northern neighbourhood immediately following the change of government and the Maastricht Treaty with the demonstration of an integrationist attitude. The crisis in the Balkans developed nationalistic sentiments which overshadowed Greece's European orientation. Greece not only lost ground in its attempt to overcome the negative reputation of the 1980s and once again created tensions with its European partners, but also created problems with its Balkan neighbours instead of becoming a stabilising factor in the region. The new government in 1996, after the change of leadership in the socialist party, improved Greece's foreign policy in the Balkans by ending Greece's tensions with its northern neighbours and adopting new policies of cooperation. From its relations with Albania and Bulgaria to the normalisation of Greece's relationship with Macedonia and its involvement in Kosovo, Greek foreign policy started to demonstrate signs of coherence and contribution to stability. However, Greek-Turkish relations remain the question mark for Greek foreign policy. Although there have been signs of improvements, the policy of Greece on the issue still remains defensive and strongly based on nationalistic considerations.

In-depth Case Studies

A good insight into the policies and attitudes of Greece and Spain in foreign policy can be achieved by two specific case studies. Each one is a foreign policy issue of national importance for the Member State. The analysis of the way that Greece and Spain have dealt with these issues provides an evaluation of their behaviour and attitude towards common European foreign policy. The points which are discussed are the domestic consequences of the issue or the domestic sources of the foreign policy attitudes, its exclusion or inclusion in the European agenda, and the manner in which this was done. The issues of Macedonia and Gibraltar both have implications to the European Union. The dispute on the Macedonian issue undermined stability in the region which was in the vital interests of the EU to preserve. Similarly, the solution of the Gibraltarian issue could end a conflict between two Member States and the problems that this creates in EU decision-making. The purpose of this section is to offer the historical details of the two cases which are points of several references in the next chapters. The extent of the study of the two cases looks unbalanced, however this is the result of the extent to which the case of Macedonia formed part of the European foreign policy agenda and is not, in any way, a qualitative judgement of this book.

The Case of Macedonia

The disintegration of Yugoslavia in the early 1990s brought the Macedonian question into the spotlight. From early 1991, the Yugoslav Socialist Republic of Macedonia started to make steps towards independence, though in the beginning Skopje was happy to remain within a sort of Yugoslav Confederation. On 25 January 1991, the Assembly of the Republic adopted the 'Declaration on Sovereignty' according to which the laws and the Constitution of the Socialist Republic of Macedonia were to be supreme over the federal legislation of Yugoslavia. In April, and after the election of Kiro Gligorov to the Presidency, the word 'Socialist' was dropped from the State's name.[64] It was only after the armed conflict in Croatia and Slovenia that Macedonia realised the impossibility of the maintenance of Yugoslavian unity and decided to call a referendum for independence on 15 September 1991. The referendum resulted in a 90% support of an independent Macedonia. From mid-1991, Greece was confronted with the prospect of having at its northern border an independent Slav-Macedonian state. The Greek diplomacy seemed to be surprised at this development and there had been conflicting views and positions on the existence of the new state.

The first reaction of Greece was to try to contribute with whatever means to the maintenance of unity in Yugoslavia. It seemed that Greece was afraid that the new state, by its independence, would serve to destabilise the Balkan region and was perceived as a threat to Greek national security. The threat for Greece consisted of the fact that she neither existence of a separate Macedonian national identity. The problem of minorities in Greece is so extensive to the point that Greece is unwilling to recognise any ethnic minority within its border. The refusal to recognise the Turkish minority in Thrace as Turkish and Greece's insistence to call it Muslim, illustrates the problem of insecurity that Greece feels with ethnic minorities. This of course does not prevent Greece from supporting the Greek minorities in Albania and Turkey. In fact, the perception that minorities would work to destabilise the unity of the Greek State, has been an artificial threat and something that particularly is illustrated in the case of the Turkish minority in Thrace where Greece has always been afraid of a possible claim for annexation from Turkey. This threat from inside, in addition to the one from outside, has added to the importance of the development of the Greek 'national issues' in foreign policy.

After the first reaction of Greece, and when it was obvious that Yugoslavian disintegration was an irreversible fact, the Greek foreign minister Antonis Samaras presented a Memorandum on Yugoslav Macedonia to his fellow European ministers on 27 August 1991, only a few days before the referendum in Macedonia. The Memorandum had two main parts. In the first, the Greek minister outlined possible scenarios of instability in the region from a possible declaration of independence and recognition of Macedonia, none of which came true. In the second part, it summarised the Greek reservations about the use of the name Macedonia by a Slavic nation. Despite the negative spirit in which the memorandum was written, a basic characteristic of it is that it refers to the people of the Yugoslav Macedonia as Slav-Macedonians. It also states that: 'The Greeks believe that the Macedonian name is part of their own historical heritage and should not be used to identify, in an ethnic sense, another nation.' The inclusion of the phrase 'in an ethnic sense' is defined as the new state can use the name Macedonia in a geographical sense. The term 'Slav-Macedonians' has been used throughout the twentieth century by Greece to refer to the Slavic population of Macedonia.[65] It is obvious that Greece had not yet adopted a hard-line policy on the issue of Macedonia, and its policy was about to change. In the Cabinet decision of 4 December 1991, the Greek government put forward the conditions for the recognition of the 'Republic of Skopje'.[66] The decision asks Skopje to:

- Change the name 'Macedonia', which has geographic and not ethnic substance.

- To recognise that it does not have any territorial claims against Greece.
- To recognise that there is no 'Macedonian minority' in Greece.[67]

The diplomatic strategy, which Prime Minister Mitsotakis followed, was to leave the question of the name open for negotiations and a possible compromise, while having a strict approach to the issue of the minority. On 16 December 1991, in the Council of Ministers on foreign affairs in Brussels, the issue of the dissolution of Yugoslavia, which was prominent after the results of the Badinter Committee on 7 December, and the issue of recognition of the independence of the different Yugoslav Republics. The final declaration of the meeting states that 'the European Community and its Member States agree to recognise the independence of all Yugoslav Republics that fulfil all pre-conditions described below' and that 'the implementation of the decision will be made on 15 January 1992'.[68] In that meeting and after the insistence of Samaras, Greece managed to include in the prerequisites for recognition three conditions: to provide constitutional and political guarantees that will safeguard the Republic from any territorial claims from any of its neighbouring countries; to make sure that it does not realise hostile propagandistic campaigns against its neighbours; and not to use a name which might suggest territorial claims. For the inclusion of these three conditions, Greece gave its consent to the dissolution of Yugoslavia, which up until then she was fighting against. However, although Greece celebrated the decision, it was soon made clear that not all of the Member States had the same interpretation as Greece on the third condition. On 13 January 1992, the findings of the Badinter Committee found that the Republic of Macedonia satisfied all the conditions and prerequisites of the 16/12/91 decision of the EC, and that the use of the name 'Macedonia' did not suggest any territorial claim against another country, since Macedonia had renounced any territorial claim of any kind according to international law. The findings of the Badinter Committee were a big blow to Athens bringing a premature end to the celebrations that followed the 16/12/91 decision.

The immediate reaction of Greece to a chain of recognitions of the 'Republic of Macedonia'[69] was the cultivation of a nationalistic hysteria in the Greek society, which resulted in a huge rally in Thessaloniki, on 14 February 1992, in which one million people participated with slogans such as: 'Macedonia was, is, and always will be Greek', 'Macedonia is Greece', 'Macedonian history is Greek history', 'No recognition of the Skopian

Republic under the Hellenic name Macedonia'. Three days later, in the ministerial meeting of Lisbon, the foreign ministers agreed that the Portuguese Presidency should take an initiative to achieve a compromise between Skopje and Athens. Pinheiro, the Portuguese foreign minister, was about to prepare a package agreement agreed by Greece, which was to be offered to Macedonia on a 'take it or leave it' basis. In the case that Skopje rejected the agreed solution, there would have been no recognitions from any Community Member State.

In March 1992, the developed international climate was very hostile towards Greece. The Americans were willing to proceed with recognition and were pressing the Europeans to act accordingly. This was made clear during the joint EU-US summit of foreign ministers, in which the term 'Republic of Macedonia' was used in Baker's speech, when the US foreign secretary asked for the prompt recognition of the new state. On 1 April, Pinheiro met Samaras in Brussels and he submitted his proposals for Greek consideration. Samaras compromised both with Pinheiro and with the summit of foreign ministers in Luxembourg on 6 April, agreeing that a package deal according to Pinheiro's proposals was possible. Pinheiro's proposals consisted of four points: alteration of the Constitution of the new state according to the Greek proposals; signing of a framework treaty between Greece and Macedonia for the safeguard of the existing borders between the two states; a declaration on the issue of the existence of a Macedonian minority in Greece; and the use of the term 'Macedonia' with the addition of an adjectival complement as 'New Macedonia'.

Despite the optimism which the compromise of the Greek foreign minister created between Greece's fellow members, the Greek government dismissed the proposals and declared that it would not accept any inclusion of the term 'Macedonia' in any form in the name of the new state. It was after a meeting of the leaders of all Greek political parties on 13 April 1992 that the consensus to a Greek hard-line policy was achieved. Following that meeting, the Greek government began a campaign of 'information' in order to persuade its fellow members of the validity of its arguments and the 'falsification' of history made by 'Skopians'. On 5 May, during the ministerial meeting in Guimaraes, Mitsotakis, who since the party leaders meeting had dismissed his foreign minister and taken on the responsibility himself, managed to gain a concession from his European colleagues. The declaration of the Presidency stated that: 'the EC and the Member States are willing to recognise this state (FYROM) as a sovereign and independent state, in its existing borders and under a name which can be accepted by all parties concerned'. This statement made the Greek consensus to the name a pre-requisite of recognition. The euphoria that this decision created in Greece was broken just a week later in Brussels when some Member States, with the British lead, threatened unilateral recognitions if Community recognition could not be achieved. The Greek dissatisfaction with the developments and the rise of nationalistic feelings in the Greek society were expressed with mass demonstrations both inside and outside Greek borders. The most important of these that took place abroad, was the rally of the Greek-American community in the US outside the White House in Washington, on 31 May 1992. With the American elections coming up, the Greek-American community was using a powerful weapon.

At the end of June 1992, just before the summit of Lisbon, Mitsotakis sent a letter to all EC leaders (23 June 1992) concerned with the Macedonian issue, which illustrated the change in the Greek strategy. Greece was no longer trying to persuade the EC members of the validity of its historical arguments. In the letter, Mitsotakis made known the danger that a decision contrary to the Greek position could lead to the destabilisation of his government, arguing that he could not control the nationalistic sentiment in the Greek society. At the Lisbon summit of 26-27 June, the declaration of the European Council stated the repetition of Guimaraes, but altered the phrase 'with a name that can be accepted by all parties concerned' to 'with a name that will not include the term Macedonia'. To a large extent, this decision can be attributed to the letter by the Greek Prime Minister and to the removal of the Greek veto for the EC financial protocol for the Mediterranean non-member countries. This actually meant the Greek consensus to financial aid to Turkey in exchange of the support of the Community to the Macedonian issue.

The escalation of the tension, the Greek hard-line policy and the Lisbon declaration had a negative impact on Macedonia. The moderate government of Gligorov was struggling to keep down the nationalists of VMRO, but it seemed that help could neither be found in Greece or in Europe. On 2 July, and in reaction to the Lisbon decision, the Macedonian Parliament voted for the maintenance of the name 'Macedonia' and also decided to adopt as a national symbol in the flag, the sun of Vergina.[70] The Greek reaction to this was the imposition of an oil embargo. The opportunity for the Greek action was given following condemnations that Greece was not respecting the oil embargo imposed by the UN to Serbia. The Greek argument was that Skopje was actually selling oil to Serbia while spreading the rumours that Greece was not respecting the embargo.

This first Greek embargo[71] towards the Republic of Macedonia was imposed on 21 August 1992 and although during the first months created big problems to Macedonia, these were soon solved by the contribution of Bulgaria and Turkey who offered their help. The Greek government was forced to withdraw the embargo in face of the need to secure the maintenance of the Lisbon decision during the Edinburgh summit of the British Presidency in December 1992. Just before the Edinburgh summit, a second mass rally took place in Greece, this time in Athens, in which almost one million people demonstrated the Greek slogans. Ultimately, Edinburgh was no different from Lisbon. The difference came with the Macedonian strategy after Edinburgh. After its disappointment with the European Community, the Republic of Macedonia applied for accession to the United Nations on 17 December 1992. It was an unexpected development for the Greek diplomacy, since it could not block such an accession. After a long period of hard campaigning by Greece against the Macedonian accession to the UN, a proposal came from the Security Council,[72] which was accepted by both parties, and the Republic of Macedonia entered the UN under the name 'Former Yugoslav Republic of Macedonia' on 24 March 1993. After the conclusion of the initial negotiations between Greece and FYROM in New York under the auspices of Cyrus Vance and Lord Owen, they put a proposal on the table. This proposal, which was made on 14 May 1993, was for an agreement on the issues of the existence of a Macedonian minority, the use of Slavic names for locations in Greek Macedonia, the use of symbols like the sun of Vergina, the irredentist propaganda from any source, and also proposed the name 'Nova Makedonija' (New Macedonia). The Greek government did not express an opinion, since the proposal was dismissed by Gligorov on the grounds of the change of name and the ambiguity of the reference to the use of Slavic names for locations in Greece. The negotiations did not go too far because of the internal political problems which the Macedonian issue had created in Greece. Samaras, the ex-foreign minister who created his own party based on nationalistic grounds, led to the fall of the government and to general elections in October 1993. Papandreou, as Prime Minister after the elections, took the decision to withdraw from the UN negotiations on 5 November 1993.[73] The result of this development was the immediate recognition of Macedonia by the other EU states on 16 December. Following the decisions for recognition, Greece closed its border to Macedonia and on 16 February 1994 imposed a unilateral economic embargo.

Greece, who held the Presidency of the European Council during the first semester of 1994, received the condemnation of its fellow Europeans for its decision and the issue was brought to the Court of Justice by the Commission on 22 April 1994 (C-120/94R). The ECJ refused to apply interim measures against Greece (29 June 1994). Article 224 of the Maastricht Treaty can provide an interpretation against 'state-sovereignty', but this interpretation requires an activist ruling by the ECJ, something which in this case did not happen.[74] It would have been very interesting to see the final decision of the Court, but the lifting of the embargo after the signing of the Interim Accord between Greece and Macedonia, on 13 September 1995, ended the Court proceedings. The imposition of the economic embargo was one of the most damaging acts of Greece for its own interest and reputation since the first five years of its membership of the EC.[75] One of the worst criticisms expressed during the Greek embargo, was that of the *Times* 8 April 1994. It called upon Greece to give up its presidency of the European Union in order to prevent even greater damage to Europe than it had already caused. It said Greece had placed its own interests above those of the Union by introducing the embargo against Macedonia, thus abusing its position and damaging the Union's reputation.[76] Greece tried to get its partners' support on the issue of Macedonia by campaigning its position based on historical arguments. However, Greece completely ignored the political realities that were the main considerations of the EU Member States in their attempt to stabilise the region. That is why Greece ultimately failed in its objectives, despite the fact that it temporarily succeeded to gain the sympathy of its partners.

By September 1995 the American attempt to find a common ground for the solution of the dispute resulted in the signing of the Interim Accord in New York. This agreement is referred to as 'a small package' because it excludes the issue of the name. Due to the exclusion of that issue, the Interim Accord does not make a reference to Greece or Macedonia. Greece is named as 'the Party of the First Part', and Macedonia as 'the Party of the Second Part'. In Article 1 of the Accord, Greece, recognises Macedonia (with no name) as an independent and sovereign state. The agreement foresees, among others, the establishment of diplomatic relations between the two states, the inviolability of their international border (Article 2), the respect of the sovereignty, territorial integrity and political independence of each other (Article 3), and the removal of the sun of Vergina from the Macedonian flag (Article 7.2). Greece lifted the embargo and agreed to the future settlement of the name issue under negotiations.

The Case of Gibraltar

The issue of Gibraltar goes back to 1713 when, after the conquest of the Rock by Great Britain, Spain signed Article X of the Treaty of Utrecht which conceded the sovereignty of the peninsula to the British Crown. Article X gave the UK the right of sovereignty for an indefinite time. However, according to the article, if ever the UK wanted to renounce sovereignty on Gibraltar, Spain has the first right of its acquisition. The problem of Gibraltar was developed after the Second World War and the process of decolonisation. Since 1830, Gibraltar was officially named as Crown Colony, which included it in the list of colonies to be decolonised according to the United Nations Charter. In the 1950s, the UK gradually gave the colony auto-governance rights. The Franco regime in Spain was not pleased with that development because its aim was the decolonisation of the Rock and its incorporation into Spain, according to Article X of the Treaty of Utrecht. Its response was to close down the Spanish consulate in Gibraltar in 1954 and to impose several restrictions on the colony. Some of these restrictions have included refusing to issue new work permits to Gibraltarians, imposing restrictions on Spanish visitors and making the acquisition of products and materials from Spain difficult. The start of bilateral negotiations between Spain and the UK in the UN in July 1966 for the resolution of the conflict did not go far and in 1969 the Gibraltarian Constitution tranformed it into a colony of the British Crown with an internal auto-governance. The governor of Gibraltar was to be elected and form his own government instead of being appointed by Britain. However, this event worsened the conflict with Spain as it looked like the UK was pushing for independence for the peninsula.

The UK's accession in the EC in 1973 marked the incorporation of Gibraltar into the European Community as a dependent territory of a Member State. For the next decade, the British government used its ascent to Spanish adhesion in the EC as a tool to achieve the withdrawal of the Spanish restrictions on Gibraltar. The democratic transition in Spain brought gradual changes to the conflict. Although the Spanish arguments and claims remained the same, the policy of restrictions gradually changed. Some of the restrictions were abolished by the new democratic government in the late 1970s, namely the re-connection of telephone lines, however, it was the socialist government that removed all restrictions in 1985 and opened up the frontiers on 15 December 1982.

The first step for the normalisation of Spain-UK relations, related to Gibraltar and was made in 1980 in Lisbon. After the agreement of Spain to accept Gibraltarian participation in the negotiations as part of the UK delegation, the first meeting was arranged between the two foreign ministers, Marcelino Oreja of Spain and Lord Carrington of the UK, in Lisbon. The meeting resulted in the Lisbon Declaration. In the declaration both sides were committed to the start of negotiations for the solution of the conflict. The Spanish government expressed its willingness to remove the restrictions on Gibraltar. However, the Lisbon Declaration had no legal binding and the Spanish government delayed the removal of the restrictions. On the other hand, Margaret Thatcher made it clear that she could only accept unconditional removal of restrictions and appeared determined to block Spain's entry into the EC otherwise. In April 1982, and after the Argentine invasion of the Falklands/Malvinas islands, Spain constrained from condemning the invasion. This act created great preoccupations in Gibraltar that Spain might consider similar action. However, the socialist victory in Spain six months later, in October, and the removal of further restrictions in December ended such fears. The opening of the frontiers with Gibraltar took place in December 1982 but with certain restrictions. The crossing of the border could only be done once a day and for pedestrians only and was directed to the Spanish and Gibraltarians working in Gibraltar or Spain respectively.

Despite this gesture of goodwill on behalf of the new Spanish government, negotiations on Gibraltar did not start before September 1983. This can be attributed to the refusal of the British foreign secretary Francis Pym to negotiate with Spain.[77] After the closing of the CSCE meeting in September 1983, the new British foreign secretary, Geoffrey Howe, decided to reopen talks with his counterpart Fernando Moran. The UK was asking for the removal of all the restrictions in order to give its assent to Spanish adhesion in the EC. Spain developed a proposal, which the foreign minister Moran proposed on several occasions, to come to an agreement on Gibraltar similar to the Hong Kong arrangements. This was never accepted by the UK, whose new argument was that following accession, Spain could be forced to remove restrictions on Gibraltar by implementing the 'aquis communautaire'. The final removal of the restrictions happened with the Declaration of Brussels of 27 November 1984. In this declaration, Moran and Howe made a mutually acceptable interpretation of the Lisbon Declaration. The objectives of the Brussels Declaration can be summarised in the following:

- The reciprocity and equality of rights in relation to the 'aquis' that without a doubt implied the removal of restrictions.
- The further discussion of the sovereignty issue.
- The promotion of cooperation in the areas of culture, tourism, air transport, the military and environment.

The compromise of the Spanish government in adopting certain actions intended to permit secure and efficient air communication in the air space of Gibraltar region. The Declaration of Brussels brought an end to the restrictions imposed by Franco on Gibraltar in the 1950s. However, the declaration did not bring any solution to the conflict. After the Spanish accession to the Community the problem of Gibraltar entered into the agenda through different sets of policies. In preparation of the European Community's norms for proceeding to the liberalisation of air transport in 1987, the UK and Spain signed the London Agreement on 2 December 1987 on the joint use of the Gibraltar airport. However, this agreement is still to be implemented due to the will of a third party in the conflict, that of the Gibraltar government.

The problem of Gibraltar affected the process of Community legislation, particularly on issues of air traffic, external borders and any other which had direct relevance to the conflict.[78] One of the most important cases was the Convention on external frontiers. A proposal for such a convention was presented in Rome on 16 November 1990 by the Ad Hoc Group on Immigration. The purpose of the Convention was to determine the external frontiers of the European Community and to establish a control regime for the movement of people. The problem was created by the issue of Gibraltar being considered as inside or outside the external frontier. According to the Spanish argument, the fact that Gibraltar is not considered as an integral part of the UK, disqualifies it from being an integral territory of the Community. According to this argument, there was no disagreement on behalf of the UK. The problem was created by Article 30.5 of the Convention which extends the external frontiers of the EC to include territories for which its foreign policy is realised by a Member State. According to this article, Gibraltar is included inside the external frontier. This was unacceptable for the Spaniards, who wanted the negotiation of a special provision for the British colony in order to sign the Convention.

On 24 July 1991, a meeting of the Interior Ministers of the EC took place in Luxembourg with the purpose of proceeding to the adoption and signing of the Convention. As predicted, one of its points, Article 30.5

became the object for Spanish reservations. Spain offered to agree to a solution based on a similar arrangement with the 1987 Air Transport legislation. The Council of Ministers mandated UK and Spain to search for a compromise before the next Council meeting of 1 July 1991. The UK, however, refused to accept any solution similar to the combined use of the airport since that could be interpreted as 'joint sovereignty' on Gibraltar. During the Council of 1 July, the Luxembourg Presidency declared the adoption of the Convention and expressed its plans to put it forward for signature on the 19th of the month. This provoked furious protests from Spain who clearly expressed plans to reject the Convention. The Council did not made any final decision; the Convention remained closed and was frozen until a consensus could be reached. Such a consensus was not achieved until this time. Today, the Schengen Convention has replaced the functions of the Convention for external frontiers.[79] Spain became a signatory of Schengen but the problem of Gibraltar was not addressed since the UK has opted-out from Schengen and from its incorporation in the Amsterdam Treaty. However, a future conflict can be developed when and if the UK expresses its willingness to become part of the Schengen agreement.

Final Remarks

The cases in this chapter demonstrated that whenever Greece and Spain supported supranational solutions in EPC/CFSP decision-making, they exercised greater influence than when they disagreed. It can be suggested that constructive and cooperative behaviour enhanced state influence. As it is summarised in the above chart, the foreign policy behaviour that Greece and Spain adopted in all those different cases affected the outcome of EC/EU common position. The evidence suggests that the influence of Greece and Spain in EPC/CFSP has been enhanced by cooperative actor strategies and on the contrary has been damaged by obstructionist actor strategies. This was the case during the period of ideological confrontation in foreign policy between the EC and the Greek government during 1981-85. The cases illustrate the isolation of Greece, produced by its behaviour, which had as a consequence (a) the loss of the potential to influence European foreign policy and (b) the scepticism with which Greece's partners perceived any Greek foreign policy position. It is evident that even on issues such as the Mediterranean partnership in which Greece pursued a cooperative strategy, scepticism in the perceptions of other Member States by Greece's nationalist positions on Turkey and Macedonia overshadowed its position and Spain was presented as the only constructive initiator for this initiative. Spain on the other hand, despite evidence that suggests that it used EC/EU common policies for its advantage, demonstrated a cooperative strategy and that boosted its image and reputation allowing it to be more influential. Since 1996, it is this reputation that has started to change. After several years of cooperative behaviour, Greece slowly changed and moved from its past negative reputation. In contrast, Spain seems to have adopted a number of obstructive positions that might damage its constructive image.

Notes

[1]   Just before his first participation in the European Council summit, Andreas Papandreou declared to the press that: 'I do not have any preoccupation nor any kind of misunderstanding with our fellow-members. I will make them clear, though, that I am not going to accept any decision that damages our nation' (To Vima, 24.11.1981).

[2]   S. Nuttall, 1992 p.215.

[3]   The Greek press that was friendly to the government particularly celebrated the Greek action as the first impact of the change in Greek foreign policy. Also, see Valinakis, 1991, p.112.

[4]   S. Nuttall, 1992, p.202.

[5]   Y. Valinakis, 1987, pp.317-324.

[6]   S. Nuttall, 1992, p.194.

[7]   Interview with senior Greek official, Brussels, December 1997.

[8]   S. Nuttall, 1992, pp.207-208.

[9]   S. Nuttall, 1997, pp.33-34.

[10]   G. Edwards, 1984 pp.301-304.

[11]   S. Nuttall, 1992 p.211.

[12]   Ireland was very quite to renounce economic sanctions against Argentina and to condemn Britain for the use of force. Also Italy and Denmark withdrew their imposition of sanctions.

[13]   Interview with senior Greek official in the General Secretariat, Brussels, January 1998.

[14]   N. Winn, 1996, p.144.

[15]   J.C. Loulis, 1984, pp.374-391.

[16]   N. Winn, 1996, p.146.

[17]   See newspaper To Vima, 6/3/82.

[18]   See To Vima newspaper 3/11/81 for the enthusiastic impression of the public opinion, as illustrated in the press, on the change that occurred in Greek foreign policy.

[19]   See chapter 4 on the formation of Greek foreign policy, p.108.

[20]   R. Calduch, 1994, p.216.

[21]   C. del Arenal, 1994, pp.279-302.

22 Argument arisen from several interviews with politicians and senior officials in Madrid in May 1998 and in Brussels in December 1997.
23 S. Nuttall, 1992, p.302.
24 For more details on previous EC cooperation on terrorism, see J. Lodge (1981) and (1988) eds.
25 See chapter 2, p.21.
26 S. Nuttall, 1992, p.304.
27 S. Nuttall, 1992, p.307.
28 Interview with senior Spanish official, Madrid, May 1998.
29 E. Regelsberger, 1989, p.122.
30 E. Barbé, 1996b, p.268.
31 The Barcelona process started the Euro-Mediterranean partnership and is discussed in the next section.
32 R. Calduch, 1994, p.217.
33 Interview with Rafael Estrella, Madrid, May 1998.
34 UN resolution 2072-XX.
35 See chapter 6 for an in depth analysis of this argument.
36 E. Barbé, 1996, p.122.
37 S. Nuttall, 1992, p.264.
38 The UN was promising a continuous interest in the solution of the regional problems, including the Palestinian, while President Mitterrand proposed a plan for the peaceful withdrawal of Iraq with specific measures and guarantees.
39 R. Calduch, 1994, p.312.
40 Interview with Xavier Prats, Brussels, January 1998.
41 Interview with Enrique Barón-Crespo, Brussels, January 1998.
42 N. Winn, 1996, p.211.
43 A. Korakas, 1987, pp.17-55.
44 See chapter 6, pp.272-276.
45 E. Regelsberger, 1989.
46 Interview with A. Pierucci, European Commission, Brussels, December 1997.
47 E. Barbe, 1996, p.118.
48 See chapter 5, p.137.
49 E. Barbe, 1996, p.121.
50 A. Ortega, 1994, p.227.
51 'New Democracy' formed the government on its own after the third successive election in October 1990. Since October 1989, when the socialist lost the elections, there have been a coalition government of 'New Democracy' and the Left Coalition, and an ecumenical government after the April 1990 elections.
52 Libya was the only state absent from the Conference.
53 COM(94)427final, 19 October 1994, Communication from the Commission to the Council and the European Parliament: 'Strengthening the Mediterranean Policy of the EU: establishing a Euro-Mediterranean Partnership.'
54 The islets are called Imia by Greece and Kardak by Turkey.
55 Interview with K. Mitsotakis, Athens, March 1998, also confirmed in D. Papahadjopoulos (1998), p.39.
56 See Memorandum of Greece for the 1996 IGC.
57 See Memorandum of Spain for the 1996 IGC.

58   Ibid.
59   F. Rodrigo, 1996, p.32.
60   A posture that supports integration and majority voting but only to a level by retaining unanimity and the veto right in important issues of foreign policy.
61   E. Barbe, 1996c, p.37.
62   E. Barbe, 1995, p.121.
63   Both the main Spanish areas of interest, Latin America and Mediterranean-Middle East, have become important areas of EU involvement.
64   T. Skylakakis, 1995, p.32.
65   The ethnological map, which the government of Venizelos printed in Greece in 1918, referred to the Slavic populations as 'Macedonian Slavs'.
66   This name is extensively used in Greek literature, the media and governmental documents to refer to the Republic of Macedonia.
67   T. Skylakakis, 1995, p.48.
68   Council resolution, 16 December 1991.
69   Bulgaria was the first state, followed by Turkey, to recognise the new state as 'Republic of Macedonia'. The EC members did not hurry to offer diplomatic recognition to the new state because they were trying to understand the Greek position and to demonstrate solidarity to Greece.
70   An action that brought furious reactions from Greece, which considered the symbol as Greek national heritage. The symbol was dropped from the Macedonian flag after the interim agreement of New York between Greece and Macedonia.
71   A second embargo was imposed later, on 16 February 1994, by the Papandreou government.
72   It was actually an act of solidarity to Greece from the three EU members sited in the Security Council at that time, France, Britain and Spain, who proposed the entrance of Macedonia under conditions. The conditions were that it had to negotiate with Greece for the solution of the dispute, while entrance was to be with the temporary name 'FYROM' and no flag.
73   He sent a letter to Boutros Boutros-Ghali, in which he puts down new conditions for the continuation of the talks.
74   C. Stefanou and E. Xanthaki, 1997, p.82.
75   During the first five years of Greek EC membership, 1981-85, Greece consistently abused its institutional powers and caused hostile reactions from its fellow members.
76   J. Shea, 1997, p.295.
77   A. Marquina Barrio, 1985, p.892.
78   For more about legal issues created by the Gibraltar conflict in EU legislation, see C. Izquierdo Sans, 1996.
79   A. Boixareu, 1996, p.143.

PART II

4 Adaptation of National Foreign Policy

After looking at the history of participation of the foreign policies of Greece and Spain in the European Union's Common Foreign and Security Policy, this chapter endeavours to look at national foreign policies themselves. Membership of the EU constitutes a process of adaptation of national policy making, which in its general form is called Europeanisation.[1] This process takes place at different levels and different areas, from the administration of policy-making to the policy objectives and outcomes and the political culture of the Member State. Foreign policy is a part of the national policy- making process and so, to a certain degree, the adaptation process has an impact on it. This chapter explores whether this degree of adaptation affects the behavioural patterns of the Member State in foreign policy. The argument here is that the degree of adaptation of national foreign policies is *one* of the determinants of the nature of state participation in the CFSP. The chapter seeks to examine whether it is more likely for a state to pursue a constructive role and to limit the areas of differentiation from CFSP if the national foreign policy objectives and practices are adapted to the common framework. This chapter looks at (1) the process of adaptation through membership, (2) the degree of adaptation in any given period of time since accession to the EC and (3) the implications of this process on the national foreign policy. Adaptation of Greek and Spanish foreign policy is measured in this chapter by examining the change that occurred in them after membership. In order to facilitate the study of the adaptation process, this chapter is separated into three main sections, each one looking at an important aspect of national foreign policy. These aspects are the organisation, formation and differentiation of national foreign policy. In each of these, adaptation can be measured according to the degree of change in the organisation; to reflect the necessities of participation in the EU, in the formation of policy; to reflect the European orientation of policy makers, and the degree of differentiation; and to reflect the level of convergence of national foreign policy.

The section on the organisation of foreign policy deals with the way in which national foreign policy administrations have responded to membership and the changes in the administrative structure of the foreign ministries in order to cope with new requirements. An important aspect of the organisation is the way that changes in the administrative structure affect the nature of national participation in CFSP. The second section looks at the factors that determine the formation of foreign policy. It examines the process of formation of national foreign policy as well as the factors that influence this process. These factors may obstruct or facilitate the adaptation process. This chapter tests whether the process of formation of foreign policy within a Member State influences the convergence of national foreign policy decisions and positions to European standards. The last section deals with the differentiation of national foreign policy. Differentiation does not simply mean disagreement. It is usually a national position that differs from all other Member State positions and entails more than simply policy decisions. It has to do with policy areas that are considered vital for the national interest of the Member State and where the policy orientation and priorities of it differ from other Member States. Here it is important to look at the issue of differentiation as well as the frequency and the circumstances under which they appear. It also looks at the implications of membership of the EU on the degree of differentiation of the national foreign policy.

The comparison between the adaptation process of the national foreign policy of Greece and Spain is very useful because it can show whether the two countries achieved a different level of adaptation and whether this can suggest that this level of adaptation directly affected State influence in CFSP. Spain and Greece entered into a system of European Political Cooperation designed in the 1970s by the nine Member States, and the way they have accommodated to it demonstrates their ability to adapt, their acceptance of the system and the significance they attach to a common foreign policy. The ability to adapt is not only a matter of structure and the potential of the national administration, but also a matter of the Member State's general political culture that influences foreign policy formation. This chapter examines the degree to which Greece and Spain accepted a supranational system of European foreign policy as one of common policy, as opposed to a simple coordination of national foreign policies, and the way in which this common policy is achieved, as this might suggest the nature of their participation. The comparison of Greece and Spain can produce some interesting conclusions about the national perception of the accepted form of CFSP and the implications of this perception on the national adaptation process.

Greece and Spain are compared on three different levels. Initially, this chapter looks at the implications of membership on national foreign policy. Then it goes on to examine what need for adaptation was created and finally, to study the results which the adaptation process has had on the style of participation of these states. The implications of membership can be found in the administrative structure, the political culture and the foreign policy objectives of the two states. The administrative structure is dealt with in the organisation section, and it has to do with the structures that have been created in the national administration to deal with the demands of membership in the field of foreign policy. The policy formation section looks at the implications of membership on the political culture of Greece and Spain and studies the ways in which the factors that influence policy formation have reacted to the new environment. Finally, the chapter looks at whether the foreign policy objectives have gone through a process of redefinition as a result of membership. It is interesting to see whether these objectives were adapted to common European objectives or came into direct conflict with them.

It is argued that foreign policy in Greece and Spain is influenced by domestic political developments. In fact, foreign policy is an issue-area of domestic political debate. That is because foreign policy administration in Greece and Spain to a large extent depends on the government and does not have the independent power of a permanent design of strategy that the 'State Department' or the 'Foreign Office' has. Also, foreign policy in Greece and Spain forms part of the political parties' electoral campaign. This implies that State foreign policy is not given, despite the fact that there might be a long-term strategy. However, this chapter considers whether there is continuity of interests in Greece and Spain despite the dominance of parties in determining foreign policies, and whether this continuity results in policies. Foreign policy, like any other issue-area, is influenced by the program and the political platform of the party or the coalition in government. This is intensified in Greece where opposition parties are more likely to oppose the government's choices in foreign policy than support them for electoral benefits. The Greek particularity in this area is due to the fact of its 'securitisation' of national foreign policy.[2] This makes foreign policy a subject of domestic political debate and also an area in which the government wants to score successes. That is one of the reasons that Greek foreign policy in several cases followed public opinion instead of the advice of experts.[3] These however, are not necessarily successes of Greek foreign policy but rather they are presented as such for electoral gains. Papandreou's foreign policy in the 1980s used the blocking tactic in EPC to present an independent foreign policy to the Greek public that brought him electoral benefits. In this logic, Greece exploits the execution of its foreign policy program to gain domestic political advances in a similar way that a government tries to exploit the implementation of its program in health, education or any other issue-area.[4] The factors that influence national foreign policy are as important as the policy itself. That is because the objective behind foreign policy formation is not necessarily the 'national interest' but can be the interest of the government, the party in government or the personal political interest of a particular minister. In Spain, the change of government in 1996 brought significant changes to what was considered as foreign policy strategy according to national interest. In Greece similar changes occurred even when there was a change of foreign minister in the same government, e.g. when George Papandreou replaced Theodore Pangalos in 1999. This is as far as the different interpretation of national interest is concerned. However, there are cases, such as that of the Greek foreign minister in 1990-1992, Antonis Samaras, where he implemented a particular policy to advance his personal interests of political career. This chapter looks at the adaptation process of national foreign policy and its impact upon foreign policy behaviour, by taking into account the domestic factors that affect the adaptation process and the formation of foreign policy.

Organisation of Foreign Policy

The administrative structures of both Greece and Spain underwent important changes to cope with the demands of membership. The specific issues under consideration in this section are the actual effects of membership on the organisation of national foreign policy, the areas in which most and least adaptation has taken place and the reason for these, as well as the effect of organisational adaptation on the nature of participation of Greece and Spain in CFSP. In both countries, membership resulted in changes in the administrative structure.

Greek Administrative Structures

In Greece, the overall coordination and representation of Greek European policy was shifted from the Ministry of Coordination, later to be renamed as the Ministry of National Economy, to the Ministry of Foreign Affairs (MFA). The main reason for this was that, during the association agreement, all relations between Greece and the EC were of a commercial nature. Membership created a necessity for a coordination of the different ministries on European affairs since the EC affected more sectors. The MFA became responsible for the functions of forming, coordinating and presenting the Greek policy in the Community institutions. The MFA took on the role of 'gatekeeper' of European policy and as the Permanent Representation in Brussels was subject to it, any interaction between any other ministry and the Brussels representation had to go through the MFA. This role was passed to the MFA from the Ministry of National Economy since the relationship between Greece and the EC ceased to be a purely economic one, such as the relationship during the association agreement. Membership created the need for most of the departments' interaction with the EC institution, so a coordination of this interaction was necessary and the MFA was considered the appropriate link. The structure of the MFA has undergone significant changes several times since the accession of Greece into the EC in 1981.[5] The last time such restructuring was undertaken was with the Presidential Decree No.230 of 28 July 1998.[6] The new structure of the ministry makes a separation between issues of the first and third pillar of the EU and those of the second pillar.[7] The DG C is responsible for issues of pillars one and three, while DG A is responsible for pillar two. A reason for this is that DG C became the link between the EU and the different Greek departments, while the MFA wanted to maintain its supreme control over foreign policy and CFSP, so it kept it under DG A. Among other EU issues, the Directorate General C for EU affairs is responsible for EU external relations which are not subjects of CFSP. The C1 Directorate deals with European external relations, which are subjects of the first pillar, while the C4 Directorate is concerned with the third pillar, including the Schengen agreement. The Directorate General C (DG-C) is headed by the General Secretary for European affairs and is under the supervision of the Alternate Minister. The issues of CFSP are subjects of the A11 Directorate, which is part of the A' Directorate General for Political Affairs. This Directorate General is headed by the General Secretary for Political Affairs who has the grade of a Political Director.

However, inside the Directorate General A (DG-A) exists a separation of Directorates into two, each one a subject of a different deputy General Director. A11 is subject to the first Director, who is responsible for all issues of foreign policy except those of Cyprus (A2), the Balkans (A3) and Turkey (A4). The second deputy General Director is under the direct leadership of the Deputy Foreign Minister, who is responsible for Greece's 'national issues', that is Cyprus, Turkey and the Balkans. All three ministers are accountable to the Prime Minister, the Ministerial Council and the Greek Parliament. Although the Minister is the overall person responsible for foreign policy, the independent responsibility and actions of the two junior ministers in designated areas can create problems and conflicts in Greek foreign policy making. A serious problem that this organisation has caused is the Greek representation in the Council of Ministers. Greece is represented in the Foreign Affairs Council by the Foreign Minister and in the General Affairs Council by the Alternate Minister. This has caused problems of coordination of the Greek position in the European institutions several times.

Despite the coordination between the different Directorates, this separation that gives a special treatment to the Greek national issues, can create problems of coordination when these issues are discussed in CFSP. For instance, in a case where economic aid and humanitarian assistance for the Balkans is discussed as a joint action in CFSP, there are three different offices that deal with the issue. The subject obviously becomes an issue of A11 as it is discussed in CFSP. It also becomes an issue of A3 on Southeast Europe, which is directly linked to the Deputy Foreign Minister, and a subject of C1 on European external relations which is linked to the Alternate Minister. Another area of possible administrative problems can be the fact that the DG-A is responsible for the coordination of political issues when these are dealt by other DGs with the exception of DG-C.[8] That means, for example, that when the Directorate C1-III on EU-Turkish relations deals with the issue of the fourth financial protocol to Turkey, there is a problem of coordination and representation with A4 on Turkey and A11 on CFSP, as this issue is a highly politicised issue of foreign policy in Greece and is linked with the Greek position on Turkey in CFSP. In addition to that, the fact that Greece is the only Member State that is represented in the General Affairs Council by the junior minister (alternate) and not by the foreign minister, is an indication of the potential conflict that this situation could create. This is a product of Greece's separation of foreign policy issues from other EU policy-making.[9]

Spanish Administrative Structures

In Spain, like in Greece, membership necessitated a restructuring of the administration.[10] For the same reasons as in Greece, the Ministry of Foreign Affairs took the role of gatekeeper. After several changes in its structure, in 1998, Spain incorporated the General Secretariat for the EC/EU that was set up after the Spanish accession in the EC with the General Secretariat for Foreign Policy.[11] The difference with Greece is that in Spain the separation between EC and CFSP issues ends at the level of the Directorate General and such issues are linked under the responsibility of the General Secretary. Also, there is no separation of CFSP issues with other issues of national foreign policy. Instead, the General Secretary for Foreign Policy and the EU is in charge of coordination of all General Directorates of foreign policy for different regions and is responsible for supervising CFSP matters. In order to assist the General Secretary, a Deputy GS post was created exclusively for CFSP issues. This demonstrates the importance that Spain gave to the CFSP framework. These changes had an important implication for the efficiency of the administration dealing with European foreign policy, namely, that the CFSP issues became linked together with the general administration of Spanish foreign policy.[12] This was to ensure the successful influence of the CFSP agenda and the identification between Spanish and European interest in foreign policy. The result was the enhancement of the efficiency of Spanish European foreign policy, since the COREU system was not isolated from the general formation of Spanish foreign policy, and also in the improved representation of Spanish policy in CFSP.

Comparison   An area in which changes have occurred as a result of membership, due to administrative adaptation to European standards, is that of the nature and style of foreign policy. In both countries, foreign policy became more of a collective exercise involving a wider number of actors, such as technocrats, experts and diplomats. In Greece these actors were drawn either from inside the MFA or from other specialised ministries, according to their area of expertise. This fact has made foreign policy administration more 'open' and more 'transparent'.[13] However, this is not a direct product of membership but more of the democratisation process that developed the accountability of foreign policy-makers. Previously, foreign policy was highly influenced by the US domination. In Greece, the ministry had special envoys in the American Embassy that served as links with the

CIA.[14] As far as CFSP is concerned, the Greek administration has benefited from the huge amount of information received from other Member States through the COREU system, which covers issues of foreign policy because Greece lacks the operational capacity for its own production of that amount of information. Greek foreign policy administration is able to develop a more coherent policy and increase its negotiation skills and bargaining power as a result of being a member of the EU CFSP. This bargaining power and negotiation skills is identified in the relations of Greece with third states. An example of this has been the change of position of Pakistan from recognising the Turkish Republic of Northern Cyprus (November 1983) when Greece threatened to veto its commercial agreements with the EC in the mid 1980s. By being a member of the EU, Greece has upgraded its position in international affairs. However, the separation between normal Greek foreign policy and CFSP creates a contradiction in the Greek nature and style of foreign policy. On the one hand, there is the coherent approach and development of policies on CFSP, and on the other is an administration that presents a nationalistic foreign policy on issues that are regarded as vital for Greek interests. That is why during the Yugoslav crisis in the beginning of the 1990s the Greek government's position demonstrated a contradiction of Europeanism and Nationalism. On the one side, the Greek government was supporting the development of CFSP and adopted a constructive attitude to the development of common policies. On the other side, however, when the discussion was centred on the Greek 'national issues', the Greek attitude in CFSP rapidly changed to support what was considered as its national interest.

Spain on the other hand, has benefited from participating in the system of CFSP and from the advantages that such participation has contributed to the role and prestige of Spanish foreign policy on the international stage, but unlike Greece, she did not make an artificial separation between different foreign policy issues. On the contrary, Spain incorporated the CFSP process in all its foreign policy structures in order to add a European dimension to its own policy and to apply common European policies in all departments. It can be argued that this was a strategic decision taken by Felipe González to enhance Spain's Europeanisation. This had the advantage of sharing information and expertise from the different departments of which all come under the supervision of the General Secretary for Foreign Policy and the EU. The whole restructuring of the Spanish administration had as its purpose the adaptation of the whole diplomatic machinery to Spain's growing international role as enhanced by its participation in CFSP.[15] As a result of the development of the Political Director[16] of the MFA, the nature of Spanish foreign policy became Europeanised, with CFSP as an integral part of the foreign policy making process. This result was a product of the realisation of the opportunities for influencing in CFSP that caused the restructuring of the MFA.

Areas of More or Less Adaptation

In order to evaluate the level and consequences of the adaptation process of the administration, this chapter looks at the areas in Greek and Spanish foreign policy which were more or less adapted. In Greece, three areas can be identified that changed most significantly due to membership of the EC/EU. These areas are (1) the function of the organisation structure, (2) the information management, and (3) the negotiation skills. The new structure in the Ministry of Foreign Affairs were necessary in order for the administration to cope with the demands of membership. In order to achieve efficiency in European policy making it was modernised along the lines of the administration structures of other Member States.[17] In CFSP, Greece familiarised itself with the mechanisms of European political cooperation both in the A11 Directorate and in the Political Committee of the Council of Ministers. In the late 1990s, Greece demonstrated a large degree of adaptation in using the structures of political cooperation in the EU.[18] Alterations in the management of information were important in order to achieve efficiency in the management of CFSP issues. Greece took advantage of the large amount of information received through the COREU system from the experienced Member States in foreign policy, with more extensive networks, in order to familiarise itself with the process and to gain political importance in international relations.[19] This was in fact one of the most important benefits of EU membership in foreign policy. Indeed, on several occasions, Greece used its status as an EU member in order to increase its negotiation position against third countries, something that Greece extensively used to improve its negotiation power against Turkey.[20] Given the fact that the Greek foreign policy is part of a large network of cooperation in which national administrations are in direct interaction with each other, the European experience has been a learning process and partly accounts for the increase of the negotiation skills of the Greek diplomats. This can be seen by examining the attitude, knowledge and selection criteria of the Greek diplomats in different times from accession until today.[21]

However, there are two areas in which the adaptation process has been minimal. It can be argued that, in a way, these areas limit the benefits reaped in the areas of greater adaptation. These areas are the separation of competence on foreign policy issues between CFSP issues and Greek national foreign policy issues, as mentioned earlier, and the selection procedure of the personnel. The separation of foreign policy issues has many reasons and many consequences. The reasons for the selection of specific issues of national concern are given in chapter 5 and are related to Greece's geopolitical situation. The criteria for the selection of 'national issues', it can be argued, are their importance on Greece's territorial or ethnic integrity. That is why all such issues are related through territorial conflicts or problems of ethnic minorities. The implications of this separation for the administration are that when issues of foreign policy, which are regarded as 'national issues' for Greece, are discussed in CFSP, the administrative personnel who deal with them differ from those with experience of CFSP. This in turn, is one of the reasons for the lack of comprehension of the Greek arguments by Greece's counterparts. It may also result in the exclusion of these 'national issues' from the normal CFSP process.

The second area is that of the selection procedure of the personnel. This is a general observation of the Greek political culture, which reflects on the MFA as well. As many scholars observe,[22] the dilemma is the problematic relationship between the State and the political parties. As Dimitris Sotiropoulos argues, the Greek bureaucracy has been unable to shape policy output in the way it has in other western democracies, such as the UK and Germany, because of the problem of clientelism in the recruitment process. In turn, because of the clientelist culture, the administration is characterised by weak organisation, that is, it lacks the ability of a foreign policy élite that could act like an expert think-tank, maintaining continuity in Greek foreign policy planning and advising the Minister to avoid possible traps and mistakes. Rather, the administration is dominated by the political leadership because the personnel are selected according to political criteria and not on the basis of qualifications and expertise. This weak organisation strengthens the governing political parties' ability to dominate the State and shape it to their own needs. It is customary that each time the governing party arrives in government, it changes all the high posts of the administration in order to place people of ideological allegiance in the party. This creates the contradiction that 'the Greek State is top-heavy, mismanaged, overburdened with excess labour but understaffed in terms of technical expertise'.[23]

In Spain, the adaptation process was much more successful. However, Felipe González, who started the process of restructuring of administration in order to achieve the Europeanisation of Spanish policy, was assisted by the fact that clientelism was associated with Francoism and was successfully rejected after the end of the regime. The organisational restructuring gave Spain the opportunity for an efficient and effective preparation of foreign policy. The system of national participation in CFSP is not separate from the bilateral foreign policy decision making but each one complements each other. In that way, the Spanish administration has been able to manage the information received from the COREU system to complement its bilateral foreign policy network and also to use its own areas of expertise, such as Latin America, to complement CFSP or to develop a capacity as an acknowledged 'expert' on Latin America in the EU. Another area of successful adaptation has been the quick familiarisation of the Spanish diplomatic personnel with the function of the European institution, and in this case, of the institutions of CFSP. This resulted in a better representation of Spain in the institutions in terms of quality of participation and also the achievement of leading roles for Spanish diplomats in the EU and in particular in CFSP. Since Spain has been isolated for decades, Spanish diplomats lacked the experience of international relations. However, the quality of participation and their dedication to European integration made this achievement possible, since they were seen as impartial, promoting European rather than Spanish interests. Another advantage of the Spanish foreign policy administration has been continuity.[24] Unlike Greece, the personnel of the MFA are selected with qualitative criteria of their expertise and are working for the State, which functions independently from political parties. This process is supported by the fact that the administration does not alter with the change of government. Even in the highest posts, such as the General Directors of the MFA and the Spanish ambassador to the COREPER, the Spanish diplomats have remained the same, to a large extent, despite changes of government. This is not to argue that changes do not occur, but that they do not occur for political reasons of party allegiance. However, there is an area in which the Spanish administration has not been able to be totally incorporated into the European system, that is the Spanish foreign policy on Latin America, which is considered vital for Spain. This area is in the competence of the State Secretary for International Cooperation and Latin

America and it is not under the supervision of the General Secretary for Foreign Policy.[25] The consequence of the maintenance of Latin America as an exclusive area for Spanish foreign policy is that Spain contributed to a greater involvement of the EU in the region only in term of economic agreements since all the EU agreements with Latin America are in the sphere of economic cooperation and the region is excluded from the areas for joint action of CFSP. That is because Spain withholds the privilege of special relations with Latin America and made all links between the region and Brussels in foreign policy/CFSP to pass through Madrid.

Impact of Organisational Adaptation

The degree of administrative adaptation of national foreign policies due to membership of the EU, has an important impact on the nature of the participation in CFSP of Greece and Spain. One of the most important impacts is the familiarity of the national administration with the European decision-making process. Three areas identify this familiarity: the role of information, the processes and the bargaining. Due to the increased level of information obtained from the CFSP process, national administrations in both countries were able to alter their participation patterns, in terms of the way they negotiated and presented their views. This implies that they were able to base their national positions and proposals for common positions or joint actions on a more coherent basis, given the better information and fuller picture that they have of any case under discussion. As a result of this, national positions are based on an improved analysis of information which makes national participation in CFSP more effective. However, this does depend on the ability of the administration to effectively analyse the information received. This is an area in which differentiation exists between Greece and Spain. The superior technical expertise that Spain possesses has given her the possibility of preparing effective positions, proposals and initiatives. Due to Greece's problem of party politics in the administrative structure, the process of information and preparation of the national position has been subject to party political objectives rather than State interests. This means that because the majority of the personnel is selected on party political criteria, their objective in analysing and preparing the national position is not the State interest but the Party's ideology. During the Macedonian crisis between 1992-1995, the Greek administration was unable to form a coherent proposal in order to achieve a common policy, and instead became hostage of the party political debate that was directed at the domestic audience. Officials of the Foreign Ministry were unable to express an opinion and influence the direction of foreign policy which was left to the agreement of the major political parties on nationalistic policies moved by public opinion. However, in the case of Kosovo in 1999, Greece presented a different face which was more adapted to the European standards and was able to implement a policy of disassociation from nationalistic tensions in public opinion. This may suggest that there has been a change in Greece's approach to 'national issues' that affected all levels of foreign policy-making.

The Spanish administration, because of its relative independence from party political objectives, was able in many cases to analyse information and form positions on the long-term interest of the State and not be guided by domestic factors. One of these cases is Morocco, with whom Spain has been promoting a strong European link and support, even when domestic opinion in Spain was negative because of human rights violations in Morocco, the problem of fishing or the issue of Western Sahara.[26]

Another area is the familiarity with the processes of CFSP. A higher level of adaptation of the national administration is caused to an extent by a greater degree of familiarity with the way decisions are taken in the second pillar and the way common positions are formed. This familiarity makes cooperation and consultation an integral part of the process, since it creates the need for positive interaction with others to ensure success. From the state of isolation, where national positions are formed independently and are communicated to the others for debate, the adaptation process transforms the national administration to a state of complex interaction. This interaction makes the national position more of a product of cooperation and consultation, in which national representatives seek common ground and common proposals. Apart from the familiarity with the process of decision-making, another factor which influences this development is the familiarity that develops between national representatives. Diplomats in the COREPER and the working groups get to know one another which creates a positive environment for discussion, cooperation and compromise. This is where continuity in national representation is very important for the nature of participation of the Member State. Spain has improved its level of effectiveness and its reputation because of the continuity of its personnel in European foreign affairs, dealing with more experienced partners. Participation in CFSP procedures became a learning process for Spanish diplomats to use their achieved skills to enhance the Spanish role in European foreign policy and to achieve common policies.[27] Although the Greek administration has demonstrated signs of improvement in this familiarisation process, the changes of personnel according to the party in government has limited the potential of Greece, in promoting a consistent policy and coherent behaviour.

The final area is familiarity with bargaining in the decision-making process. By taking part in the every day process of decision-making in the working groups of the Council of Ministers and the COREPER, national representatives not only become more familiar with each other but also with the process of negotiation, bargaining and solution-seeking. This process has had important implications for the nature of participation of Member States since all issues in the EU agenda have become interrelated. Therefore, the national position on a specific issue depends upon others' positions on other issues. The accession of a new member (Cyprus) depended on EU relations with another state (Turkey), or the future of an EU policy-area (social cohesion funds) was linked in the Edinburgh Summit with another EU activity (enlargement to the East). Although this process of trade-offs can be seen as buying and selling of positions, it facilitates a mutual understanding between Member States, providing that it is not taken to extremes. The argument here is that a higher degree of adaptation to the system of European foreign policy has, as a result the Europeanisation of national policy that makes trade-offs beneficial not only for the Member State but for the whole of the Union. When the degree of adaptation is lower, the priority is the Member State's own national interest which can lead to extremes. Therefore, in order to achieve its objective in one area, a State holds the Union hostage in another.

Greece has many times traded its consent, for other gains. In foreign policy, Greece particularly used the issue of EU-Turkey relations as hostage in order to achieve benefits from its counterparts. The 1995 Greek removal of veto on the EU-Turkey customs union was subject to the unconditional start of accession negotiations with Cyprus.[28]The continuing veto of the fourth financial protocol to Turkey has also been used as a tool to achieve future concessions from the Union. This extreme practice sprung from the fact that the issues of national importance for Greece are dealt with outside the scope of the CFSP, so the objectives are purely national. However, this practice cannot benefit Greek interests, since it creates an environment of isolation which leads to decisions such as the one made by the European Commission of October 1998 that found a way to incorporate the finance to Turkey into a proposal that requires qualified majority voting, and thus, overcome the Greek veto.[29] Spain on the other hand has also used trade-off practices, but to a different extent and in a different way. When Felipe Gonzalez threatened to veto EU enlargement in 1993, during the Edinburgh Summit,[30] he did so in order to achieve the deepening of the social cohesion funds and by explaining the benefits of such a development for the Union as a whole and not for the narrow Spanish interests. This shows the importance of the way issues are presented in negotiations. The difference in the nature of negotiation, therefore, can be attributed to a large extent, to the degree of adaptation of national foreign policy to the EU structures. This degree of adaptation is illustrated by the level of administrational adaptation but also by the process of formation of national foreign policy. The next section examines whether the higher the degree of adaptation at the administration level is, the more likely for the policy formation process is to follow the same patterns.

Formation of National Foreign Policy

This section looks at factors that influence foreign policy formation, the changes in these factors (if any), the way in which these factors and processes have influenced the adaptation process and the impact they have had on the nature of participation of Member States. The purpose is to see how national foreign policy is formed and what the implications of the adaptation process have been on the policy formation. This is important because the process of policy formation and its implementation influence the actual outcome of the policy. Therefore, the degree of adaptation of the formation process has a direct impact upon the nature of the policy and the way in which it is presented in CFSP. Thus, foreign policy behaviour depends, to an extent, on the factors that influence foreign policy formation.

Factors and Changes

The factors which influence foreign policy formation can be grouped into endogenous and exogenous factors. These factors can be both actors in foreign and domestic policy or geopolitical influences. In the domestic sphere, the actors can be the government, the leadership of the government or the foreign ministry, as well as political parties. Domestic influences on foreign policy can be a particular ideology of the government, national tradition and political culture, as well as the influence of the media and public opinion. External factors can be other states as actors, particularly the neighbours, or the state's geopolitical position, its economic interests and events in the region as geopolitical influences. The adaptation process of a Member State foreign policy to the CFSP produces significant changes to the factors which influence foreign policy formation. These changes might be caused by membership of the EU and they can act as factors which influence foreign policy formation according to the degree of adaptation that occurred. Membership of the EU creates new actors who influence national foreign policy formation such as other Member States, and the European institutions for example the Commission and the European Parliament. There are also new structural influences, such as the new environment of participation in common positions and joint actions, and the different tools that are offered for the promotion of the national foreign policy in an extended framework.[31] It is important to look at these factors and changes which occurred because of membership of the EU of Greece and Spain in order to identify possible links between these changes and the degree of adaptation to European foreign policy as well as to find out the results of the adaptation process by comparing the two states.

Greece In Greece, because of the weakness of the administration that has been seen in the previous section, foreign policy formation is vested to a large degree with the government, or to put it more accurately, with the political party that is in power. The ideology of the governing party, or the leading faction in the party, is one of the main factors in the formation of foreign policy objectives. During the 1980s, that was the main reason for Greece's total differentiation for its counterparts. The New Democracy government in the early 1990s pursued its own objectives based on its neo-liberal ideology, while the intra-party conflict between nationalists and Europeanists was also demonstrated in foreign policy in the case of Macedonia. Finally, the new PASOK government of Simitis portrays its own ideology of modernisation.[32]

Foreign policy is also an area in which the government has a relative advantage over the opposition parties. The government can use foreign policy to win electoral battles at a low cost.[33] It has been suggested by many public opinion polls that whenever there is an issue of foreign policy in Greece, which takes huge proportions in the press, it becomes the most important issue of concern for the public.[34] This has to do with the Greek particularities in its geopolitical situation. These issues are then exploited either by the government or the opposition because they know that the party, which can identify itself with public demands, can gain electoral advances, particularly at election times.[35] That is why the government is very sensitive to public opinion in order to claim national victories in foreign policy issues. Often, because of the above reasons, the government's objective for responding to a foreign policy issue is not the solution to the issue itself but the electoral benefits that can be drawn from any given national position, or to avoid any electoral defeat. In this, the media plays a very important role. Foreign policy issues attract a good deal of publicity and the media acts as a pressure group, to influence the formation of national foreign policy, and is correspondingly used to deliver the government's image and positions to the public.

External factors in Greek foreign policy mainly have to do with Greece's geopolitical position, that is the Balkan environment. This is characterised by traditional conflicts and new opportunities for Greek foreign policy, particularly in the economic sphere. The traditional conflict with Turkey, in particular, has been the greatest factor that influences Greek foreign policy. This has been achieved on two levels. First, the issues related to Turkey form a significant part of the agenda, and second, the consequences of other foreign policy decisions on the Turkish issue are major considerations for the Greek government. The fact that the issue forms a large part of the Greek foreign policy agenda is a result of its securitisation.[36] This creates an environment in which tradition and political culture become very influential in foreign policy. One of the effects of securitisation is that it makes foreign policy formation conservative. Systemic changes are perceived as threatening to the status quo. For this reason, Greek foreign policy is usually conservative in relation to the changes and developments in the Balkan region. Any development in the neighbouring region is seen in terms of the implications for the Greek-Turkish dispute. The revival of Muslim groups in Albania, Bosnia and Kosovo is perceived as an increase in Turkish influence in the region which should be avoided at any cost.

In the same way, the issue of self-determination in the case of ex-Yugoslavia, and particularly Bosnia and Kosovo, has been seen as a threat to the status quo in the region, something that could have implications on the Turkish minority in Thrace or other minorities in the Greek State. In that sense, foreign policy decisions, not only in the Balkan region, but also in the CFSP and the general international stage, are made under the light of the Greek-Turkish conflict. This is revealed for example by the Greek demand during the institutional changes in the EU to include a clause in the

Treaty that guarantees the Union's external borders. This demand is influenced by the desire to create a European front at its eastern borders. To mention the Turkish argument, Greece wanted to put the European flag in each one of the thousand islands and islets of the Aegean Sea. After the signing of the Turkish-Israeli military-training agreement in February 1996,[37] Greece was quick to approach Syria and develop a series of agreements and common military manoeuvres. The perception that 'the enemy of your enemy is your friend' and vice-versa has been an important feature of Greek foreign policy. Together with traditional and cultural factors this served to develop Greek foreign policy links with Serbia, Russia, Armenia, Syria and other Arab States, as well as support for the Kurds.

Structural changes that were caused by the Greek accession to the European Community had contradictory consequences for its foreign policy. For instance, Greek foreign policy objectives came closer to the Europeans following an adaptation process that started in the late 1980s rather than immediately after accession. However, this adaptation excluded the issues perceived as 'national' for Greece. The contradiction is that Greece was now relying on the EU for support but on the other hand is using the change in its international status and the widening of its foreign policy scope to promote its own national objectives through CFSP. The widening of its foreign policy scope meant that Greece, through its participation in CFSP could form policy positions on issues that were outside its scope before membership. Given its status as an EU member, Greece also increased its negotiation power in world politics. This power proved beneficial for Greece in many cases. For instance, Greece managed to avoid the recognition of the Turkish Republic of North Cyprus, by a number of countries, by threatening to veto their association or cooperation agreements with the EU. Greece therefore used a structural change to promote its own objective and extended the Turkish factor into the new areas created by this change.

Spain In Spain, as in most European states, foreign policy has been an activity for the established foreign policy administrative elite. This means that, although the government has a significant input to the design of foreign policy, there is a large degree of continuity in the administration which creates a long term objective and strategy of Spanish foreign policy, something that is constant despite the changes of government. It has been a strategy created during the democratic transition in Spain as it moved away from the Francoist era. This move can be described as an ideology which greatly influenced Spanish foreign policy formation. It is an ideology of Europeanisation of foreign policy and a break with all the old isolationist elements which dominated the Francoist era. A foreign policy incorporated into the European system has been seen as the prime objective since that was the only way to upgrade the Spanish role in Europe and on the international stage.

Leadership in the government and in the ministry of foreign affairs is an important factor of policy formation in Spain as in every State.[38] Spanish foreign policy enjoys a large degree of consensus on the direction of policy which makes the differences between governments an issue of presentation and image rather than substance and context. The direction and objectives of foreign policy do not form part of the domestic political debate in Spain. This has facilitated the development of consistency in foreign policy formation and continuity in the administration which created an elite political culture. Unlike Greece, the influence of domestic factors, such as the media and public opinion, on foreign policy is limited by the fact that it is not a highly contested issue in Spanish politics.

However, a characteristic of Spanish foreign policy is decentralisation. Following the development of the autonomous communities and the federalisation of Spain after the Constitution of 1978, the autonomous regions are able to develop a kind of foreign policy on issues that affect them.[39] This is not *de jure* right to make foreign policy but *de facto*. Autonomous Communities have the ability to conduct their own external economic relations. This is a foreign policy capability that has political implications upon their relations to the central administration. In an informal way, their relation to the central government is collaboration by means of negotiations, in the formation of the State's foreign policy.[40] Regions act as lobby groups and for that reason their successful input depends on their power of influence in the Spanish political system. The prime example is Catalonia, which has had a significant influence on the formation of foreign policy because of the power of the Catalan political parties have acquired after being part of the governing coalition for many years and with different governments.

Tradition and culture are also very important factors in the shaping of Spanish foreign policy.[41] For this reason Latin America has been and will continue to be a very special case for Spanish policy. For similar reasons, Spanish foreign policy concerning the Maghreb and the Arab World is also of great importance. Apart from the cultural and traditional Spanish links to the Arab World, the geopolitical position of Spain influences its policies towards the Mediterranean region. Spanish membership of the EU, like in Greece, brought changes to the systemic framework and the nature of the actors. Membership placed Spain in an enhanced role in the region as well as on the international stage. The end of isolationism for Spanish foreign policy has influenced both the factors and the processes of policy formation by changing the very objectives of it. Participation in European foreign policy has offered Spain the possibility of playing a stabilising and cooperative role in the region by 'Europeanising' the Maghreb region and the South Mediterranean in general, in the sense of creating links for cooperation and development with the EU. This philosophy of cooperation and development has become the prime objective of Spanish foreign policy after membership and this has been the main difference between Greece and Spain. This difference is identified in the objective of their foreign policy in CFSP which was an important factor in the formation of their policies and attitudes. Greece was trying to take advantage of the systemic changes and the benefits which these brought to the potential influence of Greek foreign policy in order to pursue a sense of security in its region by building barriers and fortresses. Spain, on the contrary, was trying to incorporate its region into the democratic principles of the European framework and to enhance cooperation between them, thus, trying in this way to achieve stability and security.

Implications of Policy Formation Adaptation on the Nature of Participation

The factors and processes of foreign policy formation, as well as the changes to them caused by membership, demonstrate a particular degree of adaptation in the formation process of foreign policy of the Member States. The degree of this adaptation in the formation level influences the outcome of the policy or the final national position in CFSP. This in turn influences the attitude of the state in CFSP, as well as the orientation of its foreign policy which influences its participation in European foreign policy instruments. In order to facilitate the comparison between Greece and Spain the present analysis will identify three areas in which the adaptation process in policy formation has had an important impact. These are foreign policy objectives, behaviour in CFSP and national foreign policy making. As seen in the previous section, membership has influenced the foreign policy objectives of both Greece and Spain. However, the results have been different according to the degree of adaptation that occurred. In Greece, the formation of foreign policy on 'national issues', that is, those issues that are considered vital for national security, enjoys a considerably lower degree of adaptation than other issues. In these issues the European influence in the formation of policy has been kept to the minimum. The formation of foreign policy in these areas resisted any attempt to moderate the ethnocentrism of Greek foreign policy and the incorporation of European objectives in these particular issues. In contrast, membership of the EU provided a framework for the strengthening of this ethnocentrism. Particularly in the Turkish case but also in other cases in the Balkans, such as Albania and Macedonia, Greece used membership as a tool of strength to impose its own national perspective and objectives in the EU and in the region.

In the model of the two-way relationship that characterises successful adaptation to the EU, that is, the Europeanisation of national foreign policy and the incorporation of national priorities in the European agenda, Greece has only partially adapted to the first, but has put a great deal of emphasis on the second. The Europeanisation of Greek foreign policy has excluded its national issues, while the incorporation of these issues in the EU agenda became the main objective of its foreign policy in order to enhance its position. Greece's objective was to achieve the support of the whole of the EU in its arguments and was ready to block any development that was seen as unwanted for Greek interests. So, the adaptation process on the formation of foreign policy, or the lack of adaptation in respect of the Greek national issues, had implications for its foreign policy objectives, which have been the export of the ethnocentrism to the EU agenda and the development of a notion of security provided by the EU against its neighbours. It had also implications for Greek foreign policy behaviour in CFSP, which has been the support of its national position in a positive or negative way. The significance of this is that the exclusion of European influences in the process of foreign policy formation concerning its national issues has created an individualist behaviour in CFSP where, what was perceived as Greek interest, was pursued without any consideration of a common European interest. Finally, it also had implications for national foreign policy-making since it created a contradiction within the Greek foreign policy. On the one hand there were the issues for which European influence was welcomed and on the other hand, the issues were excluded. This implied the development of a nationalistic element in Greek national foreign policy and a lack of a global perspective of its strategy that makes foreign policy short-sighted.

Spanish foreign policy formation, in contrast to that of Greece, incorporated the European dimension in the whole process of foreign policy formation. Spain developed the two-way relationship by Europeanising its foreign policy process and objectives and also by putting its own priorities on the EU agenda. It also linked the Spanish interest with the common European one in the sense that its foreign policy objectives incorporated the dimension of a common European interest. This was a consequence of the high degree of adaptation achieved in the policy formation process that changed the direction of its strategy. Security was no longer seen as the defence of the integrity of the State, as in the Greek case, but as an attempt to Europeanise its neighbourhood. This new strategy is also demonstrated in the development of a new General Directorate in the Ministry of Foreign Affairs for International Cooperation and Development. This change illustrates the new direction of the Spanish foreign policy objective towards cooperation and development of its neighbouring region, as well as a global perspective, which is achieved by its adaptation to a common European interest. As a consequence of this, the Spanish behaviour in CFSP became one of constructive participation with the aim of building common positions. This was achieved because of the identification of the Spanish with the European interest, and vice versa, which was the product of the European orientation and adaptation of Spanish foreign policy. Finally, this high degree of adaptation had implications for national foreign policy-making, since it became a collective activity in which the major priorities of the Spanish foreign policy formation were to end the isolationism of a nationalist foreign policy and to incorporate Spanish foreign policy into the European framework.

Differentiation of National Foreign Policy

Both the administrative structure and the policy formation process illustrate the degree of adaptation achieved in the process of national foreign policy-making in Greece and Spain, and its implications on the nature of participation of the two countries in CFSP. The last section of this chapter examines, by means of comparison, the areas where adaptation has not taken place. These are characterised by differentiation from the common European position. The aim of this section is to find out whether and why this differentiation took place and look at the factors that influenced it. The objective is to test the proposition that this differentiation is more likely to occur when there is a low degree of adaptation, and also that a continuing differentiation from the common European position causes the isolation of the Member State and feeds the nationalist elements in its national foreign policy-making. This chapter also looks at the extent to which differentiation in national foreign policy is not necessarily against the common European position, but can exist in areas where there is not enough interest for a common EU response. However, even in these cases differentiation demonstrates a lack of adaptation as well as a lack of potential on behalf of the Member State to influence the development of a common position. In order to distinguish between different issues and the various possible implications for the foreign policy behaviour of the Member State in CFSP, this chapter looks at three groups of issues; those put on the EU agenda by the Member State; those added by other Member States; and issues excluded from the agenda. The latter may be done by the affected Member States or by its fellow-members.

Issues put on the Agenda by the Member State

Putting an issue on the CFSP agenda is on its own a sign of adaptation and influence. In order to do that, the Member State has to follow the rules and processes of EU agenda setting and managed to persuade its partners for the common interest in the issue. Sometimes, however, Presidencies have the power to impose issues on the agenda without previous consultation with others. These attempts are very unlikely to produce common policies. The difference lies in the objectives of the proposal and the considerations behind it. As the European Union consists of different and diverse Member States, difference between foreign policy priorities is normal and acceptable since the EU is a puzzle of different pieces that make up the whole picture. The problem arises when a particular Member State tries to use the common framework of CFSP in order to pursue national rather than common interests without Europeanising its national goal.

Greece On several occasions, Greece put issues on the agenda where the Greek position differed significantly from its fellow members. In most of these cases, the issues had to do with its conflict with Turkey. The questions that should be asked are why these issues were added to the agenda, is there a difference in the way they were presented that was caused by adaptation, and what have been the consequences of this development. The issues which Greece brought to the CFSP agenda in the ministerial meetings have been issues related to its dispute with Turkey, such as the request for a condemnation of the Turkish aggression, issues of human rights in Turkey including the Kurdish case, and issues related to the Cypriot problem. The main reasons for the Greek attempt to communitarise these issues were, first, to achieve sufficient backing for its arguments, creating a common European front against Turkey, and second, to make CFSP act as a pressure group for the solution of these problems. Greece decided to communitarise its conflict with Turkey because of the potential benefits it perceived from such an action. Greece saw the Community as a supporting framework which could provide her with the necessary solidarity in the case of a crisis. The Greek strategy has been one of identifying and exposing any Turkish action that was perceived by Athens as aggressive and thus, following a process of 'demonising' Turkey in front of its European counterparts. This particular strategy sprung from the fact that Greece had securitised the Greek-Turkish relations and thus made it the prime issue on its foreign policy agenda. Its willingness to create a pressure group for the solution of these disputes contradicts the 'demonising' process and as demonstrated later, it was not successful because of this contradiction.

The adaptation process of the Greek foreign policy has been successful at a very low level as far as the Greek national issues are concerned. Greece is holding on to the issues regarded as of vital national importance, for which it fears that more adaptation or inclusion of them in a supranational system of CFSP would mean the weakening of the Greek interest. Although this is true for most Member States, the difference in Greece is the extent and intensity that this happened, particularly before 1996. However, it did make a difference in the way that these issues are presented in CFSP. During the 1980s the attitude with which Greece used to present such issues in the ministerial meetings was an attitude of demand. It was an attitude of demand for *Community Solidarity* to Greece's perceived problems. Greece perceived the Community as being obliged to accept the Greek arguments and to support them. However, any attempt from Greece's partners to challenge these arguments was confronted by Greece. This attitude of demand was a product of ignorance of the European process combined with the 'independent foreign policy' rhetoric that was made for domestic consumption. The process of adaptation and its familiarisation with the European system of policy-making changed this attitude to that of attempting to persuade. Nowadays, when Greece presents an issue in CFSP relating to Turkey, it tries to present its arguments in a way which can persuade its counterparts of their validity, and thus, gain their support.[42] Despite the change in attitude, the policies themselves remain the same because of the low degree of adaptation, and that has important implications for its success. The Greek practice of 'demonising' Turkey in the CFSP ministerial meetings has two consequences that actually brings about the opposite of the desired results. First, it creates a negative atmosphere in meetings of the foreign ministers or prime ministers. Greece's fellow members see that practice as the least constructive for finding a peaceful solution to the Greek-Turkish disputes and they are also annoyed by the barrier that Greece constructs between any approach of the Union with Turkey.[43] The contradiction between solution-seeking and confrontation has actually limited the Greek possibilities of success both in making its arguments understood by its European counterparts and in finding solutions to the problems themselves. That is because any kind of solution coming from disputes requires a degree of compromise. The lack of adaptation in national foreign policy issues caused by the securitisation of them in Greek foreign policy has made compromise impossible. Greece kept its national issues away from a common European notion of dialogue and compromise and as a consequence has isolated Greek arguments even further.

Spain The contrast between Greece and Spain is largely both in the nature of the issues of differentiation and the way in which these are presented in CFSP. The issues that Spain put on the CFSP agenda, on which the Spanish position differed from the common European one, have been issues relating to the Maghreb and the Mediterranean. The objective of Spain has been to direct the interest of the Union to these areas, which are regarded by Spain as vital for European security. However, unlike Greece, Spain never tried to gain the support of the Union against its neighbours but in favour of them. Unlike the Greek policy of exclusion, Spain follows a policy of inclusion. The nature of the differentiation has been that Spain sees cooperation between the Union and the South Mediterranean, and help for their development, as an essential priority for European security, something which is not always the case for the northern Member States. The first difference between the nature of Greek and Spanish differentiation is that Spain has not tried to achieve the Union's support in order to advance its own interest, but rather what it perceived as common European interest.

The reasons for the Spanish differentiation are the geographical proximity and the traditional cultural links with the region, something which makes the stability of the region a high priority for the Spanish foreign policy. Since its membership, Spain had been trying to incorporate this Spanish priority in the European agenda. The second difference is the way that this was attempted. Spain demonstrated the validity of its arguments by trying to persuade its counterparts in CFSP of the necessity of such a development for Europe. The Spanish attitude has been one of cooperation and consultation in order to persuade fellow European Members States. This willingness to present the issue demonstrates the high level of adaptation which has occurred in the Spanish foreign policy. Spain has incorporated its foreign policy process in the broader European process of foreign policy-making so that differentiation in a foreign policy issue does not mean an isolation of the State's position.

As a consequence of this, Spain has successfully managed to persuade its counterparts of the validity of its arguments and to initiate the Euro-Mediterranean partnership initiative. Another consequence has been that even when Spain used a veto, or the threat of one in order to achieve its objective, this was not perceived as 'blackmail', as the Greek veto was perceived in many cases.[44] The adaptation of Spanish foreign policy and the link of the Spanish with the European interests created an objective which was compatible with the common European interest.

Issues put on the Agenda by other Member States

Apart from the issues that are presented by the Member States which hold a different position to the majority in CFSP, there are issues that are put on the agenda by other Member States. The argument is that when a Member State is confronted with an issue, for which its position is radically different from the rest, raised by another state in CFSP, its behaviour is highly influenced by the degree of adaptation of its foreign policy. This section tests the argument that the more the state has harmonised the objectives of its own national foreign policy with the common European policy, the more likely it is to downgrade the significance of its differentiation. In contrast, the less adapted its national policy is, the more likely it is to see a common European policy, in the issues it disagrees with, as a threat to its national interest.

Spain Due to the Europeanisation of its foreign policy objectives and the high degree of adaptation, Spain did not encounter in CFSP a case presented by another Member State in which Spain differed significantly from everybody else. The reasons for this achievement are the careful planning of its own foreign policy towards its neighbours, and particularly Morocco with which it has had several traditional disputes, and the line up with the European foreign policy objective, which is cooperation and development. Spain has encountered several points of tension with Morocco which include the two Spanish enclaves in Morocco territory, Ceuta and Melilla, the Western Sahara case, and fishing. The Spanish strategy has been to downgrade the significance of these disputes and to prioritise the importance of Spanish-Moroccan economic and military cooperation in order to avoid any kind of confrontation over the disputes. This strategy, which was developed after the Franco era and particularly after the Spanish accession in the EC, is in line with the European objective of overcoming problems and conflicts through mutual cooperation. On the fishing issue Spain avoided confrontation with Morocco, which was sometimes unpopular in the Spanish society, and rather supported an EU-Moroccan agreement on the issue. In the Western Sahara case, in which Spain traditionally supported the Polisario Front and the Saharan independence, Spain on the one hand decided to downgrade its importance in order not to damage its relations with Morocco, and on the other, when the issue was brought in EPC, agreed with France, who supported Morocco, in a neutral declaration supporting a UN solution to the dispute. Even in the very few and not so important cases of Spanish differentiation from the common European policy, Spain opted not to pursue its differentiation but rather to support the compromising solution accepted by everyone.

This is best illustrated with reference to the issue of the enlargement to include central and eastern European countries. Spain has been very sceptical about the Eastward orientation of the Union's foreign policy to the expense of the South. With a demonstrated European commitment, Spain was able to strike a balance, increasing the funds available for South Mediterranean while maintaining the majority of them for Eastern Europe. As a consequence of the adaptation of Spanish foreign policy in the two-way relationship, both from Europe and towards Europe, the Spanish differentiation was also adapted in the same way. Spain moderated its differentiation by Europeanising its foreign policy, but also the common

European position came closer to the Spanish as its priorities were included on the CFSP agenda.[45]

Greece On the other hand, because of the isolation of the Greek foreign policy on its national issues, Greece perceived any related issue in CFSP as a threat to its own interest. Any attempt by other Member States to bring up cases in CFSP on which Greece differed was seen as an attempt to impose a common European position on Greek interests. Although the case of Turkey has traditionally been the area of Greek differentiation, a new dispute came up in the beginning of the 1990s after the Yugoslavian crisis; that of the recognition of Macedonia as an independent State. This chapter does not look at the period between 1981-1986, when Greece followed a policy of total differentiation in all foreign policy issues. That was a special period of ideological confrontation, which was looked at in chapter three and is not the subject of this section since adaptation in other areas of foreign policy has progressed in Greece. What this chapter looks at is the period of the late 1980s and 1990s when differentiation was limited into what was called 'the national issues'.

The differentiation that was enhanced by the lack of adaptation and the growing nationalism in Greek society led to a behaviour that not only failed to be understood by the other members but also isolated the Greek arguments even more. In the case of Macedonia, Greece blocked the recognition of the new State by the Union by developing an ultra-nationalist posture.[46] Even after a long period of diplomacy with which the EU was trying to accommodate the Greek concerns and find an acceptable compromise, Greece was unwilling to do so.[47]

Greece's isolated behaviour is a product of the low level of adaptation of its foreign policy and as a result of that, Greece perceived any compromise which the EU supported as a defeat of its own interest. This isolation became a direct confrontation with its fellow members and the European Commission when, after the imposition of the Greek trade embargo of Macedonia, the Commission took the case to the European Court of Justice. The Macedonian issue was finally downgraded and 'desecuritised' by the Greek government because of the realisation of the deadlock in which Greek foreign policy had gone in and the eventual dying out of the nationalist hysteria. However, it is an illustration of how a lack of adaptation gives rise to nationalist priorities in foreign policy which ultimately brings confrontation between the Member State and its counterparts.

The issue that has been always 'securitised' and formed a continuing issue of differentiation and confrontation is that of Turkey. The issues related to the Turkish case which were presented by other Member States or the Commission were the issues of the Customs Union with Turkey and the fourth financial protocol. As a product of its general opposition to any approach of Turkey to Europe,[48] Greece objected to both developments, using its veto power to block them. The only way that Greece could be persuaded to abandon its veto was a trade off with something considered to be of vital Greek interest. That was the way in which Greece was finally persuaded to accept the EU Customs Union with Turkey, in exchange for the start of accession negotiations with Cyprus. However, many attempts by the Union to find a compromise for the financial protocol have been unfruitful during the twelve years of the Greek veto. The consequences of the Greek insistence on the imposition of its differentiation have brought completely different results from those intended by Greece. Evidence of these consequences can be illustrated by the November 1998 proposal of the European Commission for the financial assistance of Turkey was based on Article 130X that is subject to Qualified Majority Voting, and thus, overcame the Greek veto. The Greek behaviour achieved the delay of the process but not its avoidance. In contrast to the Spanish approach, Greece did not follow a cooperative behaviour and by being isolated in some issues of foreign policy related to its national issues, has been unable to secure even what was perhaps wrongly perceived as its own interest.

Issues Excluded from the Agenda

The issues that, by whatever means, find their way onto the agenda are issues where there is an interest of one or more Member State to Europeanise them. However, there are several issues which are of interest for a Member State, but it abstains from putting them on the CFSP agenda. These issues are not necessarily issues of differentiation but issues where a State wants to keep them exclusive.[49] The exclusiveness of an issue can also be a product of lack of adaptation of foreign policy.[50] However, as the cases of Greece and Spain demonstrate, the maintenance of an exclusive issue in foreign policy can either be because of special traditional links or because of fear of or an inability to pursue a common European approach, because of the compromises that such an approach would require. In addition, the exclusion of an issue from the agenda can mean the downgrading of an issue, where differentiation exists, in order to avoid confrontation for the common European interest.

Spain kept the issue of Gibraltar outside the CFSP. The issue was regarded as a bilateral problem between Spain and the UK and there has not been any attempt to communitarise the issue. However, because of the nature of the problem, Gibraltar could not be excluded from other EU policy areas and particularly Justice and Home Affairs.[51] Although the issue is important for Spain, the reason for its exclusion has been the Spanish willingness to avoid any confrontation in CFSP. Spain in no way wanted to damage its image as consensus builder in European foreign policy by bringing an issue that can cause conflict between its fellow members. The downgrading of the issue of Gibraltar offered Spain the possibility of building good relations with the UK and thus opened the way for an eventual solution of the problem on a bilateral level. However, that is not the case in other areas of the first and third pillar of the EU, such as Justice and Home Affairs and air transport where the Spanish differentiation created many problems in EU decision-making. Another area of exclusiveness for Spanish foreign policy is Latin America. This constitutes a prestigious area for Spanish foreign policy because of its extensive cultural links. Spain did not attempt to Europeanise the area of Latin America. However, it did endorse advancing towards a common foreign policy so long as it did not clash with Spain's essential interests.[52] Latin America was not part of the agenda of the EC in any form, before the Spanish accession. Spain promoted a greater cooperation between the EC/EU and Latin America but only to a certain extent. Latin America is not a specified area in the Treaty as one in which CFSP can adopt joint actions and Spain has objected to any such inclusion, although such a development has never been proposed by any Member State, because Spain wants to maintain the exclusiveness of foreign policy influence in that region. However, the exclusion exists only as far as joint actions of the EU are concerned because in all other areas there are several agreements of cooperation between the EU and Latin American countries or groups of states. The above evidence can suggest that Spain behaved differently in CFSP and in the rest of EU decision-making. The cases of Gibraltar and Latin America were excluded from CFSP but formed part of the other two pillars. This suggests that Spain acted with its national interest in mind in these two vital cases for Spanish foreign policy.

Greece, because of its weak geopolitical position and its objective to promote its national policies through the EU, has hardly kept an exclusive issue. When it did so, it was in the form of an initiative that Greece had not been able to pursue through the institutions of CFSP, or was afraid of the influence of other Member States. An example of such an issue was the Balkan Cooperation initiative.[53] The Balkan Conference, which started in Crete in 1997 and continued in Antalya in 1998, was a successful initiative of the Greek government that brings together the heads of States of eight Balkan States once a year.[54] It is a process that seeks to enforce stability and cooperation in the region, and although the Greek-Turkish dispute is not formally discussed, the meetings between the two countries in the sessions of the Conference can lead to a more structured dialogue. However, Greece has not tried to link the Balkan initiative to CFSP, and although the royaumont process deals with Southeast Europe, there is no link between the two.[55] The most probable reason was because by doing so, Greece would have accepted the EU's involvement in the resolution of the Greek-Turkish disputes that could be in a way that which Athens opposes.

The Greek decision to exclude the issue from the CFSP agenda, and to thus follow an independent initiative, can be seen as a product of the limited adaptation of Greek foreign policy. There are two sides to this explanation. First, because of the Greek behaviour and special interest that it promotes on its national issues, Greece's partners in the EU are very sceptical about Greek initiatives in the CFSP which relate to the Balkan region. Even if they agree on the priorities and objectives of the initiative, they would always like to have a system of institutional control in order to safeguard the exclusion of nationalistic elements and any secret agenda that Greece might promote. On the other hand, the institutionalisation of the process in CFSP could mean the creation of special links between the Balkan States and the EU, including Turkey. That is something that goes against the principle objective of Greek national foreign policy, which is to maintain control over the EU-Turkish relations. To accept and promote a CFSP initiative for the Balkans could mean that Greece would no longer have the leading role and that the views of other Member States, particularly on Turkey, would take precedence in the process.

Final Remarks

Since the majority of agreements in CFSP, as in all pillars of EU decision-making, are achieved in the working groups, the behaviour and nature of participation of national representatives depends on the organisational adaptation of the Member State. The effectiveness and efficiency of the foreign ministers depends to some extent upon the administrational structure. The evidence in the organisation section suggests that the degree of adaptation affects the behavioural patterns of the Member State in foreign policy. An administration adapted to the model necessary for the efficient administration of European foreign policy is essential for the nature of participation and effective interventions of national ministers. Both a one-country approach and a comparison of the two support the argument. In the first case, in both Greece and Spain, organisational adaptation has altered their nature of participation. The large amount of information received, the extension of the areas of interest of national foreign policy, and the negotiating power and image gained as members of the EU, made a big difference in the way they participated in CFSP. Membership has been a learning process for national administrations through which they improved both the participation of national representatives and the preparation of national positions.[56] In the second case, the comparison between Greece and Spain proves that the degree to which adaptation is achieved also determines the nature of participation. The fact that the Spanish organisational structure is characterised by a greater degree of adaptation than the Greek results in the fact that Spain's participation in the institutions of CFSP is more effective. The lack of coherence caused by the separation of foreign policy issues in the Greek administration has limited the Greek potentials of participating in a more constructive way. The extent to which administrational adaptation was achieved or not has influenced the nature of participation of national representatives in CFSP, but also the process of national foreign policy formation.

The degree of adaptation of national foreign policy also affected the formation of the policy itself. Both Greece and Spain have developed an interest in the construction of common European policies according to the level of their adaptation. Membership has enhanced the need for cooperation in the designing of foreign policy and has contributed to an interchange of opinions between Member States that has influenced the formation of the national position. However, this influence depends upon the degree of adaptation achieved. The evidence suggests that the adaptation process bring changes to the factors which influence foreign policy formation. By Europeanising its foreign policy, Spain achieved the formation of national positions which were closer to common European positions and, in that way, it benefited from its constructive behaviour towards a common policy in CFSP. Greece on the other hand failed to follow such behaviour, on a number of issues, because of its lack of adaptation in the formation of its national policy on issues of national importance for Greece. However, the evidence did not suggest that low level of adaptation in foreign policy formation results always in the nationalisation of its objectives. Rather, according to the Greek case, it affected only a limited number of objectives related to its 'national issues'.

Finally, the differentiation of national foreign policy from a common European position is also related to the adaptation process. However, differentiation does not always mean lack of adaptation. Furthermore, adaptation is directly related to the way that differentiation is presented in CFSP. The lack of adaptation at the organisation and the policy formation level can enhance differences between the Member State and its counterparts in a case of differentiation, and the contrary can make it of less significance. In the case of Greece, the lack of adaptation at all three levels during the 1980s has made Greek differentiation harsher. However, compared with the Greek behaviour in the Luxembourg Summit of 1997 it is suggested that, although the differentiation remained, the Greek behaviour was different because of the progress of the adaptation process. That was when Greece avoided vetoing the inclusion of Turkey in the European Conference but rather followed a constructive attitude by suggesting criteria for its inclusion. Spain's differentiation has been of minor significance for CFSP because of its high degree of adaptation in the first two levels, and of the lack of importance of the area of Spanish differentiation for most of the EU Member States. The Spanish achievement of foreign policy adaptation to Europe through the Europeanisation of the Spanish foreign policy has benefited Spain by offering the possibility of influencing the European agenda with Spanish priorities. This is a result of the nature of Spanish participation that was achieved because of the high degree of adaptation to the European Union.

Notes

[1] D. Rometsch and W. Wessels, 1996.
[2] See chapter 6, p.172.
[3] Interview with senior Greek official, Brussels, January 1999.
[4] J.C. Loulis, 1984/85, pp.374-91.
[5] See Annex 2 for the organograma of the Greek MFA before accession to the EC, p.227.

[6] Official Journal of the Government of the Hellenic Republic, n. 177, (1), pp. 2761-82, 28/07/98.

[7] See Annex 1 for the current organograma of the Greek MFA, p. 225.

[8] Official Journal of the Government of the Hellenic Republic, n. 177, (1), pp. 2761-82, 28/07/98.

[9] The minister of foreign affairs sits only in the Foreign affairs Council, which deals with CFSP issues.

[10] See Annex 4 for the organograma of the Spanish MFA before accession to the EC, p. 231.

[11] See Annex 3 for the current organograma of the Spanish MFA, p. 229.

[12] Interview, Enrique Gonzalez Sanchez, Council Secretariat, January 1999, Brussels.

[13] P.C. Ioakimidis, 1993b, p.415.

[14] K. Mardas, 1992, p.295.

[15] K. Saba, 1996, p.194.

[16] The General Secretary for Foreign Policy and the EU has the status of a Political Director of the Ministry.

[17] Th. Stoforopoulos and A. Makridimitris, 1996.

[18] Interviews with Community officials, Brussels December 1997 and January 1998.

[19] Interview, T. Stamatopoulos, Greek Permanent Representation, January 1999, Brussels.

[20] P.C. Ioakimidis, 1993b, p.416.

[21] Interview with K. Mitsotakis, Athens, March 1998.

[22] H. Axt, 1993, N. Diamadouros, 1993, A. Makridimitris and A. Passas, 1994, P.C. Ioakimidis, 1994, D. Sotiropoulos, 1993 and 1996.

[23] D. Sotiropoulos, 1993, p.54.

[24] Interview, F.E. de Tejada, Spanish foreign ministry, May 1998, Madrid.

[25] Royal Decree no. 1485/1985 developed in a ministerial order of 12 May 1985.

[26] R. Gillespie, 1997, p.35.

[27] Interview with I. Guardans, Madrid, May 1998.

[28] European Foreign Policy Bulletin, 95/186, Conclusions of the European Council meeting in Cannes, 26-27 June 1995.

[29] Proposal of the Commission for a Council Regulation regarding the implementation of a special financial cooperation measure for Turkey, 1/12/98, (http://europa.eu.int/eur-lex/en/com/dat/1995/en_595PC0389.html).

[30] Interview, Guillermo Casan, Spanish MP, Madrid, 21/05/98.

[31] M. Holland, 1997.

[32] Modernisation has been in the PASOK electoral campaign rhetoric ever since 1996 and has been the basic theme for justifying the government's choices in policy making.

[33] Interview with senior Greek official in the Council, Brussels, January 1998.

[34] See the recent poll on issues of concern during the 1999 European Parliament elections in Greece and the predominance of Kosovo, Oikonomikos Taxydromos, 3 June 1999.

[35] During the last few years the Imia crisis, the arrest of the Kurd leader Abdulah Ocalan and NATO intervention in Kosovo have been top priority issues for public opinion and issues for political exploitation.

[36] See chapter 6, p.169 on securitisation of foreign policy issues.

[37] P. Robins, 1997, pp.82-100.

[38] H. McClosky, 1967 and J. Rosenau, 1963.

[39] C. Garcia, 1995, p.125.

[40] Ibid., p.128.

[41] J. Grugel, 1995, pp.142-3.

[42] See the conclusions of the Luxembourg Summit in December 1997 where conditions were put on Turkish candidature for accession.

[43] Several interviews with senior officials in the European Commission and the Council of Ministers Secretariat, Brussels, December 1997 and January 1998.

[44] See Francesc Morata, 1998, p.113, on the Spanish threat to veto enlargement in the Edinburgh Summit.

[45] Interviews with Francisco Elias de Tejada, Madrid, May 1998 and Angel Viñas, Brussels, January 1999.

[46] See chapter 3, p.76.

[47] D. Tziotis, 1994, pp.226-31.

[48] Greece has always put as prerequisite for the Turkish European orientation the solution of all Greek-Turkish disputes (according to the Greek arguments) and the solution of the Cyprus problem.

[49] P. Bachrach and M. Baratz, 1962.

[50] Ibid.

[51] See in chapter 3 the section on Gibraltar, p.83.

[52] E. Barbe, 1995, p.122.

[53] See chapter 3, p.73.

[54] Newspaper 'Eleftherotypia', Athens 4/11/97, p.4-7.

[55] The Royaumont process has been a French initiative in CFSP, which started in Paris on 13/12/95 and aimed at the improvement of relations between the countries of Southeast Europe.

[56] J. Richardson, 1996.

5 Foreign Policy Action in CFSP

This chapter looks at Greece and Spain in the Common Foreign and Security Policy of the EU. Its argument is that positive behaviour and constructive participation, playing by the European rules and through the institutions of the EU, can contribute to increasing a Member State's influence in CFSP and the political orientation of the government shapes foreign policy behaviour. This chapter focuses on the participation patterns of Greece and Spain in the formation of European foreign policy (1) structures, (2) priorities and (3) actions. It attempts to examine the link between Europeanisation of national foreign policy and the success of national priorities in CFSP.

Greece has recently started to adapt itself in the functioning of European foreign policy after almost fourteen years of going alone or playing the awkward partner.[1] According to Stephen George, the definition of an awkward partner is that it is (1) in a minority of one, (2) out of step with the rest, and (3) difficult to deal with. However, the reasons for the Greek awkwardness were different from those of the UK described by Stephen George. In Greece, awkwardness was generated in the 1980s by ideology, geopolitics, and domestic traditional influences. The active and positive participation that Greece seems to pursue in the CFSP has started to overturn the negative image of the past and has increased its degree of influence in Europe. Spain, on the other hand, adopted a positive approach from its first moment as a full member of the EC. The Spanish participation soon after its accession dissolved the fears of a second Greece, based on the awkward Greek behaviour of the early 1980s, as described in chapter two. The Spanish example proves that an isolated and newly democratised state can increase its role and influence in Europe's foreign policy by following the rules and adopting a constructive approach. Such participation is more important to Greece and Spain than some other Member States. That is because states with a traditional network of external relations, whose extensive foreign policy activities are not contained primarily within CSFP, can still maintain a significant level of influence even if their behaviour is negative, e.g. the UK. Greece and Spain have found that the EC/EU has reinforced their foreign policy. Despite the traditional Spanish links with Latin America, both states have benefited enormously by participating in the institutions of EPC/CFSP and not independently. With a proactive participation, Greece and Spain can successfully catch up with the rest of the Member States and play a significant role as a full partner in European foreign policy.[2] As a Spanish diplomat argues, it is more difficult for states like Greece and Spain to maintain their achieved influence in CFSP than states like France and the UK.[3] It is because of the absence of their own extensive foreign policy networks that Spain and Greece have to work hard to demonstrate their commitment to European foreign policy and work through the institutions. That is why this chapter looks at five areas of structures, priorities and actions related to CFSP in order to evaluate Greek and Spanish participation in them and the implication of their behaviour on their role and degree of influence. These are their participation in the structures of the Intergovernmental Conferences and the Presidency of the EU, their priorities in foreign policy initiatives, and their actions in participation and interest granted to the CFSP process, and national personalities that obtain key-post positions in EU institutions and particularly in CFSP.

This chapter looks at the Greek and Spanish participation in the last Intergovernmental Conference (IGC), paying specific attention to their positions in past IGCs. Greece has participated in three Intergovernmental Conferences and Spain in two, of which all had very important significance for the development of CFSP. The second important area with which the chapter deals, is the Presidency of the European Council. The Presidency is an institutional arrangement that gives the opportunity to a Member State to take initiatives and to influence the agenda. Although the institution of the Presidency is very important to any study of the participation of a state in CFSP, it does not always reflect its real degree of influence. That is because items on the agenda of Presidencies are scheduled[4] for that particular period and thus important initiatives of a Presidency are not always its own initiatives. That is how the Netherlands had the Presidency during the signing of both Treaties in the 1990s, and Greece had it during the 1995 enlargement. Active participation can take the form of foreign policy initiatives which a state can take. However, in order to plan and to develop an initiative in CFSP, a Member State has to carefully design its moves. This is why initiatives are not just declarations or proposals of the head of government, but they include a period of planning and discussion in the working groups at different levels; in the national administration, in the COREPER, and in the General Secretariat of the Council. Finally, this chapter considers the impact of national personalities holding key-posts, not only in CFSP but also in the institutions of the EU in general.

Structures: Intergovernmental Conference

Greece's Participation in Institutional Reform

The position of Greece during the Intergovernmental Conference, which led to the Treaty of Amsterdam, was very different from the other two IGCs in which Greece participated. First, this section will look at the difference in the Greek positions, and will then evaluate the reasons for them and for the change. Finally, this section will conclude by considering the way that this change has influenced the actual role and image of Greece in Europe, and in particular in the CFSP.

The principal preoccupation of Greece has always been security. Indeed, this was the main reason for its application to join the European Community.[5] The attempt to accommodate its question of security has led Greece to a very contradictory position during the IGC that established the Single European Act in 1985. After opposing even the convening of the 1985 IGC in Milan, Greece then took a strong position against the development of a General Secretariat in the Council for European Political Co-operation.[6] This was because Greece perceived the Secretariat as a centre for decision-making in foreign policy away from the Member States. Any further development of a Common Foreign Policy was perceived by the then socialist government as a limitation of its independence to dictate its own foreign policy. However, on the defence issue, Greece supported a common European defence that can guarantee the inviolability of its external borders. During the Intergovernmental Conference for Political Union in 1991 security was again the principal preoccupation of the Greek government. This time, the pro-European conservative government, put all its effort in becoming a full member of the Western European Union. As a defence alliance, the WEU could address Greece's security problem, which the EU could not safeguard. Greece went as far as to use its consent to the new Treaty in order to gain membership of WEU. During the negotiations that led to Maastricht, Greece, several times, presented the argument of conditionality, asking for a promise on its WEU accession in order to give its agreement. This was also the case during the Maastricht Summit when the final promise was made on the Greek WEU membership. In general terms, however, the Greek position in Maastricht was in favour of institutional changes towards a common foreign policy, in which they desperately wanted to develop the defence dimension.

In the very short memorandum[7] which the Greek government submitted for the 1985 IGC, there was no mention of either foreign policy or defence. It was a document consisting of political declarations on general economic issues, in which the primary position held the issue of structural funds. A slightly larger memorandum was submitted during the 1991 IGC.[8] It consisted of some six pages and was concerned with three main issues: institutional reform, democratic deficit, and new policies and actions. In the latter, there was a reference to foreign policy and defence. With its proposal, the Greek government asked for the incorporation of EPC to the Community procedures, and thus the Communitarisation of EPC and the development of CFSP. According to the Greek proposals, the Council of Ministers of Foreign Affairs and the European Council should replace EPC meetings, and the EPC secretariat should be gradually incorporated in the Council Secretariat. Proposals that were always part of the Greek petitions in Europe, such as the recognition of the notion of external borders of the Union, the incorporation in to the joint actions of problem-issues that Member States face, and the issue of Community solidarity was also included.

The difference in the nature of the Greek contribution to the 1996 IGC was very profound. The memorandum that was submitted[9] had 20 pages covering all the issues that the IGC was concerned with, from citizenship, social dimension, institutional reforms to CFSP and the field of justice and home affairs. A three-page section dealt with the issue of CFSP. In that memorandum the Greek government critiqued the functioning of CFSP since Maastricht and proposed a genuine common foreign and security policy. In the objectives of CFSP was included the classic demand of Greece, 'the guaranteeing of the EU's external frontiers and territorial integrity, as well as the adoption of a 'solidarity and mutual defence assistance clause'.' Greece was willing to accept the extension of qualified majority voting to second pillar issues, which do not affect the vital national interests of the Member State, in order to gain the benefits of solidarity. Greece supported the 'partial communitarisation' of the second pillar. According to the Greek memorandum, the Commission should have a more active role in the fields of analysis, planning, implementation and management of common actions and the power of the Parliament in foreign affairs should be reinforced.[10] Also, CFSP expenses should be included in the Union's budget. However, the European Court was left without any jurisdiction. On the defence issue, Greece was fully supportive of the development of a common defence policy and a common defence. Its elements, according to Greece, should be the development of an EU defence identity with the gradual incorporation of WEU in CFSP. However, it was stressed that this policy should be complementary rather than antithetical to NATO.

The basic Greek proposals had been the same in all three IGCs, despite the difference in the ideological perspective of the 1985 Papandreou government. That was because the EU had not managed to address the Greek security preoccupations, and as the recent memorandum stated:

'Greece is obliged to spend a disproportionate share of its national resources on national and collective security purposes' and 'unlike the vast majority of Member States, therefore, Greece has been unable to reap the so-called 'peace dividend".

The significant difference between the Greek positions at the three Intergovernmental Conferences was the attitude and the degree of participation in the discussion. Also, there was a significant difference in the results of the Conferences and the rate of success of the Greek proposals. By looking at the differences and the success of the Greek proposals, one has to look at three important aspects. These aspects are first, the political environment of the time, second, the developments within Europe and third, the maturing of the Greek policy. During the 1985 IGC, Greece came from a period of four years of hostile behaviour towards the European Community and particularly, the notion of a common foreign policy for Europe. The proposal for a common defence and recognition of borders, which came out of the blue from Greece, created suspicion in its fellow Member States. This proposal foresaw the development of an autonomous European policy for defence in order to guarantee Europe's independence and sovereignty.[11] However, one has to recognise the political environment of the 1980s. First, it was a time when Communism still existed and ideological differences were very strong. Ideology and domestic policy rhetoric shaped Greek foreign policy. Second, the European Community had not yet developed the close Union it has now. In the mid-1980s, the first attempt to review the Treaty of Rome was made, and it was logical that some kind of suspicion would exist in countries like Greece. Finally, Greek policy makers in the 1996 IGC had the examples of past Greek involvement in such a process, and could learn from the mistakes of the past.

Nevertheless, a different result came about because of the different level of participation and attitude of the Greek government, not only in the IGC itself, but also in the general working of the EU institutions. In 1985, the hostile attitude of the Greek government, together with the lack of participation and interest in the everyday functioning of the Community, deprived it of the possibility to influence developments during the Intergovernmental Conference.[12] In 1991, when there was a change in attitude, the Greek government was still preoccupied with the membership of WEU, and was willing to jeopardise the future of the EU in order to achieve its objective.[13] This behaviour, together with the fact that Greece did not seem to care for any other issue apart from its own interests, actually weakened the Greek position in the IGC. Although Greece succeeded in entering WEU,[14] none of its principal proposals for the IGC on Political Union had any success. This is because Greece's partners were annoyed by the way that Greece was promoting its national interest at the expense of the common European interest. One of the non-written rules of partnership in the European Union is that any particular interest of a Member State should be linked with the general interest of the EU, in other words, promoting national interest through and not at the expense of the common interest. Greece was in breach of this particular Euro-rule. That is why the Greek entry to the WEU was accepted by the EU in a particular way so as to avoid any nationalistic exploitation of the institution by Greece at the expense of its fellow members. This is important for Greece because it allows for the development of defence policies of cooperation and avoiding conflicts. For CFSP, it is also important because as more EU Member States become members of WEU, it is easier to gradually develop common defence policies linked with that institution.

The Greek objectives in the 1990 IGC fell into five areas:

- The limitation of the democratic deficit by supporting the role of the European Parliament.
- The effectiveness of decision-making in the Council by the restructuring and simplification of the policy-making process.
- The strengthening of the powers of the European Commission.
- The development of European citizenship and the principle of Community solidarity.
- The communitarisation of EPC and the incorporation of defence issues in it, with the guarantee of the Union's external borders.[15]

The Greek participation in the 1996 IGC provided a signpost for three things: the incorporation of Greece as a full and respectable partner in Europe, the maturing of Greek European policy and the building of understanding between Greece and its partners.[16] Even before the start of the IGC, Greece gave signs of its changing attitude. The co-operation approach that Greece started to adopt, in contrast to the confrontation of the past, benefited the change in Greece's image and reputation. This suggests that as the European Union matures, so does the participating administration of the Member States.[17] As with other states, the Greek administration has become more and more accustomed to the European system. Finally, understanding means to speak the same 'language'. For many years, the Greek claims and arguments sounded strange to the ears of the Europeans. For the first time Greece started to explain its position and its arguments in a way that was understandable to its fellow Member States.[18] As the evidence suggests, the change in the Greek behaviour of how its priorities were presented brought changes to the ability of Greece to influence decision-making, without necessarily changing the priorities themselves.

The Greek objectives in the 1996 IGC negotiation, as illustrated in its memorandum, were based on five areas:

- The restoration of the confidence of the European society and citizens of the Union with the substantial enhancement of the European identity.
- The European concern with social and economic issues, such as unemployment, social exclusion and cohesion.
- The preparation of the Union for the next enlargement with the reform of the institutions while preserving the institutional identity of the Union.
- The deeper development of the institutional European unification, through the guarantee and development of the differences in cultural identities.
- The enhancement of the Union's external action and identity with the development of its international competitiveness.[19]

The result of these changes was the development of a Greek participation in Europe, which supports, in a moderate fashion, the Greek interests, but also demonstrates a greater understanding of general issues affecting the Union. Also the EU has started to show a greater understanding of the

Greek problems. Considering the general failure to achieve a radical revision of CFSP, the incorporation of the clause for the recognition of the Union's external borders can be considered as a Greek success. The recognition of the Union's external borders has been a major preoccupation for Greece, since the guarantee of its territorial integrity has always been the core of Greek security policy. This objective, which has been the centre of the Greek argumentation in the last two IGC's (SEA and Maastricht), was a significant part of Greece's proposals at Amsterdam, but not the core argument. This helped Greece to dedicate more time to the development of other proposals concerning a variety of EU policy-areas in need of reform.[20] In doing that, Greece demonstrated its concern for the whole development of the EU and a common interest rather than specific interests of Greece. This eliminated the suspicion that Greece's partners would have on proposals that might have to do with the Greek-Turkish conflict. The Greek proposals aimed at the clarity of the CFSP's objectives, the recognition of their complexity and the interconnectedness upon the part of policy-makers. Greece argued that by moving CFSP in this direction, it is likely to prevent failure of policy action and damage of the EU's prestige. The proposals covered *Jo's suggestion*, the protection of the Union's independence and reinforcement of its security as the ultimate goal of CFSP. In order to achieve this goal, Greece proposed that the Union should guarantee the inviolability of its external borders and territorial integrity, as well as to adopt a solidarity and mutual defence assistance clause.[21] Greece also projected this proposal as the fulfilment of another CFSP goal, which is the promoting of peace and stability in Central-Eastern Europe, the Balkan Peninsula and the Mediterranean. In contrast with past tactics, Greece in the 1996 IGC wanted to avoid being seen as promoting 'narrow' national interests through common means. That is why Greek diplomacy works hard to persuade its fellow members of the importance of these proposals not only for Greece but for all Member States, particularly those bordering third countries including the prospective Member States. The Greek diplomacy played a lot on the issue of enlargement, arguing that is impossible to consider accession of new member states from the Central-Eastern Europe without addressing the external security of the EU issue. Greek officials even suggested the development of an EU 'core group' of states willing to undertake defence commitments, under a 'Common Defence Protocol'.[22] This proposal demonstrates an offensive behaviour employed by the Greek government who wanted to achieve its objectives not by blocking others' proposals, as it used to do in the past, but by proposing more common actions. Despite the fact that Greece did not achieve its maximum (the Common Defence Protocol), at least it achieved its minimum (the clause on external borders). An advantage that led to the success of its proposals, was the fact that a number of Member States with similar concerns for the external borders, such as Finland, Austria, Spain and Italy, supported Greece's arguments. However, the main difference which, in comparison with the past, made the majority of Member States look favourably on such proposals, was the development of the Schengen agreement and increased waves of illegal refugees from the east and the south.

Spain's Participation in Institutional Reforms

Spain participated as a full member in two Intergovernmental Conferences. During negotiations for the Single European Act, Spain held an observer position since it was about to join the Community. The Spanish position regarding the integration process and the development of the European Union was mainly characterised by continuity. However, there are some points of change which have occurred after the change of government in 1996 that were noticeable during the last IGC. The popular party of Jose Maria Aznar, seemed more concerned with domestic issues like the economy and terrorism. The issue that dominated its participation in Europe was the achievement of the economic standards for the Spanish economy, to allow it to participate in the first group of Economic and Monetary Union. In a way, that was an extension of a domestic dimension. Foreign Policy was of a lesser concern. The domestic, rather than European orientation, of the new Spanish government had some very interesting implications for its negotiating stance during the 1996 Intergovernmental Conference.

Before analysing the change in attitude, it is important to note where this change has occurred. Two different levels can be identified here in the negotiation process. The first is the institutional level at which there has hardly been any change. The diplomats who were in charge of the Spanish negotiation team were the same people as before, headed by the very experienced ambassador Javier Elorza, who was head of the Spanish Permanent Representation in Brussels for many years. Elorza was also the leading figure during the Maastricht negotiations under the previous government. In addition, even the new foreign minister, Abel Matutes, had been a European Commissioner under Jacques Delors, and thus not only familiar with decision-making processes in the EU but also experienced by being part of the most active Commission to date. So, at the institutional level one can notice that there has been a great degree of continuity. Change can also be noted at the second level, which is the political level, at which there was a change of priorities and of the way of achieving them. This can be attributed to the difference in political orientation that Aznar's government brought and their perception of national foreign policy. The difference in the political attitude of Aznar in comparison with Felipe Gonzalez can be characterised as defensive as opposed to offensive, as is described below. There is also a difference in the scope of the priorities and interests of the two leaders. The government of Aznar was primarily concerned with domestic politics and as a consequence of that, its scope of interests was limited, during the negotiation, to the issues that affected Spain, while he expressed no interest on other European issues. A criticism, made by the opposition relating to that attitude, is that Aznar had no position at all but was waiting for a consensus to be formed, on issues that did not affect Spain, and then he entered into this consensus.[23] The defensive attitude of the Aznar government is also related to its priorities. This attitude is concerned with the domestic national interests and is willing to block any proposal that can be seen as threatening to the Spanish priorities. On the contrary, the offensive attitude pursued during the government of Gonzalez had as its main objective the construction of European integration. Although the Spanish interests were also important, the way to confront such proposals was not to block them but to counter-propose something else. In that way, Gonzalez managed to avoid some unwanted proposals while contributing to the construction of a common position.

During the years of the socialist government, the Spanish priority was not only to participate in the European political process, but was also to contribute to the construction of European integration. During the Maastricht negotiations, the Spanish objectives can be summarised in five points:

- a common foreign and security policy for Europe of a global and progressive nature, which would develop a security dimension that would eventually lead to a common European defence;
- democratic legitimacy with greater powers to the European Parliament both in terms of initiative and control, enhanced cooperation with the national parliaments, and a more relevant role for the regions;

- greater competencies and institutional efficiency that could extend Community activity to fields such as education, culture, public health and the environment;
- economic and social cohesion;
- European citizenship.[24]

However, an interesting point to note is the wide consensus within the political forces that supported these objectives. This is illustrated by the proposals of the mixed parliamentary committee on the European Community that adopted the above objectives and encouraged the government to pursue them. In addition to that, ten days before the European Council meeting at Maastricht, a parliamentary debate was held on 28 November 1991, called by the opposition Popular Party whose objective was to bind the government to defend the above objectives by giving it the parliamentary mandate to do so.[25] The active role played by Spain at Maastricht shows the importance that the Socialist government gave to the development of CFSP within the development of a political union. The main reason for the Spanish attitude was the changes in Eastern Europe. These changes created an eastern orientation for the European Union and Spain found itself in the periphery.[26] Spain also saw the Gulf War as a momentum that indicated the required effort to improve the coordination of the diplomacy and defence of the Europeans.[27] Accession ended Spain's isolation in international relations and there was a danger that Spain would become marginalised once more. According to Felipe González, the solution was political union and the development of a common foreign policy. In this way, Spain's foreign policy objectives could be part of the new institutionalised structure and Spain could be in its core. The Spanish proposals for the creation of the CFSP pillar were more integrationist than the final outcome, although Spain did not accept the Dutch proposals for total Communitarisation of the second pillar. Spain argued that the priority areas, which generate policy must be decided unanimously, while the decision-making itself, in the form of declarations, common positions and joint actions could be decided by Qualified Majority Voting.[28]

During the last IGC which concluded with the Amsterdam Treaty, Spain adopted a more defensive rather than offensive attitude. However, this was not solely due to the change of government, since that change occurred in the middle of the negotiations. The difference between the socialist and the conservative government is evident in the manner in which they handled and pursued the Spanish proposals, which enjoyed the agreement of both the two major parties and also the Catalan nationalist coalition, Convergencia i Unió. This was a change in process and not in substance. However, as is argued later, during the negotiations, the Spanish government deviated from its original proposals to change its position. Spain started the IGC negotiations, which led to Amsterdam with the Socialist Government, and finished with the Conservatives. The Spanish contribution to the 1996 IGC was prepared by Carlos Westendorp on 2 March 1995,[29] under his duties as General Secretary for EU affairs, and on 28 March 1996,[30] after he replaced Javier Solana as Foreign Minister, when the latter was appointed General Secretary of NATO.

The main objectives of the Spanish position in its contribution to the 1996 IGC were:

- Flexibility should be introduced in the EU but with clear limits, rejecting the 'Europe a la carte'.
- Institutional reforms, in the light of the forthcoming enlargement, particularly of the voting system in the Council and the decision-making procedures.
- Employment policy should be given the central role in the Treaty by establishing its legal basis.
- Tackling the problem of ineffectiveness of CFSP by reforming the decision-making procedures.
- The deepening of specific rights of citizens of the Union and the strengthening of the common approach on issues of internal security of the Union.[31]

The Spanish position during the IGC, as outlined in the White Paper, was the subject of wide consensus between the political forces, so, in the spring of 1996 when the Popular Party came to power, it followed the position developed by the Reflection Group presided by Westendorp and approved by the Spanish Parliament. However, Aznar prioritised the different elements of the Spanish position under his own political viewpoint. The main difference of the new government in the 1996 IGC negotiations was in the way of promoting the issues and not in the issues themselves.[32] Spain under Aznar was presented with a defensive attitude, more concerned with securing what was already there and willing to block any proposal that could challenge the status quo, rather than advocating further institutional changes towards more integration. For two reasons, Spain directed its efforts towards the deepening of the third pillar. First, because it deals with the problem of terrorism from which Spain suffers, and second because it has direct links with domestic politics and the issue of citizenship, which affect the citizens directly and also, third pillar issues are easy to use for electoral purposes. In the second pillar, the Aznar government not only failed to prioritise the proposals in the White Paper, but also in several cases it supported conflicting arguments. Two major areas can be identified in which the new government followed different positions than the ones proposed in the Spanish White Paper. The first is the area of majority voting. The paper states in Article 120 that the failure to use qualified majority voting in the second pillar is one of the causes of inefficiency and for that reason a process of extending QMV in this area should start, particularly in view of the coming enlargement. During the negotiations the Aznar government confronted any attempt, particularly by the Germans, to extend QMV in the second pillar.[33] The second area is that of the pillar structure which according to the White Paper should be eliminated, and all pillars should be incorporated into the main EC pillar with increased participation of the European Commission and the European Parliament, while maintaining a significant part of the intergovernmental process. The new government supported this argument only as far as the third pillar was concerned. On the second pillar, it refused to accept any significant change of the status quo. The reason for this change in position was a more realist political orientation which gives precedence to the concept of national sovereignty. The realist orientation is reluctant to give up national rights on foreign policy making to a supranational framework.

Structures: Presidency

Role of the Presidency[34]

Before looking at and analysing Greek and Spanish effectiveness and success in their presidencies it is essential to look at some of the characteristics of the Presidency. The institutional powers and the role that the Presidency gives to the Member State cannot be described as an increase of influence.[35] Rather, it is the achieved reputation of successful handling of the Presidency that increases the state's influence. The presiding state has to follow the rules dictated by the Treaties and to work within an agenda, of which the majority is set by the Commission and the Council Secretariat, and not by the state holding the Presidency. Most of the time, the 'big successes' of a Presidency are not initiatives that the Member State takes, but are issues put on the agenda at that particular time. Of course, by looking at the way the government has dealt with the issues on the agenda and the way it has prioritised them, one can define a successful or non-successful Presidency, according to the demands of the EU. Therefore, the issue under scrutiny is not the agenda itself, but the way it is handled by the Presidency. However, the possibility of an initiative in the sphere of the Common Foreign and Security Policy cannot be dismissed. In the area of CFSP, the EU responds to events or crises that cannot always be predicted. In such cases the Presidency might take an initiative or even prevent others from taking such initiatives, as was the case with Greece in its first Presidency. However, even in these cases, initiatives are not perceived as an increase in influence because to a certain extent they are expected by other Member States. However, a positive and successful handling of a Presidency, including initiatives in CFSP, adds to the image and reputation of a Member State.

The Greek Presidencies

In the first Summit under the Greek Presidency of the EC, in Vouliagmeni in 1983, still in the days of ideological differences, the socialist government of Papandreou wanted to make a stance on independent foreign policy. This policy meant a total opposition to the European majority. The first Presidency was used to demonstrate the Greek ideological difference to its fellow Europeans, but also to proclaim an independent Greek policy mainly for domestic consumption. During that Presidency, Greece abused its institutional powers twice, during the Polish and the Grenada crises, to avoid the issues from finding their way onto the EPC agenda.[36] Such an attitude had a very profound and negative impact upon the image of Greece in the Community and its role in European foreign policy. The second Presidency in 1988, which is characterised by Papandreou's illness and the political instability of the government, can be described as non-existent as far as initiatives in foreign policy are concerned.

During the third Greek Presidency, which ended with the European Council summit in Corfu in June 1994, the issues on the CFSP agenda were the implementation of the joint actions in the Middle East, the Stability Pact and South Africa. The Presidency can be described as successful because all these issues have been implemented. The CFSP supported the elections in Palestine by participating in the international force and implemented the Stability Pact despite the difficulties of financing and the duration of it. The Greek Presidency particularly relied on the role of the CFSP Secretariat in order to enhance its potentials. In fact, it added to the upgrade of its role, since during the Greek Presidency the CFSP Secretariat was incorporated into the General Secretariat of the Council. During the Greek Presidency the problems of accession were overcome and the eventual enlargement to Central and Northern Europe was agreed. Also, the constitution of the working group for the preparation of the 1996 IGC was decided in Corfu. One of the novelties that the Greek Presidency achieved was to produce, for the first time, a text of mixed character. That is, a text that refers to an issue that spread in more than one pillar. On the issue of Mediterranean policy Greece succeeded, despite some opposition, to include in the conclusions of the Corfu Summit a text which is referring to both CFSP and external relations under the first pillar.[37] Despite the generally positive outcome of the summit and the Greek Presidency, the Greek economic embargo on Macedonia added a bad sound to a well-delivered concert. This bad sound can be described as a mistake of Greek foreign policy and a negative impact on the image of Europe, and on the image of Greece in Europe. This was precisely a result of the separation of Greek foreign policy for its national issues, as seen in the previous chapter. The embargo on Macedonia was decided as a last resort of putting pressure both on the neighbouring state to comply with Greece's demands and on the EU to refrain from recognising it. However, this nationalistic policy was designed without studying the consequences for the Greek reputation as holding the EU Presidency.

First, in the beginning of the 1990s, Greece found itself in dispute with all its neighbours. Apart from Turkey, a big disagreement began with Macedonia after the Yugoslav crisis, then the relationships with Albania and Bulgaria went into crisis, and then even its relations with Croatia fell apart because Greece openly declared itself as pro-Serb. As a Greek senior official stated, 'this was a classic mistake of foreign policy, and the embargo was added to these'.[38] Secondly, it created a poor image for the EU since Greece was holding the Presidency and at the same time creating problems and crises. The impression was given that Europe, because of its President, was breaching international law. This was an immediate reaction from other Member States who asked Greece to withdraw the measures. However, an act condemning the State holding the Presidency was perceived as not in the best interests of the EU and the Commission waited until the end of Greece's term to refer the case to the ECJ. Thirdly, the Greek reputation was damaged once again. After eight years of a negative Greek attitude in Europe in the 1980s, when the government was dismissing any dialogue with Turkey, came a conservative government with a co-operative stance. This positive and open government was led, mainly by its foreign minister, to an ultra-nationalistic attitude that once again damaged the image of Greece. Papandreou supported this nationalist policy even before coming to power in 1993 and it was in this spirit that the embargo was implemented during the Greek Presidency. This was caused by the attempt to securitise the Macedonian issue and made nationalistic policies acceptable.[39] However, in the general administration of the Third Greek Presidency there have been many positive outcomes. In Corfu it was agreed to form the working group for the preparation of the 1996 IGC and also some problems regarding the accession of Austria, Finland and Sweden were overcome and the adhesion treaties were signed. Another success of the Presidency was the signing of the partnership and cooperation agreement between the Union and Russia, which established closer economic cooperation. However, there was not enough substance to it, regarding political dialogue with Russia. This agreement particularly illustrates the priority that was given by the Greek Presidency to improve the EU relations with Russia and other ex-Soviet republics, such as Ukraine. However, agreement could not be reached in the latter case because of the high financial implications that this would have. Despite the many positive outcomes of the Presidency, Greece lost an important opportunity to play a leading role in the prospects of co-operation and peace in the Balkans. It could have been a Greek initiative during the Presidency, but was never taken.[40]

The Spanish Presidencies

The First Presidency of Spain in 1989 came three years after its accession to the Community. Unlike the first Greek Presidency, the Spaniards, as the evidence suggests, were committed to demonstrating their European orientation and their maturity as respectable and influential actors in the European structure. The Spanish success can be attributed to three main factors that became the core of the first Spanish Presidency. The first was the learning process of the Spanish officials. As a new Member State, Spain lacked the experience and know-how to organise and administer an EC

Presidency. In order to overcome its inexperience, Spanish officials travelled throughout different capitals of older Member States in order to take advantage of their experience and knowledge in Presidency organisation and chairing of the Council of Ministers.[41] The second factor was the importance given by the Presidency to the effective administration through working groups and formal or informal meetings in order to produce a greater degree of cooperation and coordination of the different positions. A particular interest was given to foreign policy by supporting and using the EPC framework.[42] Finally, the last factor was the Spanish initiatives, particularly in the foreign policy field, and its determination in assuming its commitments to the integration of Europe. These initiatives illustrated the Spanish commitment to strengthening the links between the Community and Latin America and the Maghreb, two areas that were of particular interest for Spain. Spain used constructive behaviour to direct EPC in a Europeanist direction and also to situate Spain at the core of the European construction.[43] As a result of this attitude, Spain profited from the prestige of a successful Presidency both in Europe and in domestic politics.

The Second Spanish Presidency of the European Union during the second semester of 1995 took place straight after the recent enlargement and just before the beginning of the IGC for the revision of the Treaty. At that time, there was an environment of criticism towards the effectiveness of the EU Common Foreign and Security Policy after the Yugoslavian crisis. The timing of the Presidency gave the Spanish government the opportunity to achieve a number of objectives. The Spanish objectives in CFSP were, among others, for the EU to deal with the final stages of the Yugoslav conflict, the beginning of a political dialogue with Russia that was missing from the economic agreement, the Mediterranean cooperation that led to the Barcelona Conference and a series of agreements with Latin America. In addition a further Spanish objective was to overcome the fear of the CEESs that it would oppose the process for the start of accession negotiations. This was achieved by the special attention that was given by the Presidency to the applications for accession and the structured dialogue of the EU with the CEESs. The Spanish Presidency can be considered as successful for the EU because Spain disassociated its own objectives from the objectives of the Presidency, as the example of the CEESs illustrates. Spain gave issues of foreign policy the priority for three main reasons. First, Spain and particularly Felipe Gonzalez wanted to demonstrate its commitment to a common foreign policy for the EU and improve its effectiveness and reputation after the damage that the uncoordinated responses had produced during the Yugoslavian crisis. It was a particular opportunity for Gonzalez himself to indulge in an extensive network of foreign policy, representing the EU, which has always been his strong personal field of interest. Secondly, it was an opportunity for Spain to promote the two areas of foreign policy that are of particular interest for Spanish foreign policy: Latin America and the Mediterranean. During the Spanish Presidency, negotiations with Latin America resulted in the signing of an Interregional agreement between the EU and Mercosur, an agreement on political dialogue with Chile, an economic, political and commercial agreement with Mexico, and the beginning of conversations for a possible agreement with Cuba.[44] Possibly the greatest achievement of the Presidency, was regarding the Mediterranean in which the Conference in Barcelona on 27-28 November 1995 started the Euro-Mediterranean Partnership Initiative. Another area of significance, during the Spanish Presidency, was the EU involvement in the Middle East Peace Process with the signing of the new Plan for Tripartite Action and the active participation of the EU in different multilateral fora. Finally, the Presidency gave the Spanish government an opportunity to demonstrate its political abilities in foreign policy and its European commitment given the many domestic problems that the government faced at that time.[45]

The institutional role of the Presidency of the EU and the participation in institutional reform, examined above, are both activities within the framework of the institutional requirements of Member States. All Member States have the right to acquire the presidency for six months, currently every seven and a half years, based on fifteen Member States, and all participate in IGCs and have input in the shaping of the institutions. This chapter now goes on to look at the foreign policy activities, which have a direct link with the influence that the Member State can exercise, in the sense that no influence can mean no activity. This is because lack of activity can be regarded as lack of interest in the institution of the Presidency, and thus can create a negative reputation for the State holding an inactive Presidency. The next section focuses on foreign policy initiatives which Greece and Spain took or failed to take.

Priorities: Foreign Policy Initiatives

Initiatives in foreign policy can be an illustration of the influence and effective role of a Member State. However, in order to look at some of the initiatives that Greece and Spain took or might have taken, as well as at their consequences, some things have to be put into perspective. Greece is a small state in the EU with a weak economic structure, difficult geopolitical position and long-established and intense problems of security in its region. On the other hand, Spain is in a far better situation in terms of its security preoccupations and it also possesses a wider and more efficient network of foreign relations. The question that prevails is how easy it is for a state like Greece to take initiatives in foreign policy? As an answer to that question, a senior official of Greece to the EU argues that it is not at all easy for a small state to take initiatives.[46] He argues that in the case where large and important states in foreign policy dislike a specific initiative, proposed by a State such as Greece, they would never let it pass or be developed. In the case that they do like the idea of the initiative, they prefer themselves to be the initiators of it and not a small state. However, taking the examples of Luxembourg or the Netherlands, small states that have realised an extensive initiative activity supports the argument that the size of a state is not an important determinant of its influential activity. Therefore, this suggests that it is not only the size or the resources that allow a Member State to take initiatives in CFSP but rather its constructive participation in the institutions and its reputation as a promoter of the common European interest.

There is another aspect to the issue of initiatives that is probably more important than the ability of a small state to take them and that is how these initiatives are pursued. This has enormous implications both for the ability of the state to take them and for their effectiveness. Three factors are important in order for a Member State to pursue and succeed with any initiative. First, the Member State should have a good reputation as a cooperative partner in CFSP. It should be respectable and be regarded as a state which demonstrates an interest and cares, not only for its own national concerns, but also for the European Union as a whole. Second, the initiative that the state proposes should be a well-prepared and studied idea.[47] Finally, it should follow a path of consultation and preparative diplomacy with some or most fellow Member States, in order to prepare them for the initiative and to evaluate the level of agreement. The latter requires an effective foreign policy administration and experienced diplomats in terms of EU negotiation processes. All three factors are important to the success of an initiative.

Greek Initiatives

There were times during its membership that Greece had some constructive ideas and some of these times they were well prepared.[48] However, many of them resulted in failure. What was missing were the two remaining factors. For almost fourteen years the image and reputation that Greece created for it in Europe was largely negative. This was the reason why many times the Greek proposals did not get any attention at all, despite the fact that some of them were good. Greece's reputation was so poor that in order to persuade the majority of the validity of its arguments, it had to do more than just present evidence. It needed to change its overall behaviour in CFSP and not just in one specific case. Greece then had to change its position on existing EU issues, something which historically had oppose other members' views, and finally it had to put forward constructive initiatives that are likely to enjoy wide support. An example of a Greek failure to persuade the majority of the validity of its arguments can be found in the period during the Yugoslavian crisis. It was one day before the EU recognition of Bosnia and the commencement of hostilities there. The Greek foreign minister, Antonis Samaras, had just come back from Belgrade where Milosevic had completed a modus vivendi with Croatia, and he was going to do the same for Bosnia. Milosevic asked the EU,[49] through Samaras, for time and warned them that a civil war would follow the recognition of that state by the EU. Samaras delivered the message to his partners asking them not to recognise Bosnia. The reputation of Greece as openly pro-Serb and particularly that of Samaras who was pursuing an ultra-nationalist policy towards Macedonia was such that nobody could understand, consequently the Council became suspicious and dismissed Samaras' arguments. Another example is that of the Albanian crisis of 1997, which is discussed below. In this case, Greece proposed a plan for the resolution of the crisis but the joint action proposed failed because of the suspicion of Greece's partners of a Greek military operation under the EU umbrella in the Balkans, only a couple of years after the end of the hostility generated by the Macedonian case.[50]

There are also times that Greek proposals failed because of lack of pre-consultation with other Member States. An example of this was the case of the EU's external borders that Greece had been trying to achieve for years. This was primarily for three reasons. First, Greece believed that its views and position could not be understood. Second, it wanted to avoid any influence of other Member States that was not in line with its thinking being included in the initiative. Finally, Greece demonstrated an attitude of self-perceived superiority when it came to issues of its national interest. It was an attitude of exclusiveness in knowledge, according to which, Greece was the one who knew these issues best, and should therefore have been allowed to lecture its partners. This attitude has always caused offence with Greece's partners. Given the very sensitive position of Greece in the Balkans, if a proposal is brought to the Council without any previous consultation and is concerned with the region, it is bound to attract suspicion from Greece's partners, that there is a catch behind it. The best way to achieve a successful result would be to consult and discuss the idea with other states who might be interested, and present it to the Council with significant backing from others. Since 1996, there has been a radical change in Greek foreign policy with a significant improvement of the Greek image and reputation.[51] From a situation in which Greece had problems with all its neighbours, today Greece is looking to play a constructive role in the Balkans. The problems with Albania and Bulgaria were solved, and particularly during the Albanian crisis of 1997, Greece played an important and constructive role in the resolution of the conflict. In contrast to its attitude towards Macedonia, in this case Greece brought forward the issue in the CFSP as an issue that required immediate joint action on behalf of the Union. Greece even suggested contributing a large amount of troops to a WEU mission in Albania for the stabilisation of the situation. However, as mentioned above, because of its previous negative reputation, it was too soon for the Greek constructive proposal to succeed. The problem with Macedonia was resolved, although the question of the name remains. Even in the traditional Greek-Turkish conflict there has been some optimism after the Madrid declaration and the agreement on the restructuring of the Mediterranean command of NATO.[52] Today Greece demonstrates at times, a prudent foreign policy, which has already improved its image and helped increase its influence. It can also help in reaching a solution to its long-standing problem with Turkey, which continues to be its main security preoccupation.[53] There is a need for both Greeks and Turks to compromise their positions for a lasting mutual agreement, and that is the most difficult task. Although there have been signs of improvement, the sense of national sovereign rights that they both fear losing if they compromise to an agreement, makes the planning of this process seem impossible.

An example of the improved role of Greece as an EU member in the Balkans is the successful initiative that was implemented and had as its result the Balkan Summit that took place in Crete between 3-5 November 1997. The success of the Greek initiative consists of two aspects: the realisation of the Summit itself, after a period of long and hard negotiations, and also the fact that a common declaration was achieved. However, it was a unilateral initiative of Greece, outside the scope of CFSP. The Summit brought together the Heads of governments and foreign ministers of eight Balkan states. Apart from Greece, Albania, Bulgaria, Bosnia, Macedonia, Rumania, Turkey and Yugoslavia participated. In the final declaration it was agreed that a regional co-operation on a political, economic and social level should be the objective of all participating states. There is also a mention of human rights and ethnic minority rights. Despite the failure of the Greek proposal in the Summit to develop a permanent secretariat of Balkan co-operation, as a first step the Summit was a success.[54] The success of the initiative can also be seen from the launch of the Balkan Peace process that can bring positive results for peace and stability in the region. The second Balkan Conference was celebrated in Antalya, Turkey on 12-13 October 1998. This second Conference of the process dealt extensively with the Kosovo crisis. However, the Balkan Conference was an initiative welcomed by the EU, but outside the framework of CFSP. Greece had not yet been able to overcome the negative consequences of its previous reputation in order to succeed in an initiative within the CFSP framework. The success of the initiative, though, works to the improvement of the Greek reputation, and the fact that the Summit and its results were welcomed by the EU is a sign of the change in Greece's reputation. This was further enhanced by the prudent stance of Greece during the 1999 Kosovo crisis. Examples such as these can eventually eliminate the negative consequences of past behaviour.

Spanish Initiatives

Spain followed a very careful strategy of preparation and presentation of initiatives to make sure that they were successful. Spain followed an attitude of continuous cooperation within EPC/CFSP because it felt that this would lead to a better definition of its own interest, which in turn could meet with more understanding from its partners and be Europeanised.[55] This attitude developed a response from Spain's partners that was more transparent and predictable, and so, demonstrated Spain's capability to produce successful initiatives in foreign policy both inside and outside CFSP. This contrasted with Greece's lack of such capability, which was a result of its different attitude. However, perhaps the most important success of Spain was the ability to generate all the foreign policy initiatives through the institutions of CFSP and thus, enhance their importance and diplomatic capacity. The first step for successful initiatives was the reputation that Spain achieved since it became a full member of the European Community. This was a reputation of a consensus builder, which Spain gained because of its commitment to help achieve common positions. Spain demonstrated its commitment to common policies in two ways. First, it did its upmost to adapt its political orientation to Europe and identify its interests with the common European interest. Second, on the whole, Spain avoided confrontation and favoured a mutual compromise in order to achieve common positions. That was the case in the Middle East conflict, as well as in the ex-Yugoslavia crisis and many others. Finally, it was a reputation of able leadership and diplomatic excellence. Spain had the privilege of a world-wide respected political leadership and of a diplomatic administration, which was characterised by good organisation and efficiency. These reputations gave Spain the ability to take initiatives in foreign policy in which the Spanish mediation and leadership was not only acceptable, but required and highly regarded.

The second step was the preparation and presentation of ideas for any given initiative. It has to be stressed that Spanish foreign policy administration was weak and problematic before accession.[56] It was the process of adaptation and the commitment of Spain to achieve a modern and Europeanised administration, during the first years of membership, that developed the Spanish effectiveness.[57] With a quick and effective adaptation of its foreign policy administrative structure, Spain was able to combine its traditional foreign policy qualities with a sound understanding of the way that EPC was functioning and so, to prepare initiatives with a chance to succeed. Another strong aspect of the Spanish administration in Europe was the continuity. The Spanish diplomatic personnel both in Madrid and in Brussels have been there for years, despite the change in government, and that has added to the maturity of the Spanish know-how of the Community business. The final step was that of pre-consultation and institutional behaviour. Spain ensured that any proposal for a foreign policy initiative should be well-balanced and accepted by a number of other Member States before its presentation in the Council. Spain also demonstrated its commitment to work within the institutional framework of EPC/CFSP and play by the Euro-rules. By working through the institutions, Spain not only proved its European orientation but also strengthened its chances for success, given its limitations in structural power, collective action enhanced the Spanish influence. By playing by the rules that govern negotiations and the formation of common positions in the EU, and specifically in the field of foreign policy, Spain achieved the incorporation of its objectives in the European agenda by making the Spanish interests European interests and vice versa.

Between the many foreign policy activities that Spain was involved in during its membership of the EC/EU, perhaps the two most important and significant for Spain were the Middle East Peace Conference in Madrid of 30 October to 3 November 1991 and the Euro-Mediterranean Conference of 27-28 November 1995. Both of these events were a product of a long process and achieved reputation of the Spanish foreign policy and are not isolated issues. Although Spain was chosen by the International Community to host the Middle East Conference and was therefore not a Spanish initiative, there are five factors that influenced this selection and support the argument that the hosting of the Conference was, in a sense, a Spanish achievement. First, after its accession to the EC, Spain was distanced from the Francoist pro-Arab posture. By recognising Israel and building good relations with the Jewish State, Spain moved to an impartial position between the two sides, maintaining good relations with both Arabs and Jews.[58] This act moved Spain away from any biased position and made it trustworthy for hosting a peace conference. Second, Spain held good relations with both the US and the Soviet Union. The dependant nature of Spanish-US relations of the Franco era was moderated while the NATO membership was maintained, and the socialist government of Felipe Gonzalez also developed close relations with the Soviet Union, particularly after the coming to power of Gorbachev.[59] This made Spain an ideal place for the reunion of the two superpowers. Third, during its Presidency in 1989, Spain took a leading role on the issue of the Middle East Peace process in the EC. The European Council in Madrid on 27 June 1989 approved the Spanish initiative for a declaration of a common position on the Middle East.[60] This gave Spain the knowledge of handling the issue as well as the diplomatic skills of representing the Union in that conflict region as Miguel Angel Moratinos, an able Spanish diplomat later became the head of the EU mission to the Middle East. Fourthly, the Spanish initiative that was launched in Mallorca in September 1990 on the development of a Conference on the Security and Cooperation in the Mediterranean similar to the CSCE, despite its failure, added to the Spanish reputation and suitability for hosting the Middle East Conference. Finally,

Spain was rewarded by the US for its active and enthusiastic participation in the multinational force in the Gulf War.[61]

Perhaps the most significant initiative of the Spanish diplomacy was the Barcelona Conference of 1995 that launched the Euro-Mediterranean Partnership Initiative. Arguably, the success of the Barcelona process can be attributed to the Madrid Conference, without which Barcelona would not be possible.[62] This can be explained by the gradual accumulation of a reputation as a successful mediator, by building sound relations with both Arabs and Israelis on an impartial basis. In Barcelona, Spain made a step forward from Madrid. While the Spanish success in Madrid was due to the fact that it was through its reputation and diplomatic skills that it had achieved the hosting of the Conference, in Barcelona, Spain had been the initiator and orchestrator of the process. There are three groups of interesting issues that derive from the successful Spanish initiative and are indications of how Spain managed to achieve a significant degree of influence both in the Mediterranean region and in the EU. First, there is the issue of its foreign policy behaviour. Spain's priority in foreign policy had been the build up of excellent relations with its southern neighbours. This was not just a priority before the initiative, but a long process of more than ten years. Also these relationships were based on a stabilising role that Spain wanted to play as a member of the EC/EU in the region and on an objective of bringing these states closer to Europe. This type of behaviour was based on the belief of the Spanish officials and Gonzalez himself that any conflicting issue between Spain and its southern neighbours could be resolved or eliminated if these states would develop close links with the EU that could guarantee their economic development and democratic stability.[63] The second issue is that of the Europeanisation of Spanish foreign policy. Spain increasingly identified its own interest with the European one. By working through the institutions Spain managed to incorporate Spanish preoccupations with the stability of the region into EU concerns. On the other hand, by supporting a common foreign policy, Spain gave precedence to collective resolutions of problems and the opposition of unilateralism. Additionally, the Europeanisation of the Spanish foreign policy resulted in the counter-balance of the EU priorities which was led by the German concerns with Central and Eastern Europe. The final issue is the way in which Spain handled the initiative that resulted in this counter-balance. As Richard Gillespie characterises the Spanish diplomacy, it was a mixture of alliances, pressure and compromise.[64] In order to promote the Mediterranean aspect of European foreign policy, Felipe Gonzalez worked towards the formation of an alliance that would support this development. Working together with France proved the most beneficial. The next step was to persuade Germany of the significance of the Southern orientation. This was finally achieved in December 1994 at the Essen Summit, when Helmut Kohl accepted the significance of the Mediterranean for European security, and in June 1995 at the Cannes Summit, when a final agreement was reached on the financial matters of the project.[65]

Foreign policy initiatives are important to determine the influence that a Member State can exercise, however, they are not an everyday decision-making activity. The next section looks at the everyday participation of Greece and Spain in European foreign policy, trying to examine the link between interest and influence. The argument is that the more interest the Member State demonstrates in European common interests rather than its own interests, the more influence it can exercise in their construction.

Actions: Participation and Interest

Greek Interest in European Foreign Policy

There are two different views on effective participation in the Common Foreign and Security Policy of the EU that are often expressed by Greek officials.[66] The first is that it is a mistake for Greece to limit its participation and interest on issues, which are related to Greece directly, e.g. the Balkans, Turkey and Southeast Europe. This view argues that Greece must have an opinion on all issues concerning the CFSP and particularly to express interest, opinion and understanding on issues that are vital for other members. The second view of effective participation argues that Greece does not have the capacity and capability to over engaged itself with everything on the CFSP agenda. The argument follows that it should therefore deal with the issues that it knows the best and in which it can perform effectively, and leave the rest to states with more tradition and experience in foreign policy. The view that expresses an unlimited involvement with everything runs the danger of a shallow Greek understanding and unsupported opinions that can sometimes irritate other Member States. This danger can be caused by the fact that Greece does not have the profound and experienced administration that is needed for such engagement. On the other hand, the view of the limited involvement can give an impression of a state which is only concerned with its own interest for its individual benefit. During the last couple of years, it seems that Greece has chosen a third path. It focuses its attention on the region of the Balkans and the issues related to it as core interest. Greece has dedicated all its effort to play a leading role. Outside the core area there is an area of relative interest, which contains issues of interest to Greek foreign policy but not of vital importance, such as the Mediterranean, and the Middle East. On these issues, Greece participates in working groups and expresses interest and opinions. Finally, there are all the other issues in CFSP, for which Greece does have an opinion and interest but leaves the interested states to pursue them further. Such a case was that of the crisis in Zaire in 1997. This view of effective participation can secure an interest and opinion for all issues concerning CFSP but also concentrates its resources on the issues in which Greece has the know-how and which are vital for its foreign policy.

This philosophy of participation, which to a large extent is followed by the Greek government today, is implemented in three dimensions. First, with proposals and initiatives in foreign policy, such as the ones discussed above. Secondly, with an effective, flexible and experienced administration in the foreign ministry dealing with CFSP (directorate A11), whose basic task should be to co-operate and co-ordinate its policies with other Member States. However, there is a distinction between issues of CFSP of a general sense, which are subjects of the A11 and issues of CFSP that are considered as Greek national issues, like the Turkish case. These issues do not form part of the A11.[67] During the process of development of CFSP, the Greek administration, gradually became accustomed to the functioning and the requirements of its participation in European foreign policy. Finally, as a result of the second dimension, the Greek participation in the institutions has changed. Although there are plenty of areas which require improvement, the Greek administration has taken important steps to accommodate the needs of such participation.[68] The most important of these is the Greek participation in the working groups of CFSP and of the General Secretariat of the Council. This is the place where initiatives and proposals are tested, national positions are discussed and negotiations and state coalitions take place.[69] During the 1980s and in the then working groups of EPC before their incorporation in the Council, Greece used to appoint its representatives with political clientelistic methods. These appointments were considered more as a trip to Brussels and they were given on a clientelistic basis.[70] The Greek representatives were often ignorant about the Greek position on many issues and their pattern of behaviour rested on three alternatives. They either abstained from the discussion and the vote, or followed a specific country in all matters, or visited Brussels for shopping instead.[71] Although it can be argued that there are plenty of areas for improvement, the manner of participation of the Greek administration has changed significantly. Over the last couple of years the Greek representatives in the working groups have become well informed and prepared, having opinions on all issues, expressing interest and proposing ideas.

Spanish Interest in European Foreign Policy

One of the main objectives of Spain's membership of the EC/EU has been to be able to develop an extensive international voice. To be able to participate as a foreign policy actor in international affairs has been an achievement that brought the end of isolationism in Spain. However, there have been issues of special significance for Spanish foreign policy related to the Maghreb, Mediterranean, Middle East and Latin America. In the above areas, Spain wanted to be the initiator in addition to an expressed interest and participation in common policies. The issues of special significance for Spain were regarded as its privileged areas. In order to achieve its objective, which was to be able to participate effectively in all issues of European foreign policy, Spain had to Europeanise its privileged areas, so as to let other Member States have a say and also to guarantee the EU common action. Spain has only totally Europeanised the three of the four areas mentioned above. In the areas of the Maghreb, Mediterranean and the Middle East, Spain created a pro-Mediterranean lobby in the EU, supported the selection of these areas as liable to joint actions and worked towards the transfer of resources to Maghreb on grounds of conflict prevention mechanism. However, Spain perceived Latin America not as an area of risk but of prestige. Relations with Latin America do not affect Spain's security but rather its identity and values. Thus, Spain pressured the Community to transfer more resources to Latin America, such as the San José group efforts, but kept the Europeanisation of it in the EC pillar only.[72] Latin America is still an area for primarily bilateral relations for Spain in the issues covered by CFSP. It has never formed an area for CFSP joint action of the EU and most of the EU agreements with Latin American States or groups, like Mercosur, are described as lacking substance, if compared with States such as Central and Eastern European or even Southern Mediterranean States.[73] They express the interest for cooperation and the offering of aid but in the end, they do not provide any structure for the realisation of them. The official explanation given by Spanish officials is that Latin America is not significant for European security and therefore there is no reason for it to form part of the CFSP considerations.[74] However, there is another explanation that wants Latin America to be an exclusive privileged domain for Spanish foreign policy because of the close cultural links.

As a result of its great interest in foreign policy and its remarkable activism and greater international commitment, the Spanish image was given a boost, particularly thanks to its diplomatic skills. After a long period of isolation, Spain participated in the UN peacekeeping forces, became a non-permanent member of the UN Security Council and participated in the commitment of 'four-plus-one' for Bosnia-Herzegovina.[75]

In order to achieve the effectiveness of its participation in EPC/CFSP, Spain restructured its foreign policy administration to adjust it to that of the other Member States.[76] The issues of CFSP are the responsibility of the General Directorate for Foreign Policy headed by a Political Director and assisted by a Deputy Director for CFSP. The significance of CFSP being dealt with by the same General Directorate that deals with the bilateral foreign political relations of Spain as well, is that unlike Greece, there is not any artificial separation between issues of national and European concern in CFSP. This has increased both the efficiency of Spanish participation in CFSP and the effective incorporation of the Spanish priorities in the European agenda. Another aspect that reinforced the effectiveness of Spanish participation is the continuity of both the administration personnel in Madrid and the representation in Brussels. After the recent change of government, in the spring of 1996, the new prime minister Jose Maria Aznar, not only maintained the experienced diplomatic personnel but also demonstrated signs of continuity when he appointed Abel Matutes, the former EC Commissioner, as the new foreign minister. However, there have been growing concerns that the governing Popular Party is changing the manner of Spanish participation in CFSP, perhaps by a different perception of the European common foreign policy. This is based on the fact that Aznar has many times overruled Matutes and taken the initiative himself of expressing Spanish foreign policy.[77] However, strong leadership has been always the case in Spain and particularly during the González era.

Actions: Personalities

Despite the importance of the administrative structure, leadership continues to play one of the most important roles in the political orientation of any Member State.[78] Although a charismatic leadership can play a very important role to the image and influence of a Member State in foreign policy, it does not necessary mean that it will be positive. Andreas Papandreou was one of the most charismatic leaders in Greek politics and definitely will be a target of a large number of historical analyses. Despite his virtues and skills, his political orientation and ideology was such that he isolated Greece from the rest of Europe and deprived Greece from playing a significant role in the Community. Also, despite his charismatic personality, he based his relations with the other European leaders upon confrontation rather than partnership and co-operation.

There are also some limitations to the significance of leadership. It might be the case that a charismatic leadership is restricted from pursuing its full potentials by domestic politics. An appropriate example of that was Prime Minister Constantinos Mitsotakis at the beginning of the 1990s. Mitsotakis was very much a charismatic leader and also dedicated to the European ideal, but the domestic political correlation, mainly in his own political party, deprived him from the ability to control policy developments. So, in order for a leadership to be influential in Europe's foreign policy, a charismatic personality is not the only factor. Domestic political stability and a strong government, as well as a European political orientation are also very important.

Apart from the importance of the leadership of the state, a very important factor in the influence of it is played by personalities that hold key-posts. This can be described as a two-way process. Firstly, in order for a state to obtain key-posts for its nationals, it must follow a strategy of building its image and reputation as we have mentioned before in the book. Secondly, by obtaining such posts, the state is able to exercise more influence; depending on weather the post is administered successfully or not will affect its influence. With the exception of the European Parliament, Greece has never achieved a significant post in the European institutions. The reasons for the Greek failure in that area can be summed up in three ways. These are the general image and reputation of the state, the quality and effectiveness of the work that has been produced by Greek representatives, and the structural problems that Greece is facing in economics and geopolitics. The general image of the state, as has been discussed earlier, has enormous implications for the level of trust that is needed for a Greek personality to gain an important post in the European institutions. For many years Greece demonstrated a disregard for the institutions and the notion of collective action. This attitude had implications for Greeks, as they were not regarded as appropriate for important posts. The second important reason is the effective and responsible work that state representatives demonstrate. For many years, Greece had neither a coherent European policy nor a credible system of appointment of representatives. Also, its political orientation and ideology, mainly in the 1980s, deprived it from putting forward reliable politicians experienced and involved in European affairs, able to target and achieve such posts. An exception to this, is the European Parliament in which the Greek members have demonstrated exceptional qualities and contributed to the functioning of groups and committees.[79] Although the post of the President of the EP[80] was never achieved, Greek MEPs have become Vice-Presidents and leading figures in European political groupings, as well as chairmen of committees. Finally, the structural problems of Greece limit its potential. The economic problems and the weak infrastructure create a dependence upon the structural funds and thus limit the possibilities of a Greek personality achieving a key-post in the area of the first pillar of the EU. In foreign policy the problems are concentrated in the difficult geopolitical situation of Greece. As Greece is directly involved with many problems in the region, Greek representatives are not impartial enough to represent the Union in these conflicts. On the other hand, in issues that are not related to the region, it seems that Greeks are not well experienced. Despite the past failure of Greece in the issue of representatives, a Greek politician, Mr Panagiotis Roumeliotis recently became the co-ordinator of the Royaumont process for Southeast Europe. This development, which is the first of its kind, is a promising one and also underlines the changes that occurred in the Greek image.

For Spain, the achievement of key-positions, not only in CFSP but also in general in the institutions of the EU and other international organisations, has been a point of success. In leading missions of CFSP, the names of Miguel Angel Moratinos, Carlos Westendorp and Felipe Gonzalez were figuring. Moratinos is an experienced diplomat who had been working on the Middle East Peace process, particularly during the Madrid Conference. The Aznar government in 1996 sent him as an ambassador to Israel where, because of his knowledge and experience, he was appointed as the EU representative in the Peace settlement. Carlos

Westendorp was the General Secretary for EU affairs in Spain during the socialist government, and became the last foreign minister of Gonzalez when Javier Solana was appointed the NATO General Secretary. Westendorp was appointed as the leader of the EU representation team in Bosnia and the Yugoslav crisis. Finally, Felipe Gonzalez was appointed first as the OSCE negotiator in Yugoslavia and recently the same organisation supported by the EU, appointed him as mediator between the Serbs and the Albanians in Kosovo. To this successful list one can add key-posts achieved by Spaniards in the EU institutions, such as the two Spanish Presidents of the European Parliament, Enrique Baron Crespo and Jose Maria Gil Robles, the Vice-President of the Commission Manuel Marin, the President of the European Court of Justice Carlos Rodriguez Iglesias, the President of the Committee of the Regions Pasqual Maragall i Mira, and the EU envoy in Mostar, Pérez Casado. It is not without significance that after a successful term as General Secretary of NATO, Javier Solana has now been appointed as the first High Representative of CFSP.

This Spanish achievement can be explained by four main factors. First, Spain demonstrates an achieved degree of influence and reputation because of its European commitment and constructive participation. This reputation of an institutional player added to the trustworthiness of Spanish politicians and diplomats to lead EU joint actions. The second factor is the existence of what can be described as a positive strategy to achieve these key-positions. However, this is not a formal strategy developed by the Spanish government or the administration.[81] It is more like an informal process of support of any Spanish candidature in Europe regardless of her/his party political origins. That was the case during the socialist government and it is still the case today. The third factor is the unquestionably charismatic leadership. Felipe Gonzalez has been a personality of wide admiration and acceptance on the international stage. In contrast with Andreas Papandreou, Gonzalez chose the path of cooperation and constructive contribution in the EC/EU, and this has added to his image as an influential leader and a consensus-builder. Finally, there is also an element of quality of the Spanish political culture, particularly in Spanish politicians and diplomats that makes them respectable and adequate for international posts of responsibility. This is part of a process of building an advanced political culture, which developed after the start of the democratisation process in Spain from the mid-1970s.[82] This process was the one of two objectives that Spain wanted to achieve from membership of the EU. The first was to end its isolationism in world affairs and the second was to start a process of modernisation of its political structures. The success of the modernisation process is illustrated in the Spanish political culture.

Final Remarks

It can be argued that one of the recipes for success for a state like Greece or Spain to obtain a significant level of influence in the Common Foreign and Security Policy is to pursue a strategy of participation. Other recipes, such as the adaptation and the desecuritisation of national foreign policy are considered in chapters three and five respectively. This participation should be characterised by effective involvement at all levels from national administration and working groups in the General Secretariat of the Council to the foreign ministers and Heads of government. Additionally, a demonstration of an attitude of co-operation and interest is an important factor. It has been pointed out and explained that during the last years, Greece seems to attempt to follow this strategy, and there are signs that its role and influence in CFSP has been increased. However, using and maintaining the achieved influence is of similar importance.[83] Spain on the other hand had carefully planned its participation in order to become one of the leading countries in the shaping of European integration, and that includes the development of a common foreign policy. However, the recent change of government in Spain offers signs of a retreat from the Spanish all-positive participation. The evidence suggest that the two states adopted a pragmatic approach and shifted their behaviour in different cases according to factors discussed.

The comparison between the two states can be concluded in five very interesting observations. First, constructive participation in the building of European integration is an essential requirement for the achievement of influence over the process. This can be successfully supported both by looking at the two states in question and by looking at the changes that occurred in each state. Spain had a more significant influence over the outcome of the IGC on European Union than Greece had during the first two IGCs it participated in. This is mainly because of the level of commitment from the Spanish side and the lack of such commitment on the Greek side to contribute to the building of the EU. The failure of the Greek side can be attributed to the fact that the Greeks were preoccupied with their own narrow interests rather than the interests of Europe as a whole. In contrast, Spain promoted the common European interest as the prevailing one. An interesting comparison is one of the changes that the new governments have brought to the two countries. During the Amsterdam IGC, Simitis' government demonstrated a much more constructive attitude that played a significant part in the outcome of the Treaty. On the other hand, the new Spanish government has retreated to more sceptical positions with the defence of its national interest as first priority which has led to tensions that might prove damaging for its influence in the future.

The second conclusion is that playing by the Euro-rules, through the institutions, is very important for the incorporation of the Member State into the European system of mutual understanding. These Euro-rules derive from the provisions of Title V of the Treaty on European Union. Article J.1 outlines what the objectives of CFSP should be, which means that the Member States should respect them in their participation patterns. However, these formal rules generate informal behavioural requirements. When the formal rule states that the objective of CFSP shall be to safeguard the common values, fundamental interests and independence of the Union, it develops a requirement for a collective interest. Member States should refrain from promoting their own interests at the expense of the others and help construct a collective interest. In the event of a conflict of arguments, the informal pattern of participation requires compromises. A State that is promoting its own interests without the willingness to compromise for a common interest breaks both the informal and formal rules designed by the Treaty. Another example of a Euro-rule is the objective mentioned in Article J.1 that Member States should promote international cooperation. A Member State that strives to tackle a problem by confrontation rather than cooperation, breaks the rules. By that system it is argued that there are standard rules of conduct in the European process that facilitate the understanding between Member States. By insisting on nationalist arguments that was very difficult for its fellow members to understand Greece could not achieve the understanding and mutual solidarity since its actions were isolated and not part of a mutual cooperation. Greece was not willing to compromise its positions to achieve a consensus but rather chose confrontation. It was confronted by its fellow Member States, when it tried to use the institutional rules for its own benefit, and also it was confronted by neighbouring countries rather than to try to solve problems through cooperation. The ex-foreign minister of Greece, Theodore Pangalos, describes this situation as schizophrenic. He argues that 'despite foreign policy, Greece has a series of national problems for which, although it doesn't like to listen to the Community suggesting the behaviour that it should take, it often asks for the Community's support. If Greece demands the help of the Union, it is logical for her to be incorporated in the Community framework, and this means that Greece has to persuade as well as listen to the arguments of the others.[84] Spain on the other hand demonstrated its commitment to the European institutions. The main objective of Spain since its adhesion has been the development of common policies and positions through consensus building and compromise. This attitude of avoiding confrontation has had beneficial results for the Spanish reputation.

The third conclusion is that foreign policy behaviour can alter the results of negotiation even if the policy itself remains the same. The offensive approach that Gonzalez followed had far better results in achieving its objectives rather than the defensive approach of Aznar. This is because by blocking proposals, one creates a negative environment while by counter-proposing, one creates an atmosphere of constructive compromise. Greece vetoed the financial protocols to Turkey with no substantial explanations apart from the fact that it considers Turkey as a threat to its territorial integrity. However, The Greek behaviour in the Luxembourg Summit in 1998 has had completely different results because Greece did not veto the Turkish participation in the European Conference, but explained and achieved a consensus on why there is a need to apply conditions to such a membership.

The fourth conclusion that can be drawn is that collective action needs collective participation. What made the Spanish initiatives more successful was the fact that before their presentation, they were prepared in a collective environment with consultation and discussion with other fellow Member States. This is also another demonstration of working through the institutions and by the Euro-rules. Greece, on the other hand has, on the whole, acted unilaterally. Even the best proposal has little chance of success if it does not follow the way of institutional consultation. It is interesting to note that Greece has been more successful in its unilateral initiatives in the Balkan region, such as the Balkan Peace Process initiated by the Crete Conference, than in initiative in the framework of CFSP. However, as mentioned before, success in constructive initiatives even unilaterally, can alter the negative reputation and become beneficial for Greece's influence in CFSP in the long term. Finally, the last conclusion is that effective participation and cooperation at the administration level is very important for the promotion of the national position. The efficiency and organisation of the Spanish administration, as well as the continuity of the personnel dealing with European affairs at the administration level both in Madrid and in Brussels has been one of the factors for the successful preparation and deliverance of the Spanish position. Greece has recently demonstrated a rapid improvement in that area, which has contributed to a better understanding and presentation of the Greek position, with an example being the Luxembourg Summit of 1997. However, these conclusions are only valid as a whole and not as isolated. For example, the effective participation at the administration level, cannot produce beneficial results if the constructive participation is not in place or if the Member State breaks the rules that govern negotiation patterns in the EU.

Notes

[1]   S. George, 1994.
[2]   Interview, Enrique Gonzalez Sanchez, Council Secretariat, Brussels, December 1997.
[3]   Interview, Alberto Moreno, CFSP consultant, Permanent Representation of Spain, Brussels, December 1997.
[4]   Interview, Leonidas Evangelidis, General Secretariat of the Council, Brussels, 16 January 1998.
[5]   Valinakis, Y., 1994, p.200.
[6]   Valinakis, Y., 1993, p.263.
[7]   See Greek Memorandum on the reform of the Treaties, 1985, and Memorandum on Political Union, 1990.
[8]   Memorandum of Greece on Political Union, 1990.
[9]   Greek Foreign Ministry's Web page, http://www.mfa.gr/foreign/euro_union/ddceng.htm 17/09/96.
[10] Memorandum of the Greek government, MFA, 1996.
[11] Interview of the Alternate Foreign Minister, Th. Pangalos in *Evropaiki Epikairotita*, vol.12, 15/07/88.
[12] Interview, Pavlos Apostolides, Permanent Representation of Greece in the EU, Brussels, 9 December 1997.
[13] K. Hope, 1991, p.2.
[14] A success, which did not safeguard its security preoccupations due to the fact that Turkey was invited immediately as an observer and a clause of exemption, was added to avoid WEU involvement to a Greek-Turkish dispute.
[15] Memorandum of Greece on Political Union, Athens, MFA, 15 May 1990.
[16] S. Perrakis, 1997, p.367.
[17] R. Whitman and I. Manners, 2001.
[18] Interview, Angel Viñas, European Commission, Brussels, 8 January 1998.
[19] Greek memorandum for the 1996 IGC.
[20] Ibid.
[21] Y. Valinakis and E. Pitsarou, 1997, pp.163-4.
[22] Ibid. p.166.

23   Interview, Rafael Estrella, MP of PSOE, Madrid, 28 May 1998.

24   Spanish memorandum on Political Union, Madrid, November 1991.

25   Katlyn Saba, 1996, p.192.

26   E. Barbé, 1996b, p.260.

27   Common Foreign and Security Policy: Spanish Contribution, Madrid: Ministerio de Asuntos Exteriores, 26 November 1990.

28   Diario de Sesiones del Congreso de los diputados 155, 17 December 1991, p.7788, Speech of the Prime Minister Felipe González.

29   'The 1996 Intergovernmental Conference: starting points for a discussion', 2 March 1995: Official document Spanish Ministry of Foreign Affairs.

30   'Elements for a Spanish position at the 1996 Intergovernmental Conference', 28 March 1996: Official document Spanish Ministry of Foreign Affairs.

31   Ibid.

32   Interview with Guillermo Casañ, Popular Party, 21 May 1998.

33   Interview with Guillermo Casañ, Popular Party, 21 May 1998.

34   See C. O'Nuallain and M. Hoscheit, 1985.

35   Interview, Ramón Torrent, General Secretariat of the Council, Brussels, 7 January 1998.

36   See Chapter 3, pp. 49 and 55.

37   Interview, Pavlos Apostolides, Permanent Representation of Greece in the EU, Brussels, 9 December 1997.

38   Interview, ibid.

39   This is discussed further in the next chapter.

40   The Greek Foreign Minister Th. Pangalos acknowledged this lost opportunity in his speech in a conference organised by EKEM in Athens on 12 September 1994. The conference proceedings are published in a book by Stelios Perrakis and Nikos Frangakis in 1995.

41   Katlyn Saba, p.185.

42   E. Barbé, 1990.

43   E. Barbé, 1995, p.115.

44   'La PESC durante la Presidencia Española del Consejo de la UE', Official document: Office of Diplomatic Information, Spanish Ministry of Foreign Affairs, December 1995.

45   The Catalan nationalist party had already withdrew their support for the government and election were foreseeable for after the end of the Presidency.

46   Interview, Pavlos Apostolidis, Greek Ambassador, COREPER, Brussels, 9 December 1997.

47   Interview, Constantinos Economides, General Secretariat of the Council, Brussels, 16 January 1998.

48   Interview with Leonidas Evangelidis, General Secretariat, Brussels, January 1998.

49   Interview, Leonidas Evangelidis, General Secretariat, Brussels, 16 January 1998. The interviewee was present in Belgrade at that meeting of Samaras with Milosevic.

50   Samaras himself decided to abstain from the vote and not to block the decision of recognition.

51   Interview, Michail Vintsentsatos, CFSP Unit of the Council, Brussels, 7 January 1998.

52   The Madrid declaration was made during the NATO Summit in Madrid on September 1997. In the NATO Summit, Greece and Turkey agreed on a long dispute over the NATO commands in the Southeast Europe. Also the declaration by the two states provided for a process of peaceful settlement of their disputes.

[53] Interview, Leonidas Evangelidis, General Secretariat, Brussels, 16 January 1998.

[54] There has been an extensive coverage in the Greek press on the summit and its results. The newspapers 'Eleftherotypia' and 'Exousia', and the magazine 'Oikonomikos Taxydromos' particularly referred to it.

[55] E. Regelsberger, 1989, p.120.

[56] Interview with senior official in the Spanish Foreign Ministry, May 1998.

[57] E. Barbé, 1996, p.113.

[58] C. A. Zaldivar, 1992, p.229.

[59] Ibid., p.222.

[60] EPC Documentation Bulletin, 1989, 89/188, Statement on the meeting of the European Council in Madrid, 26 July 1989.

[61] E. Barbé, 1996b, p.268 .

[62] Richard Gillespie, 1997, p.33.

[63] F. González, 1998.

[64] Richard Gillespie, 1997, p.40.

[65] EFPB, 95/186.

[66] Interviews with Greek senior official and with officials in the Council, Brussels, 7 December 1997 and 16 January 1998.

[67] See Chapter 4 for an in-depth analysis of the administrative structure of the foreign ministry, p.97.

[68] See Annex 2 for the structure of the Greek MFA before accession and Annex 1 for the actual structure, pp.225-227.

[69] Interviews, General Secretariat and European Commission, Brussels, 7 and 8 January 1998.

[70] Interview, Ramón Torrent, General Secretariat, 7 January 1998.

[71] This is particularly true for the late 1980s when the Greek representatives did not know anything on the issue they had the directive to follow the Spanish position.

[72] E. Barbé, 1996, p.125.

[73] Interview, Ramon Torrent, Director, Council of Ministers, Brussels, 7/01/98.

[74] Interview, Francisco Elias de Tejada, Deputy Director of CFSP, Ministry of Foreign Affairs, Madrid, 19/05/98.

[75] E. Barbé, 1995, p.120.

[76] See Annex 4 for the structure of the Spanish MFA before accession and Annex 3 for the current structure, pp.229-231.

[77] Richard Gillespie, 1997, p.45.

[78] There are several works that deal with élite and personality in politics. Some of them are general and theoretical, e.g. V. Bonham-Carter, 1963, F. Greenstein, 1975, E.B. Portis, 1986, A.W. Lerner, 1990, P. Leonard, 1984, A.C. Elms, 1976, and D. Baer, 1989. Some other works focus on a personality, country or group of countries case study, such as L.W. Pye, 1962, R. Waite, 1998, D.P. Warwick, 1975, D.A, Tomasic, 1948, K.R. Minogue, 1987, R. Dahrendorf, 1968, T. Anton, 1980, S. Eldersveld, 1981, K. Deutsch, 1967 and E. Suleiman, 1974.

[79] Interview, Thomas Spencer MEP, European Parliament, Brussels, 6 January 1998.

[80] During the last election of the EP President there was a Greek candidate with a lot of potential.

[81] Interviews with various Spanish officials, Madrid, May 1998.

82   Interviews with Alfonso Diez Torres, Secretariat for the EU, Guillermo Casañ, MP for
     Partido Popular, and Ignasi Guardans, MP for CiU, Madrid, May 1998.
83   Interview, Ramón Torrent, CFSP unit of the Council, Brussels, 7 January 1998.
84   S. Perrakis and N. Fragakis, 1995, p.27.

6 Geopolitics and Foreign Policy Behaviour

After looking at domestic politics, participation patterns in CFSP, and political orientation, the final important factor that influences national foreign policy behaviour is geopolitics. The purpose of this chapter is to examine the extent to which geopolitics is an important factor in the shaping of foreign policy. In order to do this, we need to look at the nature of geopolitics and its influential aspects. Then, we look at how geopolitics is realised by Greece and Spain and in which way, if any, they influence the national political process. The argument is that the changing nature of world political economy has altered the priorities of State foreign policy and their capability to deliver something that is also enhanced by European integration. In this environment, traditional geopolitics tends to be replaced, in economically advanced states, by geoeconomics. In this process of change, traditional forces within states feel threatened and oppose the move for change by securitising certain policy areas. This chapter tests whether the extent to which such securitisation attempts exists in Greece and Spain influences their national foreign policy behaviour. The advantage of using the concept of 'securitisation' is that it demonstrates the importance of geopolitical concerns in the formation of foreign policy. It highlights the importance of geopolitical perceptions of security, which are as important as real threats. These perceptions are enhanced by 'securitisation' and they alter foreign policy behaviour.

Securitisation and Geopolitics

The objective of this chapter is to look at Greece and Spain and to identify the sectors in which a securitisation attempt exists, then to examine the success of that attempt and finally, to assess its implications on the national foreign policy. Successful securitisation in the military sector implies the influence of the traditional geopolitical logic on national foreign policy. It is a foreign policy in which the main concern of talks and negotiations with neighbours is the issue of national security, whether frontiers, national minorities, territory or any other related issue. This type of foreign policy is dominated by nationalism and irredentism, by patriots and traitors. On the contrary, desecuritisation implies the existence of the geoeconomics logic, which is characterised by a managerial foreign policy as opposed to a heroic one. It is a policy that favours political stability through economic development and co-operation. Such a policy has as its integral part the membership of the European Union as a means to promote regional co-operation.

This chapter tests whether the emphasis that the government places on one of the two logics, has important implications for the development of its behaviour and attitude in foreign policy and as an extension to that, to its degree of influence in CFSP. The geopolitics logic is the old logic of conflict and war in Europe. A foreign policy, which is dominated by that logic is bound to 'securitise' its national security because its primary concern is the borders. The implications of such an emphasis can be separated into three levels. At the national level, the government or successive governments, create a tradition of a nationalist type of foreign policy. A perception of threat to the territorial integrity of the state is created or if it already exists, it is taken out of proportion in order to justify policies under the 'securitised' issue of national security. This perception always goes together with the creation of an enemy, who has the capability and the objective of threatening the very existence of the state. The perception of a military threat by a particular enemy justifies an arms race and military build-up to balance the threat. This means that 'securitisation' of the issue is complete and the public has come to share the governments perception and is ready to sacrifice in order to swift resources to the 'national cause'. The development of a nationalist foreign policy as a 'securitised' domain has its roots in the society, mainly through education, as the development of the perception of the 'other', the enemy, is a process that takes years.

The second implication is at the regional level. An emphasis on the geopolitical logic of a state foreign policy can contribute to instability in the region it is in. This is particularly true in regions in which the question of borders and that of ethnic minorities has been a cause of conflict in the past. It is very likely that neighbouring states and especially the state perceived as the 'enemy' will follow up in the race of military build-up. The regional picture in which a conflict can explode anytime and everything is under question looks very unstable. Finally, the third implication is at the European level. As the state is a member of the European Union, by being a cause of instability in the region, it produces direct consequences for the CFSP process. This is done in two ways. First, it is the nationalistic attitude of the Member State that creates problems in CFSP decision-making, but also the image and reputation that it is developed for European foreign policy since one of its members behaves in a nationalistic way. Second, problems are developed in EU relations with the problematic region and the states, which are in an uneasy situation with the Member State.

Overall, the geopolitical logic implies the isolation of the state and contributes to its instability and that of the region it is in, bringing only conflicts and troubles rather than 'securing' its national integrity. The benefits of the geoeconomic logic can also be seen at the three levels. At the state level, it favours economic development through a stable and strong democratic system in which nationalistic elements would have been eliminated. It educates policy makers and the public on the benefits of dialogue. Solving any problems with dialogue in a civilised and co-operative environment contributes both to the stability of the state's democratic institutions, and to a sensible foreign policy based on co-operation and not confrontation. At the regional level, the geoeconomic logic favours regional co-operation and development and the overcoming of old inherited conflicts and problems. Such logic favours the development of a stable region with mutual respect, in which states can be partners for development and not competitors for territory, thus, any sense of hostility and 'enemy' feeling would be eliminated. It can also contribute to the demilitarisation of the region, shifting resources of states towards economic development. Finally, at the European level, Member States can gain the reputation of sensible and co-operative partner, contributing with their national policy to a European foreign policy of peace and development.

Securitisation does not only occur in the military sector but in the other four as well. This chapter focuses on securitisation attempts in any sector which can have an impact on foreign policy. This could be a sector of the economy that is considered as vital for the national interest and should be protected at any cost or an ethnic or religious identity which needs to be preserved and promoted. The process of integration in foreign policy itself can be a threat to national sovereignty and can produce securitisation attempts for the preservation of 'national interest'.

The Geopolitics of Greece

With the democratic transition that followed the end of the military regime in 1974, Greece began a process with which the old geopolitical logic could be replaced by a European orientated geoeconomic one. As Theodore Couloumbis argues, after 1974 Greece replaced its heroic foreign policy with a managerial one.[1] However, despite the truth of this argument, Greece is often seduced by the old geopolitical logic. Membership of the European Community served to diminish such diversions. It can best be described as a chain which holds Greece away from the traditional regional conflicts of the Balkans. However, it is true that these chains were sometimes loosened and Greece was found acting not as a catalyst to the problem but, as a troublemaker. Greek foreign policy, throughout its years of EC/EU membership, can be described as a struggle between its European and its traditional orientation.

Greece has the disadvantage of being in the most difficult and unstable region in Europe. It is a region in which states have been fighting throughout the century for territory and national identities. European Community membership offered Greece a way out of the troubles inherited by its geopolitical situation. However, successive governments have dealt with traditional problems in the region using a geopolitical logic, mainly for domestic consumption. During the 1980s, the PASOK government used foreign policy in order to establish itself in front of the Greek electorate as the party of change and of Greek independent voice. Foreign policy decisions were made for domestic consumption. There are three main considerations of the socialist government in the 1980s that reinforce this argument. First, there was the independent foreign policy consideration. The Papandreou government argued that, until then Greece had no real independent foreign policy but it was dependent from 'big power', by which he meant the UK, the US, and even the EC. Therefore, PASOK stood for an independent Greek voice, different from other voices in the West. This tactic was employed for domestic consumption since the party's rhetoric before coming to power was against membership of the EC and NATO. In government, PASOK came to accept membership of both, but had to make a stance to justify its previous positions. The second consideration was socialist ideology. As a socialist party coming to power in a right-wing dominated country, PASOK followed policies which were different from the normal Cold-War related policies of the West. This was again directed to the electorate, which saw a socialist government making a stance for its ideology. The final consideration was nationalism. Papandreou always criticised the past conservative governments for making concessions to the Turks in order to achieve friendly relations. Therefore, PASOK followed a nationalistic foreign policy towards Turkey, refusing any dialogue and favouring a more military build-up.

Sectors in which Securitisation Exists

The military sector Greece's relations with Turkey became and remained by all governments, a 'securitised' issue. The 'threat perception' that Greece developed, particularly after the Turkish invasion of Cyprus in 1974, became unquestionable in Greek society. Turkey was the number one threat for Greece and had the capacity and the will to be so. There are many arguments to suggest that this issue has been 'securitised' successfully. It has been accepted that relations with Turkey is an issue of national security. There can be no dialogue or negotiations with the neighbouring state on any problems with the exception of the Aegean seabed. All the above are not governmental policy, but enjoy the consensus of all parties, media and public opinion. In addition, debate on the issue is unthinkable. There is no political debate, at elite level, or in the public domain.

It is not the aim of the chapter to discuss the validity of any claims made by Greece or Turkey. However, the chapter does argue that because the issue in Greece has been 'securitised', Greek policy-makers have been bound to policies, which are dominated by geopolitical logic. These policies shape public opinion to the same extent that public opinion influences such policies, so, a nationalist circle is created with which any diversion can be criticised as treason. This domestic circle of nationalist behaviour has therefore important implications for the place and role of Greece in the Balkan region as well as in the process of CFSP in the EU. During the Cold War, the issue of Greek-Turkish relations was the only 'securitised' issue of Greek foreign policy. At the beginning of the 1990s, just after the end of the Cold War, the explosion of the Balkans with the Yugoslavian crisis created domestic tensions and pressure for a geopolitical logic to be applied in every aspect of Greek foreign policy.

During the period between 1991-1994 nationalistic policies were pursued towards all neighbouring countries. Relations with Bulgaria became problematic, there was a crisis with Albania that could have had very dangerous outcomes if continued, blind support of Serb forces in the Yugoslav crisis was anticipated for traditional, religious and nationalist reasons, and the issue of Macedonia was intended to become the new 'securitised' issue in Greek foreign policy. It can be argued that Macedonia became a partially 'securitised' issue or its 'securitisation' failed to be completed. There are three main reasons for that. First, the 'threat perception' was artificial. It was never rooted in Greek society and attempts to spread the nationalist feeling into a massive reaction from the Greek population, which in a way could replace normal foreign policy-making, had only a short-term effect.[2] Secondly, there was not a consensus between political parties on that line. Although the majority of the parties seemed to agree to a nationalist line, the Communist Party was openly against it. The fact that there was a difference in opinion, however small, gave rise to criticism in the press, which later spread because of the failure of such policies.[3] Finally, even the political parties that agreed openly with the mainstream, in secret feared the implications of such policies. At that time, only the Foreign Minister Antonis Samaras and the leader of the opposition Andreas Papandreou believed in the agreed policy. The remainder were forced to follow, fearing the political cost that an alternative stance could entail in front of a rising nationalist electorate.

The instability of the Balkans region and the difficult relations with Turkey had always been the main excuse of Greek policy-makers for the military orientated foreign policy which Greece pursued and still follows. During the Cold War and before 1981, Greece was isolated in the region. In the North, there were Communist neighbours from whom Greece had to be protected as a NATO member, whilst in the East was a fellow NATO member but a traditional 'enemy'. After 1981, the new socialist government perceived no threat from the North but an increased and persistent threat from the East. During that time, Papandreou developed good relations with most of the Balkan states (excluding Albania and Turkey). It is interesting to note that Greece, under Papandreou, signed an agreement of mutual military aid with Bulgaria, at a time when during the Cold War Greece and Bulgaria belonged to different military alliances. That is to say that Greece, although a member of NATO, did not share the same threat perception from the North as the alliance, but rather felt a threat from the East, from Turkey, a fellow member of NATO. After the end of the Cold War, at a time when old geopolitical conflicts arose in the Balkans, instead of being a factor of stability and co-operation in the region, Greece became one of the problems. Its relations with Albania worsened radically, in respect of the Greek-speaking minority in South Albania, and its good relations with Bulgaria were tested after the inclusion in the new conservative government in Sofia of the Turkish party. Added to these was the big crisis with Macedonia over names and symbols. It was a period in which it seemed that geopolitical logic dominated Greek foreign policy and led to behaviour which had a negative effect upon its position in the region.

Today the regional setting looks different and Greek foreign policy in the Balkans seems more 'sensible', having rejected the geopolitical logic. This is illustrated by the solution that has been given to many of the conflicts, the good relations that are being built, as well as by Greek initiatives for regional co-operation like the successful Balkan Conference in Crete. Both during the Albania crisis in 1997 and the Kosovo crisis in 1998 and 1999, Greece adopted policies of co-operation and contributed to their resolution. Greek foreign policy, therefore, moved towards cooperation and multi-lateralism. However, the issue of Turkey remains 'securitised'. After 1996 there have been many changes in the attitude of Greek foreign policy and some of them affected relations with Turkey. During the Imia crisis in 1996, the Greek government took the prudent approach and avoided any escalation that could have had dangerous consequences. The Madrid agreement[4] in 1997, during the NATO summit for the restructuring of the Mediterranean command of the Atlantic Alliance, ended a conflict that affected the South-eastern European command of the Alliance since 1974. However, Greek foreign policy has not been consistent and at times old policies emerge. The majority of these old policies have to do with the EU-Turkish relationship where Greece takes advantage of its EU membership in order to reinforce its foreign policy and negotiation power against Turkey.

Securitisation in the military sector and the perception of the 'existential threat' from Turkey has developed other securitisation attempts in two other sectors, namely the political and the societal sectors. In the political sector, given the securitised nature of Greek-Turkish relations in Greek foreign policy, political integration in Europe developed a perception of 'existential threat' for the Greek sovereignty in foreign policy making. This implies that Greece perceives the potential abolition of the veto right as a threat to its national interests. In the societal sector, the influence of tradition and religion play an important role in foreign policy and this chapter considers whether a 'securitisation' exists in this sector. In the environmental sector there has been no securitisation in Greece. Environmental issues are not yet priority issues in foreign policy. However, it will become a serious issue in the near future as the 'environmental conscience' which has been a tradition in Northern Europe increasingly, influences the Greek public. A recent example of concern for environmental issues which can affect foreign policy was the case of Belgian meat, polluted with dioxins that affected all EU Member States in the spring of 1999 and the uranium crisis in Kosovo in 2001 resulted from the NATO bombing campaign.

The societal sector The societal sector in Greece is dominated by the issue of national identity and culture. Greek society has developed a very sensitive approach to issues of foreign policy, particularly regarding perceived threats to Greece's national integrity. For this reason the societal sentiments have been exploited in several cases, as seen before, by political parties, organisations or the press. A particular case of a non-state actor that has an important influence on the society and has used that influence to promote nationalistic sentiments is that of the Greek Orthodox Church. The Church maintains a significant level of influence in the Greek political system. This creates tensions in Greek foreign policy-making for a special relationship with countries that have major Orthodox populations. During the Yugoslav crisis in the early 1990s, these circles favoured an open support of Yugoslavia.[5] However, despite some evidence of its existence, this never became official Greek policy. These tensions can be attributed to a general conflict in the Greek society between Europeanists and Traditionalists. The former favour total integration of Greece in the European Union, in all aspects of its society, while the latter sees it as a threat to traditional Greek values and religion, and sees Greece as part of the East European group of Orthodox countries. However, Traditionalists have not managed to achieve high posts of governance and thus their influence in the policy process is kept to a minimum.

Despite the failure of the Traditionalists and the Greek Church, which is its main mechanism for achieving direct influence in government, their influence in the society has functioned as a tool of pressure for nationalist policies. The newly elected head of the Greek Orthodox Church Archbishop Christodoulos has on many occasions expressed political views with nationalist and irredentist intentions and has caused discomfort with the political leadership.[6] It is worth noting that in recent polls on popular ratings for leaders, Archbishop Christodoulos holds the first place enjoying a more popular support than political leaders. The change of leadership of the Greek Orthodox Church in 1998 signified a change in the way that the traditional nationalistic ideals were transmitted to the public. The new leadership is developing a kind of a Greek Orthodox fundamentalist movement. This is evident for three reasons: involvement in politics, mass public support and a nationalist message. The Church, and particularly the new leadership, has been involved in Greek politics by commenting on political developments and using its influence as a pressure tool. In the recent crisis in Kosovo, the Archbishop of the Greek Church used religious meetings to transmit anti-NATO and anti-Western messages. He has also been active in giving interviews to the press expressing the Church's political opinion. The message that the Church transmits to the public has been that the Catholic and Protestant West is fighting against the Orthodox people and their tradition in Yugoslavia.

The second reason has been the Church's success in getting its message across. The Orthodox Churches that were almost empty before are now starting to fill up with people from all age groups.[7] The characteristic of this development is the fact that these people are attracted, not by a plain religious message, but from a message of reviving their 'lost' national identity. This is linked to the third reason, which has been the Church's involvement in promoting Greek nationalism. There have been several occasions when Church delegations or social and political groups influenced by the Church's ideals have visited Belgrade using the Kosovo crisis in order to demonstrate their solidarity with the Serbian people. The nationalist messages that the Church transmits take an anti-European character. According to the Church, the EU is responsible for the loss of the traditional Greek Orthodox culture. Greece is seen by the Church as closer to the 'Orthodox brotherhood' of Eastern Europe than to the Catholic-Protestant dominated EU. These arguments found fertile ground during the NATO intervention in Kosovo.

The Success and Impact of the Securitisation Process

The effect of Greece's geopolitical position on European foreign policy has generally been to skew Greece's interests in such a way as to reflect its concerns with Turkey. For a short period (1991-1994), the Yugoslavian crisis and Macedonia played an important role. The Greek-Turkish dispute has always been a stumbling block in Athens' relations with its European partners. Although security was the main Greek consideration when it applied for membership of the EC, its European partners were never willing to get involved in the conflict. During the accession negotiations, Karamanlis stated that the dispute is a bilateral one, and should not affect the EC, yet things turned out differently. Particularly after the coming to power of Papandreou, Greece started to block any development of EC-

Turkish relations and used EPC summits as a forum in which Greece could condemn its neighbour. Greek foreign ministers developed a reputation of repeating the same condemnations against Turkey in every Council meeting, so that everybody knew what they were going to say.[8] Anti-Turkish rhetoric became more than a habit, it became a passion for Greek politicians. Domestic reasons of a geopolitical nature, which were mentioned earlier, can explain that behaviour, but there is one more factor that influenced the Greek attitude in European summits and councils. Since the domestic pressure was created by 'securitising' the issue, this pressure was reflected to Europe by a government willing to win national battles and claim the victory in front of the electorate. Furthermore, Greece was trying to overcome its insecurity by using its membership of the EC in order to strengthen its geopolitical position and also to damage the position and reputation of Turkey in Europe and its relations with the Community.

In the 1990s, EU-Turkish relations were put into a new dimension. A customs union was agreed and implemented by finally curbing the Greek veto, offering Cyprus accession negotiations. In 1996, the new Simitis government moderated Greece's behaviour on the issue and although Turkey was refused participation in the accession negotiations by the application of special conditions, these conditions were not presented as a Greek demand. However, the new Greek strategy, which seems more successful does not mean a change of policies. The issue of Turkey continues to be a 'securitised' issue in Greek politics and as the continuing Greek veto towards the EU-Turkey financial protocol demonstrates, it is still an issue of conflict between Greece and its partners.

Despite the short period of time in which the Macedonian issue became a problem for Greek participation in the EU, one thing that it demonstrated is the easiness with which geopolitical logic can dominate Greek foreign policy, and create a nationalistic delirium. The Yugoslav crisis was a failed first test for CFSP as a whole so, although the Greek support of the Serb forces came to opposition with every other European Member State, it did not have any serious consequences mainly because of the mistakes and failures of all European Member States' foreign policies. However, the Macedonian case did have a big impact on Athens' reputation since it seemed that Greece was fuelling instability and conflict while the EU was trying to resolve the crisis and stabilise the region. In the case of Macedonia, Greece did what it had been doing for years in the case of Turkey. It 'exported' to the EU the Greek domestic situation. With this we mean that an issue of foreign policy was, at least attempted to be, 'securitised' and presented in Europe with the aim of achieving national victories for domestic consumption. There are three reasons that can explain the attempt to 'securitise' the issue of Macedonia and develop a nationalist foreign policy. First, the Yugoslavian crisis developed a perception of threat to Greece from the increasing instability in the region. That perception was based on the historical conflicts over borders in the Balkans. Every question of reshaping borders in the region was perceived as having knock-on effects which could be dangerous for Greece's territorial integrity. In addition, the question of Macedonia itself had, in the past, been the cause of two Balkan wars. This perception created a state of alarm that justified the attempt for the issue to be 'securitised'. A second reason can be the popular feeling in the societal sector that Greece's vital national interests were threatened. Strong public support for nationalistic policies was soon created with its zenith being the two huge rallies in Thessaloniki and Athens which gathered together almost a quarter of Greece's population. These two reasons are linked together because one influenced the other. Both the perception of policy makers and the press fuelled public opinion and public demand made foreign policy.

The Implications for Greek Foreign Policy

Turkey and Macedonia have been the two issues of foreign policy which have been fully or partially 'securitised' during Greece's membership of the EC/EU. An important impact of 'securitisation' that affects its behaviour, has been Greece's development of the sense of 'national issues'. This sense has separated normal foreign policy from the 'national issues', which have been securitised. Normal foreign policy only includes the issues that do not affect Greece's interest, thus, foreign policy has been degraded. All issues of Greek national interest such as the Balkans, Turkey and Cyprus have been upgraded to 'national issues'. This upgrade entails, to a larger or smaller degree, the attempt to 'securitise' them, in other words to take them out of the party political debate. This attempt was successful in the case of Turkey, and partially successful for a limited time to the Macedonian case.

The impact of 'securitisation' of the issue of Turkey can be seen in three areas. First, it creates a lack of flexibility. Greek governments are not flexible to adopt policies that they might see fit on the issue because of a generally conceived strategy that sees moderate policies as concessions to the Turks. It is very interesting to note that even the removal of the veto to the EU-Turkey customs union was heavily criticised by the opposition, and the government had to come with a very good excuse, which in that case was Cyprus' accession negotiations. In another case, after the peaceful disengagement of the Imia crisis,[9] the government was even criticised for treason, however, the positive results of a peaceful settlement were stronger than any opposition. Although until now in extreme situations the moderate position prevailed, there is no guarantee that this will continue to happen in the future. As long as the issue remains 'securitised' there will be a lack of flexibility in foreign policy making.

Secondly, it creates an inability to negotiate. By 'securitising' the issue, Greece refuses to accept that there is a Greek-Turkish dispute, with the exception of the seabed. Greece declares that there is not a real dispute but only Turkish claims over Greek sovereignty. Since negotiations mean compromise, Greek governments are not willing or able to negotiate because if they do, they are negotiating Greek sovereignty. Finally, it creates a lack of public debate. The perception of a threat from Turkey, the validity of the Greek position and the strategy to be followed are unquestionable. It is like questioning the integrity of the Greek State. Every reference to Greek-Turkish relations is made in the political, academic or media environments, in order to explain and discuss the situation by praising the Greek position and reinforcing the threat perception, or criticising the government for not being patriotic enough. Any alternative and critical view is suppressed and dismissed as anti-Hellenic or Turkish-friendly.

Perhaps a good case to study the impact of the geopolitical logic and the 'securitisation' that it implies is the case of Macedonia. As in the Turkish case, the three results of 'securitisation' can be identified, although the third was only partially achieved and was one of the main reasons for its short-life span. The lack of flexibility of the government was obvious. The Greek Prime Minister Mitsotakis was forced to implement policies he did not want or believe in. The nationalistic climate that was evident in the Greek society, the actions of his foreign minister and the partial consensus between the political forces (except for the Communist Party), forced him to go along with policies he described as damaging to the national interest.[10] The most striking example of a 'securitisation' attempt was the informal Council of political leaders. Neither in the Greek constitution nor in the political tradition of Greece does such an institution exist. The leaders of political parties represented in the Parliament came together three times under the President of the Republic to discuss an issue of foreign policy that is normally the responsibility of the government.

Although the Council had a consultative function, in reality it turned out to be executive. No one had the political will to go against the agreed position by the Council. Although Mitsotakis did not want the Council to replace the responsibility of the government in foreign policy, he was forced to do so by the increased public opinion fuelled by the press, the opposition and his foreign minister Samaras.

The inability to negotiate was a product of the binding decisions of the Council of political leaders and of the scale that the issue had taken in the public opinion. Mitsotakis was forced to participate in talks both at a bilateral level in New York and at the European level at the European Council and Councils of Foreign Ministers.[11] At these talks he had to negotiate but without changing even a letter of the official Greek position, and as to negotiate is to compromise, Greece was unable to negotiate. As in any 'securitisation' process, there was an attempt to create 'enemies'. In a period that lasted about two and a half years, Macedonians or 'Skopjans' as the Greeks used to call them, were becoming enemies of Greece. They developed an evil image of a neighbouring nation that wanted to plunder Greek national history, heritage and territory. This process had a short-term impact on the public debate. At that time it was unthinkable to express alternative opinions. Groups in Northern Greece which openly declared themselves to be part of the Macedonian minority were faced with the threat of imprisonment. However, soon debate on the issue started, and moderate views prevailed in the end.

In the case of Macedonia, there were two issues which affected Greece's participation in the EU: the question of recognition of the Republic of Macedonia by the EU, and the Greek economic embargo. The externalisation of Greece's domestic nationalistic climate led to a crisis in the relations between Greece and its fellow-members in the European Union. The nationalistic foreign policy which had no outcome, became a negative contribution for Greece within the framework of CFSP. Greece used any means, including the veto, to avoid any recognition of the new state by the European Union, and also by individual states. Macedonia became an issue for the European Council in almost all meetings from December 1991, when the Council discussed the issue of recognition for the ex-Yugoslav republics, until September 1994, when the signing of the Interim Accord eased the tensions. Popular foreign policy of rallies and public demonstrations replaced diplomatic negotiations. Apart from the two big rallies in Greece, public gatherings have been held in different places in Europe, North America and Australia. These gatherings were organised by the Greek communities in those countries and were supported by the Greek embassies and the Greek Orthodox churches. These public demonstrations were actually playing the role of the Greek foreign ministry. The nationalistic hysteria, which characterised the domestic life in Greece, was exported with every opportunity by any means. A characteristic example was the post office campaign for the inclusion in all addresses in North Greece (Greek Macedonia) of the word 'Macedonia' before 'Greece'.[12] In addition, many names were altered to include the term 'Macedonia' or 'Macedonian', such as the new name for Thessaloniki's airport, which was renamed 'Macedonia airport'.

In the case of Turkey, Greek participation was affected even since its accession in the Community. Greece used to block any development of EC-Turkish relations with the fear that any closer relationship of the Community with Turkey would be damaging to Greek interests. The Greek reservations for the EU-Turkey Customs Union were finally overcome, but the implementation of it is subject to the financial protocol, which will provide Turkey with EU financial assistance to deal with the issues of the Union. Greece blocks this protocol. Although the government of Simitis has introduced many changes to the Greece attitude, the continuation of the blockade is increasingly bringing back old tensions between Greece and its fellow members.[13] A veto with no significant substance driven by nationalistic arguments, as seen by the EU, can only damage the Greek reputation, which in recent years has been trying to recover from the negative past.

The Geopolitics of Spain

The democratisation process that started in Spain in 1975 after the death of Franco developed as its main objective the 'ruptura' (the break) with everything associated with the regime. One of the areas where change was required was the foreign and defence policies. Franco's foreign policy was dominated by the geopolitical logic. Spain was governed by a military regime and its relations towards the neighbouring region were based on conflict and competition for power. Its policy towards Morocco and Algeria was that of maintaining a security balance, using their disputes to achieve the security of its frontiers, particularly the territory of Ceuta and Melilla that is claimed by Morocco. The democratisation process abandoned this realist policy of balance of power in the region. Instead a new policy of cooperation for peace and stability was adopted. This was a policy of desecuritisation which means a policy that focused on solving security problems through cooperation, integration and economic development, rather than through confrontation.[14]

Sectors in which Desecuritisation has taken place

In the military sector As mentioned above, the Spanish democratisation process developed the logic of geoeconomics. Military security ceased to be a vital national interest for the protection of Spain's territorial integrity. This was a gradual process, which coexisted with the Europeanisation process of Spain. In fact, military security itself was Europeanised. The objective of Spain in entering the European Community was to Europeanise Spanish foreign and defence policy.[15] Before its accession in the EC, Spain became a member of NATO in 1982, however, although the European orientation for Spain enjoyed a consensus between the political forces and the society, membership of NATO had divided views. The Centrist government of Calvo Sotelo that signed the accession treaty in June 1982 was replaced by PSOE and Felipe Gonzalez in October of the same year. Many people voted for the Socialists in the belief that they would take Spain out of NATO, as they had promised to do after a referendum.[16] Felipe Gonzalez finally made the referendum he had promised, but only after a three and a half year delay and with a different position. The referendum took place in March 1986 with the Socialist government campaigning in favour of NATO membership. The victory was achieved with 52.5%. However, it was a victory that can be attributed to the three conditions for the continuation of membership. These conditions were:

- continued membership without Spain's integration in the military structure;
- prohibition of installation, storage and introduction of nuclear weapons in Spain;
- reduction of the US presence in the country.[17]

These conditions illustrated the anti-militarism logic which was developed in post-Franco Spain, as well as an anti-American feeling in the Spanish society. For years, Spain negotiated the system of its participation in NATO with the eventual agreement signed in 1992. The fact that Spain was a member of the EC made desecuritisation a feasible and rational strategy for Spain. Although Spain was reluctant to participate in integrated military operations, it did not follow the French model. Unlike France, Spain was to be present in the Military Committee, the Defence Planning Committee and the Nuclear Planning Group.[18] The third condition was finally achieved in January 1988 when, after a period of negotiations, the first reduction of US forces took place. In the same year, Spain made another step towards its objective to Europeanise its foreign and defence policy, and that was its integration in the WEU in November 1988. Despite the problems of the Spanish refusal to allow nuclear weapons on its territory, its full agreement with the main WEU guidelines and its willingness to participate in their implementation made the Spanish accession to the WEU possible.[19]

Spain not only attempted to Europeanise its security policy but also intended to develop an integrated European security framework. Its main objective was to reinforce WEU by incorporating it into an EU common defence. The gradual Europeanisation of Spain had important impact on the anti-NATO and anti-American feeling in the Spanish society. As was mentioned earlier, in 1982 public opinion in its majority opposed NATO membership and in 1986 half of the population accepted it, only before conditions. In the next six years, from 1986 to 1992, the first years of Spanish membership of the EC, there was a radical change in Spain's public opinion on NATO. Although its main priority was the Europeanisation of WEU, Spain followed a 'prudent' security policy that always wanted complementarity with NATO and not adversary.[20] In 1990, for the first time Spain participated, in democracy, in a military operation. Spain's participation in the naval blockade organised by the WEU during the Gulf War illustrated a change in public opinion. More than 48% of the Spanish public was in favour of Spanish military participation. Also, it served to overcome the mistrust of Spain's allies on defence issues, given the fact of the conditions for NATO membership and the nuclear-free policy.[21] There were three main reasons for Spain's participation in the Gulf War: a military, a political and an economic reason. The military was the fact that Spain has disputed frontiers in Ceuta and Melilla and it was preoccupied by any attempt to alter frontiers with the use of force. The political reason was that the crisis affected the Arab World significantly, with which Spain has special relations. Finally, the economic reason was that the use of force by Iraq to increase its influence in the oil market could not be ignored.[22]

The issue of reluctant participation in NATO was decreased even more in 1995, when Spain participated in the NATO bombing of the Bosnian Serbs and in the peacekeeping operations in Bosnia. With the appointment of Javier Solana as the General Secretary of NATO in the same year, this issue, in practice, ceased to exist.

In the political sector   In his speech at the CSCE Summit in Paris in November 1990, Felipe González pointed out the main security priority for Spain. Its objective was to formulate a policy based on the close relationship between security in Europe and stability and progress in the Mediterranean region.[23] The link between European security with the Mediterranean stability was the argument that it is vital for Europe to resolve explosive problems in North Africa because they affect the economic, social, political and military dimensions of security. The philosophy behind the Spanish objective was not the geopolitical logic of securitisation that is to build a fortress around Europe's frontiers, but the geoeconomic logic of cooperation for development. It was the belief that democratisation and economic development in the South Mediterranean could solve the problem of security in its different dimensions. The purpose of Spain to Europeanise its security preoccupations and avoid their securitisation is illustrated by the several initiatives it took on the issue of the Mediterranean at the European level. In 1989, Spain and Italy proposed the development of a Conference for the Security and Cooperation in the Mediterranean. In 1990, it promoted the dialogue and cooperation in the Western Mediterranean by contributing to the creation of the 'four plus five' group, that included four Europeans, Spain, Italy, France and Portugal, (Malta entered later in 1991), and five Maghreb countries, Algeria, Morocco, Libya, Tunisia and Mauritania. The purpose of this forum was to develop a dialogue for cooperation on economic development, in which the issues of security in all its forms were in the centre.

In the other two sectors, the societal and environmental, Spain followed the policy of desecuritisation, which means that problems can be solved only with cooperation and at the supranational level. There is no evidence to suggest that the Spanish society and culture have been threatened by European integration. On the contrary it can be argued that Spanish society used Europe's multi-culturalism to promote its own culture. Spanish foreign policy has been particularly active in this area since the *Instituto Cervantes* and the *General Directorate for cultural realtions* were incorporated into the Spanish Foreign Ministry.[24] In the environmental sector, similar to

Greece, there has not been a prioritisation of environmental issues in foreign policy.

The Success and Impact of Desecuritisation

The importance of economic cooperation and desecuritisation to achieve stability and to solve problems caused by securitisation is illustrated in Spain's relations with Morocco and the case of Western Sahara. The problem with the former Spanish colony was caused by Franco's policies, which were dominated by the geopolitical logic.[25] In a letter to the UN in 1976, Spain declared the end of its presence in Western Sahara. The latter was to be administrated together with Mauritania and Morocco. However, Spain made clear its position on the self-determination process of its former colony. Decolonisation could not be complete unless the Sahrawi people exert their right to self-determination.[26] The Spanish socialist party, which came to power in 1982, in particularly had close links with the Western Sahara Polisario Front and up until 1984 Spain followed a hard line policy, and even abstained in the UN resolutions calling for direct negotiations between the Polisario Front and Morocco. Since November 1984, Spain seems to have changed its behaviour and strategy. It has voted favourably in the UN for negotiations and peaceful resolution and requested the two EPC declarations on the conflict, in 1988 and 1991 in order to welcome and support the peace agreement between Polisario and Morocco and to confirm EC support for the UN peace plan.[27] An illustration of the change of Spanish attitude is the fishing agreement with Morocco. In 1977 the Spanish Parliament refused to ratify the fishing agreement with Morocco because its text implied the recognition of Moroccan sovereignty over the territorial Sahrawi waters. This position, which was held by PSOE, changed after the Spanish accession in the EC. The agreements of 1988 and 1992 found a way to overcome the problem by making a distinction between 'waters of Moroccan jurisdiction' and 'waters of Moroccan sovereignty'.[28] When in 1991 the European Parliament blocked the fourth financial protocol with Morocco on the basis of violation of human rights and non-implementation of UN resolution for Western Sahara, Spain did not welcome the EP's attitude. On the contrary, the Spanish foreign minister Fernández Ordóñez went to Rabat to negotiate compensations for the action of the EP. In the late 1980s Spain developed a strong geoeconomic logic and perceived its relations with Morocco based on economic development and co-operation, as one of its primary objectives.

Relations with Morocco have been a prime concern for all Spanish governments. Felipe González made his first trip as Prime Minister to Rabat as a demonstration of the importance that Spain gives to its Southern neighbour. Apart from the issue of Western Sahara, the big dispute between Spain and Morocco is the Spanish enclaves of Ceuta and Melilla. However, Spanish foreign policy has been kept free from geopolitical logic, and the continuation of good economic and political relations with Morocco has been the main concern for Spain. It is interesting to note that there is military co-operation between the two countries, in fact, Morocco is the main purchaser of Spanish arms.[29] However, it would be very interesting to see the reaction of Spain to a future claim of the enclaves by Morocco, which is possible to follow an agreement for the reintegration of Gibraltar to Spain. In the EU, Spain has promoted every aspect of improving co-operation and dialogue with the Maghreb, promoting regional stability and development. Evidence of this is the inclusion of the Maghreb region to the list of areas of possible joint actions for CFSP.

The Implications for Spanish Foreign Policy

After a long term of isolation, Spain found in Europe a way to achieve its lost international voice. Participation in European foreign policy became for Spain an enhancement of its own policy. The impact of the Spanish geopolitical position has been its preoccupation with the Mediterranean region. The Spanish transition to democracy brought total changes to Spanish foreign policy and the behaviour of Spain in pursuing its objectives. The 1980s were characterised by the entrance of Spain in NATO, the EC and the WEU. As Professor Felipe Sahagun described it, Spain started to have a global model of coherent foreign policy. In Spain, for the first time there was a high level of concordance between the internal context and the international scene. Also, for the first time, Spanish words and deeds started to coincide.[30] On 28 August 1985, a Spanish Royal decree created the Secretary of State for International Co-operation and for Latin America. This act institutionalised the perception of Spanish foreign policy of being a policy for peace, development and co-operation, particularly towards Latin America, the Mediterranean and the Arab world, which have been the prime Spanish objectives of foreign policy. In that sense, Spain opted for geoeconomic logic in order to deal with the regional disputes. Spanish behaviour in the region can be seen at two levels: the bilateral and the multilateral. The bilateral level deals with the prime

Spanish priority in foreign policy, which is its relations with Morocco. Instead of confrontation with Morocco in the cases of Ceuta and Melilla and Western Sahara, Spain chose to build a network of economic and military co-operation with its neighbour in order to down-play the importance of the disputes.[31] In that way the two countries could build up close links of co-operation through which they may find acceptable solutions to both sides in the future. Spain also used its position as a member of the EU to promote co-operation and economic development in Morocco. At the multilateral level, Spain has worked for a greater involvement of the EU in the Maghreb area. The highlight of this was the successful Spanish initiative for the Euro-Mediterranean partnership which began with the Barcelona Conference in 1995, during the Spanish Presidency of the EU.

To summarise the impact of the Spanish geopolitical situation to its behaviour in foreign policy, one can argue that regional security has been its main concern. However, the difference is the way that security is pursued. The Spanish philosophy can be described as that of co-operation rather than confrontation. There are three important aspects of that philosophy. First, the building of good relations and co-operation with the neighbouring countries is more important than any regional dispute. By taking any dispute out of proportion and 'securitising' it, the tensions which are created can bring about the opposite of the desired results. The foreign policy of the democratic Spain in the 1980s and 1990s is dominated by the principle of co-operation. Good relations with Morocco were more important, even when it seemed that the contrary was in line with the Spanish interest. Even in the case of Gibraltar where there has been a degree of 'securitisation' of the issue, good relations with the UK is the prime objective of Spanish foreign policy. The second aspect is the importance of economic development. To tackle the root of the problem is more important than fighting its consequences. For that reason, Spanish foreign policy has been directed towards promoting economic development for the Mediterranean region, to tackle the socio-economic problems which are the cause of any security unrest in the region. The Euro-Mediterranean partnership initiative was particularly directed towards that objective. To accommodate the security preoccupations in the Mediterranean, the best way was to provide aid and co-operation for economic development for the North African States in order to avoid any future problems, rather than building military fronts. Finally, the last aspect is that any dispute can be solved, at the appropriate level, by dialogue and peaceful negotiations. In that sense, Spain favoured the dialogue between the parties in any dispute as the way of overcoming conflicts. This took the form of bilateral negotiations, like the Polisario-Moroccan for Western Sahara, Spanish-Moroccan for Ceuta and Melilla or Spanish-British for Gibraltar, or as multilateral talks such as the Barcelona Conference.

The Spanish accession to the EC completed a period of transition not only towards democracy, but also towards a coherent and reputable foreign policy. Spain benefited from its geopolitical situation in the sense that it could provide an asset for the EC as a member at the West End of the Mediterranean. Due to its positioning away from regions of conflict, Spain did not pose any significant problem for European foreign policy. Despite its traditionally good relations with the Arab world, the first foreign policy action that Spain took as an EC member was to establish diplomatic relations with Israel and work to build up good relations with the Jewish State. However, with the excellent diplomatic work of Foreign Minister Ordoñez, Spain managed to retain its good relations with the Arabs. The building of good relations with both Arabs and Israelis transformed Spain into a facilitator for the resolution of the crisis.[32] The first step was made in October 1991, when Spain hosted the International Conference for the Middle East in Madrid. Although Spain was not the initiator of the event, the fact that it was chosen to become the host of it both signifies and also enhances its facilitator status. In the EC, Spain reinforced its foreign policy towards the Middle East since the Madrid declaration of the European Council on 27 June 1989 which was made during the first Spanish Presidency. The following year, in September 1990, Spain in coordination with Italy also took the initiative of launching the idea of a Conference on Security and Co-operation in the Mediterranean in Mallorca, similar to the CSCE. Finally, the Spanish reputation as a respectable mediator climaxed with the placement of Miguel Angel Moratinos as the EU representative, of CFSP, to the Middle East. After that, the Spanish mediation practices continued with the leading of the EU mediation in Bosnia by Carlos Westendorp, and in Belgrade and Kosovo by Felipe González.

However, the most important achievement of Spanish foreign policy was the Euro-Mediterranean partnership initiative. Spanish Mediterranean policy is an example of how Spain turned its security preoccupations in the region into an important asset for its participation in European foreign policy. Soon after joining the EC, Spain demonstrated a significant interest in the Mediterranean region. The objective was to develop further the existing, and inadequate, EC Mediterranean policy. In 1989-90, the Spanish

Commissioner, who became Foreign Minister under the Aznar government, Abel Matutes, introduced the Renovated Mediterranean Policy (RMP). Even this development was not satisfactory for the Spaniards and in 1990 the proposal came for a Conference on Security and Co-operation in the Mediterranean. This proposal can be largely attributed to the Spanish initiative.[33] The CSCM failure to be realised diverted the Spanish priorities to the Maghreb region where it put all its efforts into the development of close EU-Maghreb links. However, the events in the Balkans in the early 1990s, the coup in Algeria, and the failure of the fourth financial protocols with Morocco after the EP's veto, furthered the need for a partnership between the EU and the Mediterranean non-member states. This partnership could encourage co-operation and development and in that way promote security and stability in the region. The Barcelona process that started the Euro-Mediterranean partnership was the main success of the second Spanish Presidency of the EU. Spain managed to incorporate and develop a strong Mediterranean policy dimension in the EU during a time when the prime consideration of the Northern Member States was Central and Eastern Europe. This development has been an implication of the Spanish behaviour in promoting co-operation as a means of solving regional security problems.

The only negative implication of Spanish behaviour in the European Union made by its geopolitical situation is in the case of Gibraltar. Although it is a bilateral dispute between Spain and the UK, Gibraltar created a lot of problems and tensions in the process of policy making in the EU.[34] Gibraltar joined the EC with the UK under Article 227(4), relating to European territories for whose external relations a Member State is responsible. However, Gibraltar does not have full responsibilities of EU membership as it is exempted from EU law in regard to VAT and the Common Customs Tariff.[35] The status of Gibraltar in the EU has been the cause of major tensions. The key policy areas affected by the dispute have been the definition of the EU's external borders, the liberalisation of air transport, and border controls. In the case of external borders, Spain refused to sign the EU External Frontiers Convention. The Spanish argument is that the Spanish border with Gibraltar is the actual external border of the Union. In that sense Spain denies Gibraltar the right of free movement throughout the Union.[36] As Gibraltar is not an integral part of the UK, but a colonial administrative unit, Spain refuses to accept it as an integral part of the EU. This Spanish position not only caused problems to the above Convention, but also to any EU legislation in which there are references to external borders. Another point of dispute was the EC directive 416/83. This directive is concerned with the liberalisation of air transport in the European territories of Member States for which the Treaty is applicable. The Spanish and the British interpretation of that were different since for the Spaniards, Gibraltar was not part of these territories. However, despite the problems that this caused for the implementation of European legislation, the solution of the Spanish-British disagreement on the issue found an obstacle in the refusal of Gibraltar itself. The Hispano-British agreement of 2 December 1987 signed in London, on the joint use and administration of the Gibraltarian airport failed in front of a strong opposition by the Gibraltarians.[37] Finally, the last of the major problems created in the EU policy-making process by the Spanish behaviour on Gibraltar is the issue of border controls. This issue has mainly affected the Schengen agreement, but because the UK does not wish to sign the agreement, the problem is kept to a minimum. However, the Spanish claims on drugs and tobacco smuggling to Spain by Gibraltarians strengthens its position to maintain strong border controls. This underlines the Spanish fear, which influences its attitude on the issue, and that has been the possibility of the enhancement of the status of Gibraltar in the EU which undermines the Spanish claims on its sovereignty.[38]

Comparison between Greece and Spain

It can be said that security considerations in Greece and Spain greatly influence foreign policy strategies. In Greece, the dispute with Turkey forms a major part of its foreign policy planning. Any issue which is raised has to be studied in light of the implications it can bring to the Greek position on the dispute. Thus, any related issue in CFSP or in the EU in general, is handled by Greece on the basis of the advantages or disadvantages it can bring to the Greek position. In Spain this is also the case, although in a different way. Spanish foreign policy strategy has incorporated a European dimension. This means that Spanish foreign policy strategy, which is highly influenced by its regional security considerations, has as its objective the 'Europeanisation' of its priorities, thus, Spanish security concerns become concerns of CFSP. Greece has tried to do the same. Its main objective since its adhesion was to obtain a sense of security by Europeanising its dispute with Turkey. However, this attempt failed and there are three main reasons for this. Firstly, unlike Spain, Greece has 'securitised' its regional security considerations. The 'securitisation' process created a nationalist foreign policy, which was very different from what was perceived as acceptable European foreign policy,[39] and many times came into direct conflict with the foreign policy interests of its fellow members. Spain, on the other hand, did not try to create an EU front against its neighbours, but rather contributed to their aid. This was indeed the case, to the extent that Spanish domestic opposition regarded the Spanish policy as being against traditional Spanish interests. Examples of this are the case of Western Sahara, when Spain favoured more its relations with Morocco than human rights in its ex-colony, and the case of the EU-Morocco fishing agreements, when Spanish fishermen felt on the losing side. The second reason is the different nature of security threats. In contrast with Spain, Greece's security threat comes from a big regional power whose role is highly important both in NATO and the EU. Greece's partners cannot afford to get involved with the Greco-Turkish dispute since relations with Turkey are perceived to be highly important. As long as Greece presents the choice of 'either us or them' and continues to block any further development of EU-Turkish relations, the result will continue to be alienation and lack of interest on behalf of Greece's EU partners. The final reason has been Greece's peculiar behaviour, particularly during the 1980s which created suspicion in the minds of its fellow members that a secret agenda was behind any Greek involvement or initiative in EPC/CFSP related to Turkey. In contrast, Spain's constructive and inclusive behaviour changed the attitudes of its fellow members from the scepticism upon entry that Spain would be a 'second Greece', to one of enthusiasm for a respective and reliable partner.

Greece and Spain have had similar geopolitical situations, despite the differences in the degree, nature and intensity, and these situations have influenced their foreign policy-making. However, the two countries have followed two very different paths and developed quite different behaviours. The difference in behaviour can be described in three opposing ways: degree of nationalism versus Europeanism; degree of co-operation versus confrontation; and degree of compromise versus national victory. Greece has developed a nationalist foreign policy towards its regional disputes. The 'securitisation' of foreign policy issues, such as its relations with Turkey or Macedonia created an environment in which battles for vital national importance had to be fought and won. Although one can find many excuses for Greece's behaviour towards Turkey, the Macedonia case, however short, illustrated a nationalist foreign policy that can find any excuse to be developed. Also, Greek foreign policy can, to an extent, be described as confrontational. This means that in any dispute, Greek behaviour is directed towards confrontation. This entitles the creation of an 'enemy' and the need to confront 'him' in order to avoid any loss of vital national interest. Also, confrontation has as its integral element the sense of national victory. Greece exercises foreign policy over regional disputes in order to win national battles and claim victories. Therefore, in line with this behaviour, Greek foreign policy in the region has been renamed as 'national issues'. These are issues of national importance at which Greece has to produce national victories.

On the other hand, Spain's foreign policy is to an extent characterised by Europeanism. However, this does not mean that Spain disregarded its national interest, but rather that it pursued it by using a behaviour that is acceptable according to the EU rules of partnership. Since its accession in the EC, Spain's objective was to Europeanise its foreign policy and to put the Spanish priorities on the European agenda. Its policy towards the Maghreb and the Mediterranean, with its highest point being the Barcelona Conference, particularly illustrate the success of such an attempt. Spain chose the way of co-operation as the means by which solutions to its security problems could be found. Spanish foreign policy strategy is dominated by the philosophy that by developing friendly relations with its neighbours and not confronting them as enemies, and by demonstrating care for their development and well being, it makes any disputes of lesser importance and directs them to a different level. Finally, peaceful negotiations and compromise, which is an inseparable element of negotiations, was the only way of finding long-term solution to disputes. However, it has to be said that the case of Gibraltar does not follow the same path as the other foreign policy issues in the sense that Spain has demonstrated its difficulty in accepting compromises on the issue.

The implications for Greek and Spanish foreign policy in terms of political behaviour can be compared along three levels: the domestic, regional and European. On the domestic level, Greece created an environment of 'securitisation' in foreign policy that makes the government hostage to its own priorities. Spain, on the contrary, in most cases avoided the exaggeration of the importance of foreign policy cases. The great national importance attached to the Greek cases made nationalism inevitable. At the regional level, Spain achieved the reputation of a cooperative partner and, as an EU member, a pole of stability. What was particularly rewarding for Spain, was that narrow national interest did not obstruct its policies of cooperation and development towards its neighbours. On the contrary, this was the issue which made Greece a part of the problem in the Balkans. However, in the late 1990s, the change of attitude brought positive implications for Greece's role in the Balkan region. Finally, the 'national issues' of Greece, which is essentially the Greek foreign policy towards its neighbours, has been a cause of tension for the Greek participation in EPC/CFSP. Although this has had negative implications upon the role and influence of Greece in European foreign policy, the evidence suggests that this is partially an inability to adapt, since Greek foreign policy has demonstrated its adaptation to the European standards in all other areas apart from those that are 'securitised'.

Notes

1   Th. Couloumbis, 1994b, p.90.
2   It is a very interesting issue that has not yet been researched into who were behind the massive public demonstrations in Thessaloniki and Athens on Macedonia. There are speculations that the then Foreign Minister encouraged them, to the ignorance of the Prime Minister, for personal political exploitation, but nothing has been proved yet.
3   Interview, Konstantinos Mitsotakis, Athens, 26 March 1998.
4   In Madrid, Greece and Turkey agreed to the responsibilities of NATO air commands in Larissa and Izmir. Also the Prime Ministers of the two states issued a statement with which they express their willingness for dialogue and committed to peaceful resolution of any dispute.
5   I.K.Pretenderis, 'The Party of Orthodoxy', Newspaper 'To Vima', Athens, 11 April 1999, p.A16.
6   Ibid.
7   Report by D. Galanis and N. Karagiannis on 'Why the young are returning to the Church', newspaper 'To Vima', Athens, 8 April 1999, p.A24-25.
8   Interview, Enrique González Sanchez, Council of Ministers, Brussels, 11 December 1997.
9   See chapter 3, p.72.
10 His public declarations on his disagreement on the nationalistic line were probably one of the major factors for losing the elections of October 1993.
11 After the third Council of political leaders, Mitsotakis dismissed his foreign minister and took over himself the Ministry of Foreign Affairs.
12 In Greek addresses, the broader region is not mentioned, and it was the first time that such an action was introduced.
13 Interview, Angel Viñas, European Commision, Brussels, 8 January 1998.
14 C.A. Zaldivar, 1992, p.228.
15 Interview of the Spanish foreign minister during the 1980s, Francisco Fernando Ordóñez, published in the *Politica Exterior*, F.Fernandez Ordóñez, 1987, pp.14-15.

16 R. Mesa, 1988, p.173.
17 E. Barbé, 1998, p.149.
18 F. Rodrigo, 1995, p.64.
19 A. Cahen, 1989, p.53.
20 E. Barbé, 1998, p.151.
21 A. Zaldívar and A. Ortega, 1992.
22 A. Zaldívar, 1992, pp.213-214.
23 E. Barbé, 1991.
24 See Annex 3, p.229.
25 See chapter 3, p.64.
26 M. Salomon, 1996, p.100.
27 Ibid., p.101.
28 Ibid., p.102.
29 Ibid., p.104.
30 F. Sahagun, 1994, p.242.
31 Interview, Alberto Moreno, Permanent Representation of Spain in the EU, Brussels, 8 December 1997.
32 Interview, Alfonso Diez Torres, Secretaría del Estado para la Unión Europea, Madrid, 20 May 1998.
33 R. Gillespie, 1997, p.34.
34 Off the record interview with Spanish and EU officials realised in Brussels, January 1998 and Madrid, May 1998.
35 Treaty of Rome, article 227.
36 A.J.R. Groom, 1997, p.33.
37 C. Izquierdo Sans, 1996, p.233.
38 Interview, Francisco Elias de Tejada, Ministerio de Asuntos Exteriores, Madrid, 19 May 1998.
39 Interview, Ramón Torrent, Council of Ministers, Brussels, 7 January 1998.

7 Conclusion

This book looked at the national foreign policies of Greece and Spain with the purpose of studying the factors which determine their influence in European foreign policy. Chapter two explored the developed framework of European Political Cooperation and the eventual framing of Common Foreign and Security Policy. It also examined the input which Greece and Spain have had in that process. This chapter outlined the importance of collective action for European foreign policy and concluded that common foreign policy is for the benefit of all Member States and was developed because there is an understanding that one common voice was far better than six, nine, ten, twelve or fifteen individual voices. Chapter three continued the historical analysis by focusing on Greece and Spain. This chapter serves to conclude that the two Southern Member States could better achieve their objectives through the European common policy. In addition, through CFSP they could gain an important international role. Then in chapter four, this book went on to explore the domestic politics and the adaptation process of national foreign policies into Europe, showing that the more adaptive the national policy and process becomes, the more effective and influential role the State can play in CFSP. This is because of the Europeanisation of national priorities and the inclusion of them in the European agenda.

Chapter five examined national foreign policy participation in CFSP and concluded that influence can be gained by a built-up reputation of constructive participation. This allows the Member State to promote the common European interest, which is also national interest, because of the Europeanisation process. This process has to take place in order for the Member State to play a constructive role. Finally, chapter six studied the impact of geopolitics on foreign policy and the implication of securitisation that might take place in a foreign policy issue. This chapter concludes with the argument that it is the geoeconomic logic and desecuritisation that can increase the State's influence in European foreign policy and also guarantee regional security and stability.

The study of the foreign policies of Greece and Spain in the European foreign and security policy has produced three major themes in which the two countries demonstrated their behavioural patterns. These are state positions in foreign policy approach, objective and process.

Foreign Policy Approach

The theme in foreign policy approach is that of realism versus liberal internationalism. Realist foreign policy is dominated by the notion of balance of power. It is a constant pursuit of military power and influence which states are involved in. In this environment, states compete for strategic advantage and exploit their respective spheres of influence.[1] From the analysis of this book it can be concluded that Greek foreign policy followed a *realist* approach in the areas of policy considered as 'national issues'. However, this is not the case for the rest of Greek foreign policy, except from the period 1981-1985. For Greece, there exists a regional balance of power in the Balkans. Every alteration of power structures in the region can develop regional conflicts. The solution to Greece's security consideration comes from an attitude of building up its armed forces to develop military power of deterrent. Greece has been fighting a constant struggle for strategic advantage in its military capabilities and in its diplomatic efforts. The latter is the development of alliances with like-minded states, who consider themselves enemies of Turkey, developing a sphere of influence. Also, its main priority has been to become a member of security alliances, such as the WEU, and regional integrated regimes, such as the EU, in which Turkey is not a member. This offers Greece a strategic advantage that can be used to increase its position against Turkey, including the exclusion of it from membership of these fora. However, as evidence suggests, there has been a change in the above attitude and after 1996 Greece increasingly adopts a more cooperative behaviour in relation to Turkey.

Liberal Internationalism is concerned with collective security for all rather than individual security at the expense of the neighbours, which is why it sees the achievement of security through institutionalised international regimes. Democratisation and economic development are the 'weapons' for ending wars rather than military build up. Economic interdependence and mutual assistance not only achieves collective security but also guarantees the well-being of the societies of both states.[2] As is concluded from the analysis, Spanish foreign policy has had a mainly liberal approach. During the democratic transition, democratisation was seen as possible only with the accession of Spain in the European structure and the Europeanisation of its policies and processes. Europe can be seen as an institutionalised international regime which promotes economic development and collective security, in all five sectors as seen in chapter five. According to the Spanish practice, the achievement of regional peace and stability can only be possible through inclusion rather than exclusion of neighbours, and through cooperation for development and partnership rather than adversity and conflict. However, the evidence suggests that at times the Spanish national interest was pursued in such a way that can suggest the existence of *realist* considerations in Spanish foreign policy. This is particularly true after the change of government in 1996. The evidence suggest that no state behaviour could effectively be explained by any of these two theories since both Greece and Spain shifted from one to the other at different times.

Foreign Policy Objective

The theme in foreign policy objectives is that of national versus European interest. Greece followed, to an extent, an ethnocentrist approach in its foreign policy objective, which involved pursuing its strict national interest at any cost and many times at the expense of the interests of others. This objective is based on the realist perspective, analysed above, since the pursuit of interest is considered as a zero-sum game. In any given conflict there can be only one winner. The ethnocentric approach puts the realist perspective of the national interests at the heart of its foreign policy objective. Greece's objective has been to fight battles for national victories and that was seen as supportive of its national interest. That is why Greece has been reluctant to allow the development of a majoritarian CFSP, since the common interest might be contrary to its national interest. However, as mentioned earlier this picture started to change in the late 1990s which can suggest that by abandoning some of its *realist* preoccupations, Greece altered its behaviour in CFSP and this in turn implied the improvement of its influential ability.

For the most part, during its period of membership of the EU, Spain has followed a eurocentrist approach to foreign policy objectives. The Spanish objective during the period of the Socialist government has been that of pursuing its national interest through the collective European interest. This was because of the liberal internationalist approach which to an extent characterised Spanish foreign policy at that time. The collective interest which is achieved by working through the institutions of the EU, serves all national, including the Spanish interest. In doing that, Spain identified its own interests with the European one. In contrast with the realist approach, in the liberal view, the pursuit of interest is not a zero-sum game. Since the common interest was also Spanish interest, majority voting was desirable for Spain. Effectiveness and efficiency are vital for the functioning of CFSP and therefore they are for the benefit of all Member States. However, the Conservative government that came to power in 1996, moderated the Spanish Europeanism and adopted some realist policies confronting common positions because of the perceived Spanish interest.

The different focus in foreign policy objective developed a difference in the level of adaptation, as seen in chapter three. For a European priority, more adaptation to Europe enhanced the identification between national and common European interest. For a national priority, there are areas in which adaptation is essential or desirable in order for the national administration to function effectively in the European structure and pursue its interest. However, there are areas in which adaptation is perceived as against the national interest and should be avoided.

Foreign Policy Process

The final theme is that of securitisation versus desecuritisation. As a consequence of its priority for the national interest in a realist perspective, Greece followed a process of securitisation in the areas regarded as its 'national issues'. This is because the areas which are considered as vital for Greece's national interest, in a securitised situation, cannot be under any negotiation or compromise. The only chance for them to be included in the areas of common positions of CFSP was for Greece's partners to adopt its policies without trying to alter or negotiate them. This was an approach which puts certain issues that are securitised in the domestic sphere, on the European agenda, only to serve the purpose of enhancing the Greek position, or excluding them from it if there is a chance that they could be altered by another Member State. Although the issue of Turkey is still 'securitised' to a large extent, the way that Greece handled it since 1996 demonstrated a change of behaviour that brought positive results.

Spain, on the other hand, followed a process of desecuritisation. This was because of its priority for the common European interest from a liberal perspective. Spain developed policies of regional and European importance based on partnership and development. Its main priority has been to desecuritise the issues of security concern by building up relations of partnership with its neighbours and thus, eliminating security threats whatever their intensity and the sector they are in. In doing so, Spain tried to Europeanise its neighbouring region by enhancing its links with the EU, so as to develop its priority, which was the identification of its national interest with the European interest. For that, Spain worked for the collective interest not only of the EU, but also of its neighbouring region. However, the evidence suggests that there were times that Spain insisted in promoting its national interest, but it did so in a behavioural pattern so it would not alienate the arguments and interests of its partners.

The outcome of the different foreign policy processes in Greece and Spain has been the contrast between confrontation and cooperation. Greece's securitisation attempts developed an environment of confrontation, which maintains hostile relations between Greece and its neighbours. However, the new government in Greece that was elected in 1996 limited the areas of securitisation. The changed Greek behaviour towards its northern neighbours was illustrated in recent years. During the recent crisis in Kosovo and the NATO intervention in March 1999, Greece followed a prudent policy of supporting NATO, condemning Milosevic, while not participating in the military action against a neighbour. After the peace agreement in June, Greece committed more than 1000 troops to the peace operation. However, the issue of Turkey remains a securitised one, despite the changes in Greek foreign policy.

Spain's attitude of cooperation with the development of its regional environment developed a spirit of partnership that maintained relations of respect and of cooperation for mutual development. In the area of foreign policy process, Spain did not change its attitude towards its neighbouring countries despite the shift of focus on national interest made by the new government. On the contrary, Spain still supported the regional policy of cooperation and continues in its attempt to enhance the Mediterranean dimension of European foreign policy. However, because of the change of focus and the slight disassociation between European and Spanish interests, there is a danger that national interest in Spain could deviate from the common European interest with implications on Spain's Mediterranean initiatives.

Conclusions

The historical analysis of chapters two and three helped in identifying the necessity of Greece and Spain working through the supranational framework of the EU in order to increase their degree of influence in foreign policy. However, that is under the condition that the State favours the development of common positions and joint actions in CFSP, in other words, that the Europeanisation of its national interest has taken place. The best example of such a development has been Spain under the Socialist government of PSOE, between Spain's accession in 1986 and the 1996 elections when the Conservative Party of PP came to power. It was a period when Spanish interest became identical with the European. This is how Spain became an important actor in European foreign policy and enhanced its potential to influence policies and process. Working through the institutions but with the purpose of promoting strict national interests rather than a common interest can have the opposite results, as illustrated by the case of Greece, particularly in the Macedonian issue.

Integration benefits Greece and Spain because it gives them relatively more power to influence decision-making in a supranational structure than in an intergovernmental framework. However, in order for them to have an effective influence in the making of European foreign policy they need to work on gaining the reputation of promoting common policies for a collective interest. This constructive behaviour could help Greece and Spain to increase their influence by incorporating their national priorities in the European common policy. This is not to say that they can still serve nationalistic aims, since in order to achieve this behaviour, they have to gain a high level of adaptation to Europe. The Europeanisation of their priorities means that their incorporation into the European agenda would favour a collective interest rather than a strict national interest.

It can be argued that the domestic environment of the State to the EU is the most important factor that shapes foreign policy behaviour. This is because in a democracy the most important preoccupation of any government is to stay in power, so domestic sources and implications of foreign policy are very important factors for its development. The political orientation of the government is also important. That is because a European or national orientation of foreign policy has a major impact on the patterns of participation in European foreign policy. The different approaches of the different governments in both Greece and Spain prove the fact that it matters which political party forms the government. That is to say that the

State foreign policy behaviour is neither given nor permanent but can fluctuate according to the ideology of the party in government. However, a long-term foreign policy strategy can be achieved when there is a consensus between the political forces on an issue. This consensus can either be achieved by securitising the issue, giving national importance to it, or by desecuritising it, creating a tradition of cooperation. Finally, the geopolitical situation is an important factor but only in its negative perception, because when a Member state succeeds in the Europeanisation process and desecuritises any issues of security concern, geopolitics becomes less important in an environment of cooperation and mutual assistance. However, it can be important in shaping foreign policy behaviour in areas where securitisation exists. This is because in these areas the national interest that is served by securitisation takes precedence over anything else.

The most important changes that the adaptation process can bring to the three factors argued before, are found in the influence of geopolitics. First, Europeanisation, which is the stage of total adaptation, results in the irrelevance of geopolitical concerns. Second, it brings important changes in the other two factors. Third, it develops a continuity of European orientation in governmental policy since national priorities have been Europeanised and national interest identified with the common European interest. Finally, it brings changes to the domestic political environment. This does however depend upon the extent of Europeanisation in the domestic society, since successful adaptation of the administration process and foreign policy-making can be limited at the governmental elite level. This might in turn develop minority opposition in the society which could be interpreted in anti-European political movements. Therefore, foreign policy adaptation does not necessarily mean important changes to the domestic political environment. This depends upon the level of adaptation of the political culture and society of the Member State.

Notes

---

[1] S. Burchill, 1996, pp.67-92.
[2] S. Burchill, 1996, pp.28-91.

Bibliography

Primary Sources

Agence Europe (1990), *Belgian Memorandum of 21/3/90*, Europe Documents, no.1608, 29 March 1990

Agence Europe (1990), *Conclusions of the Dublin Summit of 25-26 June 1990*, 27/6/90

Agence Europe (1992), *Petersberg Declaration*, Europe Documents, no.1787

Aznar, José Maria (1995), *España en la apertura de la Conferencia Intergubernamental*, Speech, Brussels, 29 March 1995

Benelux (1996), *Memorandum*, March

Bolletín Oficial del Estado (1979), *Royal Decree no.984*, Madrid, 27 April 1979

Bolletín Oficial del Estado (1985), *Royal Decree no.1485*, Madrid, 12 May 1985

Bolletín Oficial del Estado (1998), *Royal Decree no.2601*, Madrid, 4 December 1998

Bulletin of the EC (1970), *Conclusions of The Hague Summit*, no.1, pp.11-16

Bulletin of the EC (1970), *Luxembourg (Davignon), Report*, no.11, pp.9-12

Bulletin of the EC (1973), *Copenhagen Report*, no.9

Bulletin of the EC (1976), *Tindemans Report*, Supplement, no.1, pp.14-22

Bulletin of the EC (1976), *Opinion of the European Commission on Greek application for membership*, Supplement, no.2, p.7

Bulletin of the EC (1981), *London Report*, Supplement, no.3

Bulletin of the EC (1983), *Solemn Declaration of Stuttgart*, no.6

Bulletin of the EC (1986), *Single European Act*, Supplement, no.2

Communication from the Commission to the Council and the EP (1994), *Strengthening the Mediterranean Policy of the EU: establishing a Euro-Mediterranean Partnership*, Brussels, COM(94)427final, 19/10/94

Conference of the Representatives of the Governments of the Member States (1996), *CFSP decision-making procedures*, CONF 3824/96, 24 April

Conference of the Representatives of the Governments of the Member States (1996), *Security and Defence, CFSP, Article J.4 of the TEU*, CONF 3828/96, 26 April

Conference of the Representatives of the Governments of the Member States (1996), *Memorandum by the UK, CFSP planning cell, Terms of Reference*, CONF 3894/96, July

Conference of the Representatives of the Governments of the Member States (1996), *Proposals for Treaty Amendments: security and defence, from the Finnish and Swedish delegations*, CONF 3946/96, 8 October

Conference of the Representatives of the Governments of the Member States (1997), *Compilation of texts under discussion: an effective and coherent foreign policy*, SN 541/97, May

Congreso de los diputados (1991), *Diario de sesiones del Congreso de los diputados 155*, Madrid, 17/12/91

Council of Foreign Ministers (1991), *Resolution of 16 December 1991*, Brussels

Council of Ministers (1973), *EPC declaration, 6/11/73*, Brussels

Council of Ministers (1974), *Communiqué on Cyprus, 16/7/74*, Paris

Council of Ministers (1974), *Communiqué on Cyprus, 22/7/74*, Brussels

Council of Ministers (1975), *Declaration of the 18th EPC ministerial meeting*, Dublin, 13/2/75

CSCE (1975), *Declaration on the completion of the final Act*, Helsinki, 30/7/75

Dutch Presidency of the EU (1997), *Draft Treaty*, Brussels, October 1997

EPC Documentation Bulletin (1986), *Report from the European Council on European Union: Progress made with EPC*, vol.2, no.1, 85/341

EPC Documentation Bulletin (1986), *Statement on the Combating of International Terrorism*, vol.2, no.1, 86/061

EPC Documentation Bulletin (1986), *Statement on International Terrorism and the crisis in the Mediterranean*, vol.2, no.1, 86/119

EPC Documentation Bulletin (1987), *Joint Political Declaration on Political Dialogue and economic cooperation between the European Community and its member states, and the countries of Central America and of the Contadora Group, issued at the ministerial conference in Guatemala City*, vol.3, no.1, 87/096

EPC Documentation Bulletin (1988), *Council Statement on the period in office of the Greek Presidency*, vol.4, no.2, 88/204

EPC Documentation Bulletin (1989), *Statement on the meeting of the European Council in Madrid*, 89/188, 26/7/89

EPC Documentation Bulletin (1989), *Statement concerning the term of office of the Spanish Presidency and concerning the forthcoming Madrid European Council*, vol.5, no.1, 89/126

EPC Documentation Bulletin (1989), *Statement on the meeting of the European Council in Madrid and on the term in office of the Spanish Presidency*, vol.5, no.2, 89/188

EPC Documentation Bulletin (1990), *Joint political declaration of the Dublin ministerial Conference on political dialogue and economic cooperation between the European Community and its member states, the countries of Central America and Panama, and Colombia, Mexico and Venezuela as cooperating countries, held on 9 and 10 April 1990*, vol.6, 90/177

EPC Documentation Bulletin (1990), *Statement concerning the Gulf Crisis*, vol.6, 90/469

Europe Documents (1991), *Conférence Intergouvernamentale sur l'Union Politique: Le 'communiqué conjoint' franco-allemand-espagnol*, Europe Documents 1737, 17 October

European Commission (1992) *Lunch of Ministers of Foreign Affairs, 6 April*, Brussels 7/4/92

European Commission (1995), *Commission Report for the Reflection Group*, Brussels, May 1995

European Commission (1996), *Commission opinion on the 1996 IGC: Reinforcing political union and preparing for enlargement*, Brussels, February 1996

European Commission (1998), *Proposal of the Commission for a Council Regulation regarding the implementation of a specific financial cooperation measure for Turkey*, 1/12/98,
(http://europa.eu.int/eur-lex/en/com/dat/1995/en_595PC0389.html)

European Council (1973), *Document on the European identity*, Copenhagen, 14/12/73

European Council (1974), *Communiqué of the Paris Summit*, Paris, 10/12/74

European Council (1995), 'Conclusions of the European Council in Cannes' *EFPB 95/186*, June 1995

European Council (1997), *Conclusions of the Luxembourg Summit*, 12-13 December 1997, Brussels, SN 400/97

European Parliament (1990), *Report on the IGC on Political Union*, 14/3/90, A3-270/90

European Parliament (1997), *Resolution on the general framework for a draft Treaty review*, b4-0040/97, Brussels, 16 January

Finish Ministry of Foreign Affairs (1995), *Memorandum concerning Finnish points of view with regards to the 1996 IGC of the EU*, Helsinki

Foreign and Commonwealth Office (1996), *A partnership of nations: the British approach to the EU IGC 1996*, Cm 3181, London: HMSO

General Secretariat of the EU Council (1995), *1996 IGC Reflection Group Report*, Brussels, December 1995

Government of Greece (1985), *Memorandum on Greece's views on the issues of the IGC*, Athens, 11/10/85

Government of Greece (1990), *Memorandum of Greece on Political Union*, Athens, 15 May 1990

Government of Greece (1994), *Decision of the government on measures against FYROM*, Athens, 16/2/94

Government of Greece (1996), *Memorandum of Greece for a European Union with Political and Social Content*, Athens, 22/3/96

Government of Spain (1990), *Common Foreign and Security Policy: Spanish contribution*, Madrid, 26/11/90

Government of Spain (1991), *Memorandum of Spain on Political Union*, Madrid, November 1991

Government of Spain (1996), *The 1996 IGC: starting points for a discussion*, Madrid, 2/3/96

Government of Spain (1996), *Elements for a Spanish position at the 1996 IGC*, Madrid, 28/3/96

Hellenic Republic (1974), *Presidential Decree no.0115/7/AS207*, Journal of the Government of the Hellenic Republic, 20 June 1974

Hellenic Republic (1975), *Presidential Decree no.010/700/AS206*, Journal of the Government of the Hellenic Republic, 12 July 1975

Hellenic Republic (1998), *Presidential Decree no.230*, Journal of the Government of the Hellenic Republic, 28 July 1998

High-Level Expert Group on CFSP (1994), *European Security Policy Towards 2000: ways and means to establish genuine credibility*, Brussels, 19 December

High-Level Expert Group on CFSP (1995), *European Security Policy Towards 2000: ways and means to establish genuine credibility*, Brussels, 25 October

Irish Presidency of the EU (1997), *A general outline for a draft revision of the Treaties*, Council of the EU, Brussels, February 1997

Italian Presidency of the EU (1996), *Convening of the IGC*, Brussels, July 1996

Memorandum from Finland and Sweden (1996), *The IGC and the security and defence dimension: towards an enhanced EU role in crisis management*, Helsinki-Stockholm, 25 April

Ministerio de Asuntos Exteriores (1995), *Reflection document on the WEU contribution to the IGC of 1996*, Dirección General de Asuntos Internacionales de Seguridad y Desarme, Madrid, 4 July

Ministry of Foreign Affairs (1991), *Memorandum on Yugoslav Macedonia*, Athens, 27/8/91

Nouvelles Atlantiques (1996), *OTAN/Espagne: Le gouvernement de Madrid cherche l'appui du parlement national pour negocier l'integration dans une nouvelle structue militaire alliée. Le probleme de Gibraltar*, no.2486, 13 September

Office of Diplomatic Information (1995), *La PESC durante la presidencia española del consejo de la UE*, Madrid, Ministerio de Asuntos Exteriores, December 1995

Office of Diplomatic Information (1995), *Declaration of the Presidency in the name of the EU on the Helms-Burton project*, Madrid, 13/10/95

Official Journal of the EC (1993), *Decision of the Council 93/603/CFSP on 8/11/93*, L.286, 20/11/93

Official Journal of the EC (1993), *Joint Action 93/728/CFSP of 20/12/93*, L.339, 31/12/93

Official Journal of the EC (1998), *Common position of 14 December 1998*, 98/725/CFSP

Press Information Office (1974), *Texts relating to EPC*, Bonn

Press Information Office (1982), *Texts relating to EPC*, 4th ed., Bonn

Treaty of Rome establishing the European Community, Rome, 25 March 1957

Treaty on European Union, Maastricht, 7 February 1992
Treaty on European Union (revised), Amsterdam, October 1997
UK Presidency of the EC (1981), *London Report*, London, 13/10/81
UN, *proposed plan Vance-Owen*, 14/5/93
UN, *Interim Accord between FYROM and Greece*, New York, 13/9/95
UN Resolution 2072-XX
WEU (1954), *Brussels Convention*, Paris, 23/10/54
WEU (1992), *Petersburg Declaration*, Bonn, 19/2/92

Secondary Sources

Alapuro, R. (1985) (ed.), *Small States in Comparative Perspective - Essays for Erik Allardt*, Oslo: Norwegian University Press
Aldecoa, F. (1984), 'La política exterior de España en perspectiva histórica. De la autocracia al Estado de derecho', *Sistema*, no. 63
Algieri, F. and Regelsberger, E. (eds.) (1996), *Synergy at Work: Spain and Portugal in European Foreign Policy*, Bonn: Europa Union Verlag
Allen, D. (1982), 'Political Cooperation and the Euro-Arab dialogue', in Allen, D., Rummel, R., and Wessels, W., *European Political Cooperation*, London: Butterworth
Allen, D., Rummel, R., and Wessels, W. (1982), *European Political Cooperation*, London: Butterworth
Álvarez-Miranda, B. (1994), 'Greek Membership in the European Community: Modernisation, Democratisation and Foreign Policy', *Research Institute for European Studies*, Athens, Research Paper No.8, December
Álvarez-Miranda, B. (1996), *El sur de Europa y la adhesión a la Comunidad: los debates políticos*, Madrid: CIS Siglo XXI
Anton, T. (1980), *Administered Politics: elite political culture in Sweden*, London: Nijhoff
Archer, C. and Butler, F. (1996) 2nd ed., *The European Union: Structure and process*, London: Cassel
Armero, J.M. (1988), *Política Exterior de España en Democracia*, Madrid: Espasa-Calpe
Axt, H.J. (1993), 'Αποτελεσματική διοίκηση ως προϋπόθεση συνεπούς ευρωπαϊκής πολιτικής' (Effective administration as a prerequisite of consistent European policy), in L. Tsoukalis (ed.), *Η Ελλάδα στην Ευρωπαϊκή Κοινότητα. Η πρόκληση της προσαρμογής (Greece in the EC: the challenge of adaptation)*, Athens: Papazisis
Bachrach, P. and Baratz, M. (1962), 'Two faces of power', *American political science Review*, vol. 52, no. 3, pp. 947-62
Baer, D. (1989), *Elite cadres and party coalitions: representing the public in party politics*, London: Greenwood

Baldwin, D. (ed.) (1993), *Neo-Realism and Neo-Liberals: a reader*, New York: Columbia University Press

Barbé, E. (1990), 'El año español de la Cooperación Política Europea', in *Anuario Internacional CIDOB 1989*, Barcelona: CIDOB, pp. 109-120

Barbé, E. (1991), 'España y el Mediterráneo en el nuevo equilibrio europeo', in *Anuario Internacional CIDOB 1990*, Barcelona: CIDOB, pp. 75-82

Barbé, E. (1994), 'Spanish responses to the security institutions of the New Europe', in A. Williams (ed.), *Reorganising Eastern Europe: European institutions and the refashioning of Europe's security architecture*, Aldershot: Dartmouth

Barbé, E. (1994a), 'España y la construcción europea: Mirando al Norte', *Centre d'Estudis sobre la Pau*, Barcelona

Barbé, E. (1995), 'European Political Cooperation: the upgrading of the Spanish Foreign Policy', in R. Gillespie, F. Rodrigo and J. Story (eds.), *Democratic Spain: Reshaping external relations in a changing world*, London: Routledge

Barbé, E. (1996a), 'Spain: the uses of foreign policy cooperation', in Ch. Hill (ed.), *The Actors in Europe's Foreign Policy*, London: Routledge

Barbé, E. (1996b), 'Spain: Realist Integrationism', in F. Algieri and E. Regelsberger (eds.), *Synergy at Work: Spain and Portugal in European Foreign Policy*, Bonn: Europa Union Verlag

Barbé, E (1996c), 'The Barcelona Conference: Launching Pad of a process', *Mediterranean Politics*, vol. 1, no. 1, Summer 1996

Barbé, E. (1997), 'De la ingenuidad al ragmatismo: 10 años de participación española en la maquinaria diplomática europea', *Revista CIDOB d'afers Internacionals*, no. 34-5: 9-30

Barbé, E. (1997a), 'La política exterior y de seguridad común en la reforma del tratado de la Unión Europea', *Revista Española de desarrollo y cooperación*, no.1, pp.7-21

Barbé, E. (1998), 'Spanish security policy', in Eliassen, K. (ed.), *Foreign and Security Policy in the European Union*, London: Sage

Benavides Orgaz, P. (1988), 'La Cooperación Política Europea', in Instituto de Cuestiones Internacionales, *Un examen de la política exterior española*, no.40, October

Benavides Orgaz, P. (1991), 'Política exterior española y cooperación política europea', *Notocias*, CEE, no. 75

Beyers, J. and Guido, D. (1998), 'The working Groups of the Council of the EU: Supranational or Intergovernmental negotiations?', *Journal of Common market Studies*, vol. 36, no. 3, pp. 289-317

Bloes, R. (1970), *Le plan Fouchet et le probleme de l'Europe politique*, Bruges: College of Europe

Bluth, C., Kirchner, E. and Sperling, J. (eds.) (1995), *The future of European Security Policy*, Aldershot: Dartmouth

Boixareu, A. (1996), 'Las fronteras exteriores de la Unión Europea y la cuestión de Gibraltar', *Política Exterior*, vol. 10, no. 49, pp. 134-146

Bonham-Carter, V. (1963), *The impact of personality in politics*, Oxford: Clarendon Press

Bonino, E. (1995), 'La réforme de la politique étrangere et de sécurité commune: aspects institutionnels', *Revue du Marché unique européen*, 3: 261-78

Bull, H. (1977), *The anarchical society*, London: Macmillan

Bulmer, S. and Wessels, W. (1987), *The European Council*, London: Macmillan

Burchill, S. (1996), 'Liberal Internationalism' and 'Realism and Neo-realism', in S. Burchill and A. Linklater (eds.), *Theories of International Relations*, Basingstoke: Macmillan

Burgess, M. (1989), *Federalism and European Union, 1972-87*, London: Routledge

Burghardt, G. (1995), 'Politique étrangere et de sécurité commune: garantir la stabilité a long terme de l'Europe', *Revue du Marché unique européen*, 3: 261-78

Buzan, B. (1997), 'The timeless wisdom of realism', in S. Smith, K. Booth and M. Zalewski, *International theory: positivism and beyond*, Cambridge: Cambridge University Press

Buzan, B., Waever, O. and de Wilde, J. (1998), *Security: a new framework for analysis*, London: Lynne Rienner

Cahen, A. (1989), *The WEU and NATO: Building a European Defence Identity within the context of Atlantic solidarity*, Brassey's Atlantic Commentaries 2, London: Brassey's

Calduch, R. (ed.) (1994), *La Política Exterior Española en el Siglo XX*, Madrid: Ciencias Sociales

Camps, M. (1966), *European Unification in the Sixties: from the veto to the crisis*, New York

Caporaso, J. (ed.) (1989), *The elusive State*, London: Sage

Carlsnaes, W. (1987), *Ideology and foreign policy: problems of comparative conceptualisation*, Oxford: Blackwell

Carlsnaes, W. and Smith, S. (eds.) (1994), *European Foreign Policy: The EC and changing perspectives in Europe*, London: Sage

Carr, E.H. (1946), *The twenty years' crisis, 1919-1939*, London: Macmillan

Cartwright, D. (1965), 'Influence, Leadership, Control', in J. G. March (ed.), *Handbook of Organisations*, Chicago: Rand McNally

Churruca, C. (1997), 'Una aproximación al estudio de la política exterior común desde las relaciones internacionales', *Cuadernos Europeos de Deusto*, no. 17/1997, pp. 39-69

Coffey, P. (1976), *The external economic relations of the EEC*, London: Macmillan

Coffey, P. (1993), *The EC and the United States*, London: Pinter

Coffey, P. and C. Angarita (1988), *Europe and the Andean countries: a comparison of economic policies and institutions*, London: Pinter

Coffey, P. and L.A. Correa do Lago (1988), *The EEC and Brazil trade, capital investment and the debt problem*, London: Pinter

Couloumbis, Th. (1994a), 'Introduction: the impact of EC (EU), membership on Greece's foreign policy profile', in P. Kazakos and P.C. Ioakimidis, *Greece and EC Membership Evaluated*, London: Pinter

Couloumbis, Th. (1994b), 'Οι στόχοι της Ελληνικής Εξωτερικής Πολιτικής στα Βαλκάνια' (the objectives of Greek foreign policy in the Balkans), in D.K. Constas and P.I. Tsakonas, *Ελληνική Εξωτερική Πολιτική* (Greek Foreign Policy), Athens: Odysseas

Couloumbis, Th. and Yannas, P. (1996), 'Greek foreign policy priorities for the 1990s', in K. Featherstone and K. Ifantis, *Greece in a changing Europe*, Manchester: Manchester University Press

Couloumbis, Th. and Dalis, S. (1997), *Η Ελληνική Εξωτερική Πολιτική στο κατώφλι του 21ου Αιώνα* (Greek Foreign Policy in the threshold of the 21st century), Athens: Papazisis

Cox, R. and Jacobson, H. (1974), *The anatomy of influence: Decision-Making in International Organisations*, New Haven: Yale University Press

Cram, L. and Richardson, J. (1998), *Policy Styles in the EU*, London: Routledge

Dahl, R. A. (1963), *Modern Political Analysis*, Englewood Cliffs, N.J.: Prentice-Hall

Dahrendorf, R. (1968), *Society and democracy in Germany*, London: Weidenfeld and Nicolson

Dalby, S. (1991), 'Critical geopolitics: discourse, difference and dissent', *Environment and Planning D: Society and Space*, vol. 9, pp. 261-83

Dalis, S. (1995), 'Το συμβούλιο της ΕΕ στις Κάννες - Επιθετική πολιτική για εσωκομματική κατανάλωση' (The Council of the EU at Cannes - Offensive policy for intra-party consumption), *Anti* vol. 582, 7 July, pp.18-19

Danforth, L. (1995), *The Macedonian conflict: ethnic nationality in a transnational world*, New Jersey: Princeton University Press

De Gaulle, C. (1970), *Discours et Messages. Pour l'effort Août 1962-Décembre 1965*, Paris: Librairie Plon

De Schouthéete, P. (1986), *La Cooperation Politique Européenne*, Brussels: Labor

De Schouthéete, P. (1997), 'The creation of the CFSP', in Regelsberger, E., de Schoutheete, P. and Wessels, W., *Foreign Policy of the European Union: From EPC to CFSP and Beyond*, London: Lynne Rienner

De Vree, J.K., Coffey, P. and Lauwaars, H. (eds.) (1987), *Towards a European foreign policy: legal, economic and political dimensions*, Dordrecht: Nijhoff

Deutsch, K. (1967), *France, Germany and the Western alliance: a study of elite attitudes on European integration and world politics*, New York: Scribner

Deutsch, K. (1974), 'Between Sovereignty and Integration: Conclusion', *Government and Opposition*, vol. 9, no. 1, Winter

Dezcallar, J. (1988), *Un examen a la política exterior española*, Madrid: Instituto de Cuestiones Internacionales

Dezcallar, J. (1990), *La cooperación política europea y el proceso de paz en oriente medio*, Informativo no. 4, Madrid: Ministerio de Asuntos Exteriores

Diamadouros, N.I. (1993), 'Τα διλήμματα του εκσυγχρονισμού' (the dilemma of modernisation), in L. Tsoukalis (ed.), *Η Ελλάδα στην Ευρωπαϊκή Κοινότητα. Η πρόκληση της προσαρμογής (Greece in the EC: the challenge of adaptation)*, Athens: Papazisis

Diedrichts, U. (1996), 'National views and European cleavages', in Algieri, F. and Regelsberger, E. (eds.), *Synergy at Work: Spain and Portugal in European Foreign Policy*, Bonn: Europa Union Verlag

Dinan, D. (1994), *Ever closer Union? An introduction to the European Community*, Basingstoke: Macmillan

Doyle, M. (1986), 'Liberalism and world politics', *American Political Science Review*, vol. 80, no. 4, pp. 1151-69

Doyle, M. (1995), 'Liberalism and world politics revisited' in C.W. Kegley Jr (ed.), *Controversies in International Relations Theory*, London: Macmillan

Duff, A., Pinder, J. and Pryce, R. (eds.) (1994), *Common Foreign and Security Policy in Maastricht and Beyond*, London: Routledge

Dunn, J.F. (1992), 'Europe's troubled corner: How to overcome instability and tensions in the Balkans', *Wilton Park Paper 66*, London: HMSO

Edwards, G. (1984), 'Europe and the Falkland Islands Crisis, 1982', *Journal of Common Market Studies*, no. 4

Edwards, G. (1997), 'The potential and limits of the CFSP: the Yugoslav example', in Regelsberger, E., de Schoutheete, P. and Wessels, W., *Foreign Policy of the European Union: From EPC to CFSP and Beyond*, London: Lynne Rienner

Edwards, G. and Pijpers, A. (eds.) (1997), *The politics of European Treaty reform: the 1996 IGC and beyond*, London: Cassel

Edwards, G. and Regelsberger, E. (eds.) (1990), *Europe's Global Links: The European Community and Inter-Regional Cooperation*, London: Pinter

Elderveld, S. (1981), *Elite images of Dutch politics: accomodation and conflict*, Ann Arbor: University of Michigan Press

Eliassen, K. (ed.) (1998), *Foreign and Security Policy in the European Union*, London: Sage

Elms, A.C. (1976), *Personality and Politics*, New York: Harcourt Brace Jovanovich

Featherstone, K. (1988), *Socialist Parties and European Integration. A comparative History*, Manchester: Manchester University Press

Featherstone, K. (1990), 'Political Parties and democratic consolidation in Greece', in G. Pridham (ed.), *Securing Democracy: Political parties and democratic consolidation in Southern Europe*, London: Routledge

Featherstone, K. (1996), 'Introduction', in Featherstone, K and Ifantis, K., *Greece in a changing Europe*, Manchester: Manchester University Press

Featherstone, K. and Ifantis, K. (1996), *Greece in a changing Europe: between European integration and Balkan disintegration?*, Manchester: Manchester University Press

Feld, W. (1967), *The European common market and the world*, Englewood Cliffs, N.J: Prentice-Hall

Feld, W. (1976), *The European Community in World affairs: economic power and political influence*, Port Washington, N.Y: Alfred Pub. Co.

Feld, W., Jordan, R.S. and Hurwitz, L. (1983), *International Organisations: a comparative approach*, New York: Praeger

Fernández Fernández, J.J. (1998), 'El fortalecimiento de las relaciones entre la Unión Europea y América Latina: nuevas perspectivas para una PESC global, coherente y autónoma', *Revista de Estudios Políticos*, no. 99, January-March, pp. 217-226

Fernández Ordóñez, F. (1987), 'Política exterior de España 1987-1990', *Política Exterior*, vol. 1, no. 1, Winter 1987, pp. 14-27

Folliot, D. (ed.) (1955), *Documents on International Affairs 1952*, London: Oxford University Press

Frankel, J. (1963), *The making of foreign policy: An analysis of decision-making*, London: Oxford University Press

Frankel, J. (1970), *National Interest*, London: Pall Mall

Frankel, J. (1973), *Contemporary International Theory and the behaviour of States*, Oxford: Oxford University Press

Fuentes, J. (1982), 'Carácter global de la política exterior española', *Revista de Estudios Internacionales*, vol. 3, no. 2, April-June

Fukuyama, F. (1992), *The end of history and the last man*, London: Penguin

Galtung, J. (1973), *The European Community: a superpower in the making*, London: Allen and Unwin

Galtung, J. (1989), *Europe in the making*, London: Crane Russak

Garcia, C. (1995), 'The autonomous communities and external relations', in R. Gillespie, F. Rodrigo and J. Story (eds.), *Democratic Spain: Reshaping external relations in a changing world*, London: Routledge

Gardner, R.N. (1990), 'The comeback of liberal internationalism', *The Washington Quarterly*, vol. 13, no. 3, pp. 23-39

George, S. (1994), 2nd ed., *An awkward partner: Britain in the EC*, Oxford: Oxford University Press

George, S. (1996) 3rd ed., *Politics and Policy in the EC*, Oxford: Oxford University Press

Gillespie, R. (1997), 'Spanish protagonismo and the Euro-Med Partnership Initiative', *Mediterranean Politics*, vol. 2, no. 1, Summer 1997, pp. 33-48

Gillespie, R. (1997a), 'The Mediterranean dimension to Spanish influence in Europe', *Second UACES Conference*, Panel 2, Loughborough, 10-12 September

González, F. (1998), 'El euro lleva a la unión política', *El País*, Sunday 3 May 1998

Goodwin, G.L. (1974), 'The erosion of external sovereignty', *Government and Opposition*, vol. 9, no. 1, Winter

Greenstein, F.I. (1987), *Personality and Politics: problems of evidence, influence and conceptualization*, Princeton: Princeton University Press

Groom, A.J.R. (1997), 'Gibraltar: a pebble in the EU's shoe', *Mediterranean Politics*, vol. 2, no. 3, Winter 1997, pp. 20-52

Grugel, J. (1995), 'Spain and Latin America', in R. Gillespie, F. Rodrigo and J. Story (eds.), *Democratic Spain: Reshaping external relations in a changing world*, London: Routledge

Haas, E.B. (1958), *The uniting of Europe: political, social and economic forces 1950-1957*, Stanford: Stanford University Press

Haas, E.B. (1964), *Beyond the nation-state: functionalism and international organisation*, Stanford: Stanford University Press

Hallstein, W. (1972), *Europe in the Making*, London: George Allen and Unwin Ltd.

Hanrieder, W.F. (1967), 'Compatibility and Consensus: a proposal for the conceptual linkage of external and internal dimensions of foreign policy', *American Political Science Review*, December 1967, pp. 971-82

Hanrieder, W.F. and Auton, G.P. (1980), *The foreign policies of West Germany, France, and Britain*, Englewood Cliffs: Prentice-Hall

Harryvan, A.G. and Van der Harst, J. (1997), *Documents on European Union*, Basingstoke: Macmillan

Hayward, J. and Page, E.C. (1995), *Governing the New Europe*, Cambridge: Polity Press

Hermann, C.F., Kegley, C.W. and Rosenau, J.N. (eds.) (1987), *New directions in the study of foreign policy*, Boston: Allen and Unwin

Hill, C. (ed.) (1983), *National foreign policies and European Political Cooperation*, London: George Allen and Unwin Ltd.

Hill, C. (1993), 'The capability-expectation gap, or conceptualising Europe's international role', *Journal of Common Market Studies*, 31 (3): 305-28

Hill, C. (ed.) (1996), *The actors in Europe's foreign policy*, London: Routledge

Hill, C. (1998), 'Closing the capabilities-expectations gap?', in Peterson, J. and H. Sjursen (eds.), *A common foreign policy for Europe? Competing visions of the CFSP*, London: Routledge

Hinsley, F.H. (1962), *Power and the pursuit of peace*, Cambridge: Cambridge University Press

Hinsley, F.H. (1969), *Sovereignty*, London: C.A. Watts

Holland, M. (ed.) (1991), *The future of European Political Cooperation*, London: Macmillan

Holland, M. (1993), *European Integration: from Community to Union*, London: Pinter

Holland, M. (1995), *European Union Foreign Policy: from EPC to CFSP joint action and South Africa*, Basingstoke: Macmillan

Holland, M. (ed.) (1997), *Common Foreign and Security Policy: The record and reforms*, London: Pinter

Hope, K. (1991), 'Greece threatens Maastricht Veto', in *The Times*, 29 November 1991

Hull, C. and Rhodes, R.A.W. (1977), *Intergovernmental relations in the European Community*, Westmead: Saxon House

Hurd, D. (1981), 'Political Cooperation', *International Affairs*, Summer 1981, vol. 57, no. 3, pp. 383-393

Ifestos, P. (1987), *European Political Cooperation: towards a framework of supranational diplomacy?*, Aldershot: Avebury

Ioakimidis, P.C. (1980), *Ο Διεθνής ρόλος των μικρών χωρών και η ένταξη της Ελλάδας στην ΕΟΚ* (the international role of small states and the accession of Greece in the EEC), Athens: Papazisis

Ioakimidis, P.C. (1990), *Η Ευρώπη σε μεταλλαγή. Η ΕΚ και η Ελλάδα στη νέα προοπτική (Europe in transformation. The EC and Greece in the new perspective)*, Athens: Themelio

Ioakimidis, P.C. (1991), 'Η Ευρωπαϊκή πολιτική της Ελλάδας 10 χρόνια μετά την ένταξη στην ΕΚ' (The European policy of Greece 10 years after its accession in the EC), *Epilogi*, special issue, June, pp.16-17

Ioakimidis, P.C. (1993), 'Η Ελληνική διοίκηση και η διαμόρφωση της εξωτερικής πολιτικής' (the Greek administration and the formation of foreign policy), in L. Tsoukalis, (ed.), *Η Ελλάδα στην Ε.Κ.: η πρόκληση της προσαρμογής*, (Greece in the EC: the challenge of adaptation), Athens: Papazisis

Ioakimidis, P.C. (1993b), 'Greece in the EC: policies, experiences and prospects', in H.J. Psomiades and S.B. Thomadakis, (eds.), *Greece, the new Europe, and the changing international order*, New York: Pella

Ioakimidis, P.C. (1995), *Η αναθεώρηση της συνθήκης του Μααστριχτ*, (the revision of the Treaty of Maastricht), Athens: Themelio

Ioakimidis, P.C. (1995a), 'Measuring Ensomatosis: the case of Greece in the EU', *The Southeast European Yearbook 1994-95*, Athens: ELIAMEP

Ioakimidis, P.C. (1996), 'Contradictions between policy and performance', in K. Featherstone and K. Ifantis (ed.), *Greece in a changing Europe: between European integration and Balkan disintegration*, Manchester: Manchester University Press

Ioakimidis, P.C. (1996a), 'The role of Greece in the development of EC Mediterranean policy', *Mediterranean Politics*, vol. 2, pp. 67-81

Ionescu, G. (1974), *Between Sovereignty and integration*, London: Croom Helm

Izquierdo Sans, C. (1996), *Gibraltar en la Unión Europea*, Madrid: Tecnos

Jaworski, H. (1989), *Perspectivas y posibilidades de la Política Española de cooperación al desarrollo*, Madrid: Aiti-Cedeal

Jordan, R.S. and Feld, W. (1986), *Europe in the balance: the changing context of European international politics*, London: Faber

Kaminaris, S. (1999), 'Greece and the Middle East', *Middle East Review of International Affairs*, vol. 3, no. 2

Kargakos, S. (1996), 'Δυτικισμός και αντιδυτικισμός - Ευρωπαϊστές και αντιευρωπαϊστές' (Westicism and anti-Westicism - Europeanists and anti-Europeanists), *Oikonomikos Taxydromos*, (2176), 18 January, p. 3

Keohane, R. and Nye, J.S. (1977), *Power and Interdependence: World Politics in Transition*, Boston: Little Brown

Kerremans, B. (1996), 'Do institutions make a difference? Non-Institutionalism, Neo-Institutionalism and the logic of Common decision-making in the EU', *Governance*, vol. 9, no. 2, pp. 217-40

Kintis, A.G. (1997), 'The EU's Foreign Policy and the war in former Yugoslavia', in Holland, M. (ed.), *Common Foreign and Security Policy: The record and reforms*, London: Pinter

Kirchner, E.J. (1992), *Decision-making in the EC*, Manchester: Manchester University Press

Kohler-Koch, B. (1996), 'Catching up with change: the transformation of governance in the EU', *Journal of European Public Policy*, vol. 3, no. 3, pp. 359-80

Kouskouvelis, I. (1995), *Διπλωματία και στρατηγική της Ε.Ε.* (Diplomacy and strategy of the EU), Athens: Papazisis

Laffan, B. (1992), *Integration and cooperation in Europe*, London: Routledge

Landau, A. and Whitman, R. (1996), *Rethinking the European Union*, Basingstoke: Macmillan

Leonard, P. (1984), *Personality and ideology: towards a materialist understanding of the individual*, London: Macmillan

Lerner, A.W. (1990), *The manipulators: personality and politics in multiple perspectives*, Hillsdale, N.J.: L.Erlbaum Associates

Lindberg, L. and Scheingold, S. (1970), *Europe's would-be polity*, Englewood Cliffs: Prentice-Hall

Lindberg, L. (1971), *The political dynamics of European economic integration*, Stanford: Stanford University Press

Lodge, J. (ed.) (1981), *Terrorism: a challenge to the State*, New York: St Martin's

Lodge, J. (ed.) (1988), *The threat of Terrorism*, Boulder: Westview

Lodge, J. (1994), 'Negotiating the SEA in the EC', in W. Zartman, (ed.), *International Multilateral Negotiations: Approaches to the management of complexity*, San Francisco: Jossey Bass

Lodge, J. (ed.) (1998), 3rd ed., *The European Union and the Challenge of the Future*, London: Cassel

Loulis, J.C. (1984), 'Papandreou's foreign policy', *Foreign Affairs*, vol. 63, no. 2, Winter 1984-85, pp. 374-391

Ludlow, P. (ed.) (1993), *Europe and the Mediterranean*, London: Brassey's

Makridimitris, A. and Passas, A. (1994), *Η Ελληνική διοίκηση και ο συντονισμός της Ευρωπαϊκής πολιτικής (The Greek administration and the coordination of European policy)*, Athens: Sakkoulas

Marks, G., Liesbeth, H. and Kermit, B. (1996), 'European Integration from the 1980s: State-Centric v. Multi-level Governance', *Journal of Common Market Studies*, vol. 34, no. 3, pp. 341-78

Marks, P.M. and Verney, S. (1995), 'Influence and Institutions: EU relations with Spain and Greece', *Annual meeting of the American Political Science Association*, Chicago, 31/8-3/9/1995

Marquina-Barrio, A. (1985), 'Gibraltar en la política exterior del gobierno socialista', *Revista de Estudios Internacionales*, vol. 6, no. 4, October-December

Martis, N. (1984), *The falsification of Macedonian History*, Athens: Euroekdotiki (translated by John Philip Smith)

Maxwell, K. (1991), 'Spain: From Isolation to Influence', in K. Maxwell (ed.), *Spanish Foreign and Defence Policy*, Boulder: Westview Press

McClosky, H. (1967), 'Personality and Attitude Correlates of Foreign Policy Orientation', in J.N. Rosenau, *Domestic Sources of Foreign Policy*, London: Collier-Macmillan

Meerts, P. (1997), 'Negotiating in the EU: Comparing perceptions of EU negotiators in Small Member States', *Group Decision and Negotiation*, vol. 6, pp. 463-82

Mesa, R. (1988), *Democracia y política exterior en España*, Madrid: Eudema

Mesa, R. (1996), *La reinvención de la política exterior española*, Madrid: Centro de Estudios Constitucionales

Middlemas, K. (1995), *Orchestrating Europe: the informal politics of European Union 1973-1995*, London: Fontana Press

Minogue, K.R. (1987), *Thatcherism: personality and politics*, Basingstoke: Macmillan

Miret, G. Siotis, J. and Tsakaloyannis, P. (1981), *The Mediterranean Challenge: VI Spain, Greece and Community Politics*, Sussex: Sussex European Research Centre

Moran, F. (1980), *Una política exterior para España*, Barcelona: Planeta

Moran, F. (1984), 'Principios de la política exterior española', *Leviatán*, no. 16

Morata, F. (1998), 'Spain: Modernisation through integration', in Hanf, K. and Soetendorp, B., *Adapting to European integration: small states and the European Union*, Harlow: Longman

Moravcsik, A. (1991), 'Negotiating the Single European Act', *International Organisation*, vol. 45, no. 1, pp. 19-56

Morgenthau, H. (1951), *In defence of the national interest*, New York: Knopf

Morgenthau, H. (1978), 5th ed. *Politics among Nations*, New York: Knopf

Mitrany, D. (1948), 'The functional approach to world organisation', *International Affairs*, vol. 24, pp. 350-63

Myers, J.A. (1993), *The WEU: Pillar of NATO or Defence Arm of the EC?*, London: Brassey's

Nicoll, W. and Salmon, T. (1994), 2nd ed., *Understanding the new European Community*, London: Harvester Wheatsheaf

Nugent, N. (1994), 3rd ed., *The government and politics of the EC*, Basingstoke: Macmillan

Nuttall, S. (1992), *European Political Cooperation*, Oxford: Clarendon Press

Nuttall, S. (1997), 'Two decades of EPC Performance', in Regelsberger, E., de Schoutheete, P. and Wessels, W., *Foreign Policy of the European Union: From EPC to CFSP and Beyond*, London: Lynne Rienner

Nye, J.S. (1990), 'The changing nature of world politics' *Political Science Quarterly*, vol. 105, no. 2, pp. 177-92

O'Nuallain, C. and Hoscheit, M. (eds.) (1985), *The Presidency of the European Council of Ministers*, London: EIPA/Croom Helm

Ó Tuathail, G. (1997), 'At the end of geopolitics? Reflections on the plural problematic at the century's end', *Alternatives*, no. 22, pp. 35-56

Ó Tuathail, G. (1998), 'Postmodern Geopolitics? The modern geopolitical imagination and beyond', in G. Ó Tuathail and S. Dalby (eds.), *Rethinking Geopolitics*, London: Routledge

Ortega, A. (1994), *La razón de Europa*, Madrid: El País/Aguilar

Palmer, S. and King, R. (1971), *Yugoslav Communism and the Macedonia Question*, Connecticut: The Shoe String Press

Papahadjopoulos, D. (1998), 'Greek Foreign Policy in the Post-Cold Era: Implications for the EU', *Paper No. 72*, Brussels: Centre for European Policy Study

Parker, G. (1983), *A political geography of Community Europe*, London: Butterworths

Passas, A. (1993), 'Η οργανωτική και λειτουργική προσαρμογή της ελληνικής διοίκησης στις κοινωτικές της υποχρεώσεις' (The organisational and functional adaptation of the Greek administration in its Community duties), in N. Fragakis et al. (ed.), *Εθνική διοίκηση και κοινοτικό δίκαιο (National administration and Community law)*, Athens: Sakkoulas

Perrakis, S. (1997), 'Το ισοζύγιο της Συνόδου του Άμστερνταμ' (the balance of the Amsterdam Summit), in Dalis, S. (ed.), *Απο το Μάαστριχτ στο Αμστερνταμ* (from Maastricht to Amsterdam), Athens: Sideris

Perrakis, S. and Fragakis, N. (1995), *Η τρίτη Ελληνική προεδρία της ΕΚ-ΕΕ: ένας απολογισμός* (the third Greek Presidency of the EC/EU: a review), Athens: Sakkoulas

Perrakis, S. and Grigiriou, P. (1994), *Η Ελλάδα στις διαδικασίες της Ευρωπαϊκής Ενοποίησης 1981-1994* (Greece in the processes of European integration 1981-1994), Athens: Sakkoulas

Petersen, N. (1977), 'Adaptation as a framework for the analysis of foreign policy behaviour', *Cooperation and Conflict*, 12: 221-50

Peterson, J. (1993), *Europe and America in the 1990s*, Aldershot: Elgar

Peterson, J. (1995), 'Decision-Making in the EU: towards a framework for analysis', *Journal of European Public Policy*, vol. 2, no. 1, pp. 69-93

Peterson, J. and Sjursen H. (eds.) (1998), *A common foreign policy for Europe? Competing visions of the CFSP*, London: Routledge

Piening, Ch. (1997), *Global Europe: The EU in World Affairs*, London: Lynne Rienner

Pijpers, A., Regelsberger, E., Wessels, W. (eds.) (1988), *European Political Cooperation in the 1980s: A common Foreign Policy for Western Europe?*, Dordrecht: Martinus Nijhoff

Pinder, J. (1970), 'Positive integration and negative integration: some problems of economic union in the EC', in M. Hodges (ed.), *European Integration*, Harmondsworth: Penguin

Pinder, J. (1991), *European Community: The building of a Union*, Oxford: Opus

Pollack, B. and Hunter, G. (1987), *The paradox of Spanish foreign policy: Spain's international relations from Franco to democracy*, London: Pinter

Portis, E.B. (1986), *Max Weber and political commitment: science, politics and personality*, Philadelphia: Temple University Press

Poulton, H. (1995), *Who are the Macedonians?*, London: Hurst and Company

Prevelakis, G. (1996), 'The return of the Macedonian Question', in Carter, F.W. and Norris, H.T., *The Changing Shape of the Balkans*, London: UCL

Pryce, R. and Pinder, J. (1994), *Maastricht and beyond*, London: Routledge

Pye, L.W. (1962), *Politics, personality and nation-building: Burma's search for identity*, New Haven: Yale University Press

Ramet, S.P. (1996), *Balkan Babel: the disintegration of Yugoslavia from the death of Tito to ethnic war*, Oxford: Westview Press

Regelsberger, E. (1989), 'Spain and the European Political Cooperation - No *Enfant Terrible*', *The International Spectator*, vol. 24, no. 2 April-June, pp. 118-124

Regelsberger, E. (1997), 'The set up and functioning of EPC/CFSP', in Regelsberger, E., de Schoutheete, P. and Wessels, W., *Foreign Policy of the European Union: From EPC to CFSP and Beyond*, London: Lynne Rienner

Regelsberger, E. and Wessels, W. (1996), 'The CFSP institutions and procedures: a third way for the second pillar', *European Foreign Affairs Review*, July 1996, vol. 1, no. 1, pp. 29-54

Regelsberger, E., de Schoutheete, P. and Wessels, W. (1997), *Foreign Policy of the European Union: From EPC to CFSP and Beyond*, London: Lynne Rienner

Richardson, J. (1996), *European Union: power and policy-making*, London: Routledge

Robertson, A.H. (1973), 3rd ed., *European Institutions*, London: Stevens and Sons Ltd.

Robins, P. (1997), 'Turkish foreign policy under Erbakan', *Survival*, vol. 39, no. 2, Summer 1997, pp. 82-100

Rodrigo, F. (1995), 'Western Alignment: Spain's security policy', in R. Gillespie, F. Rodrigo and J. Story (eds.), *Democratic Spain: Reshaping external relations in a changing world*, London: Routledge

Rodrigo, F. (1996), 'The Spanish debate', in The Royal Institute of International Affairs, *Discussion Paper 67, The 1996 IGC- National debates* (2),

Rometsch, D. and Wessels, W. (eds.) (1996), *The EU and member states: towards institutional fusion*, Manchester: Manchester University Press

Rosenau, J. (1963), *National Leadership and Foreign Policy*, New York: The Free Press

Rosenau, J. (1967), 'Foreign policy as an issue-area', in J.N. Rosenau, *Domestic Sources of Foreign Policy*, London: Collier-Macmillan

Ruiz Miguel, C. (1995), *El Sahara Occidental y España: historia, política y derecho: análisis crítico de la política exterior española*, Madrid: Dykinson

Rummel, R. (ed.) (1992), *Towards political Union: planning a common foreign and security policy in the EC*, Baden-Baden: Nomos

Sabá, K. (1996), 'Spain: evolving foreign policy structures - from EPC challenge to CFSP management', in Algieri, F. and Regelsberger, E. (eds.), *Synergy at Work: Spain and Portugal in European Foreign Policy*, Bonn: Europa Union Verlag

Sahagún, F. (1994), 'España frente al sur', in Calduch, R. (ed.), *La Política Exterior Española en el Siglo XX*, Madrid: Ciencias Sociales

Salomon, M. (1996), 'Spain: Scope enlargement towards the Arab World and the Maghreb', in Algieri, F. and Regelsberger, E., (eds.), *Synergy at Work: Spain and Portugal in European Foreign Policy*, Bonn: Europa Union Verlag

Sbragia, A.M. (ed.) (1992), *Euro-Politics: Institutions and Policy-Making in the 'New' E.C.*, Washington DC: The Brookings Institution

Sekeris, G. (1995), 'Τα αντίμετρα των Σκοπίων' (the measures against Skopje), *Epetirida ELIAMEP*, Yearbook 1995

Shea, J. (1997), *Macedonia and Greece: the struggle to define a new Balkan nation*, North Carolina: McFarland

Sjovaag, M. (1998), 'The Single European Act', in Eliassen, K. (ed.), *Foreign and Security Policy in the European Union*, London: Sage

Skylakakis, Th. (1995), *Στο όνομα της Μακεδονίας* (in the name of Macedonia), Athens: Elliniki Euroekdotiki

Sotiropoulos, D. (1993), 'A colossus with feet of clay: the state in post-authoritarian Greece', in H.J. Psomiades and S.B. Thomadakis (eds.), *Greece, the new Europe, and the changing international order*, New York: Pella

Sotiropoulos, D. (1996), *Populism and Bureaucracy, The case of Greece under PASOK, 1981-1989*, London: University of Notre Dame Press

Spaak, P-H. (1971), *The Continuing Battle. Memoirs of a European 1936-1966*, London: Weidenfeld and Nicolson

Spence, A.andD. (1998), 'The CFSP from Maastricht to Amsterdam', in Eliassen, K. (ed.), *Foreign and Security Policy in the European Union*, London: Sage

Stefanou, C. and Xanthaki, H. (1997), *A Legal and Political Interpretation of articles 224 and 225 of the Treaty of Rome: the FYROM cases*, Aldershot: Ashgate

Stein, A. (1990), *Why nations cooperate*, Ithaca: Cornell University Press

Stoforopoulos, Th.X. and Makridimitris, A.P. (1996), *Το σύστημα της ελληνικής εξωτερικής πολιτικής: Η θεσμική διάσταση, διαμόρφωση και παρακολούθηση, συντονισμός και συνοχή, ανάλυση και σχεδιασμός πολιτικής (The system of Greek foreign policy: the institutional dimension, formation and observation, coordination and cohesion, analysis and design of policy)*, Athens: EKEM

Stopford, J. and Strange, S. (1991), *Rival States, Rival Firms: competition for world market shares*, Cambridge: Cambridge University Press

Story, J. (ed.) (1993), *The New Europe*, Oxford: Blackwell

Strange, S. (1994), *States and Markets*, London: Pinter

Strange, S. (1996), *The retreat of the State*, Cambridge: Cambridge University Press

Suleiman, E. (1974), *Politics, power and bureaucracy in France: the administrative elite*, Princeton: Princeton University Press

Svein, A.S. and Eliassen, K.A. (1993), *Making Policy in Europe: The Europeification of National policy-making*, London: Sage

Taylor, P. (1983), *The limits of European integration*, London: Croom Helm

Taylor, P. and A.J.R. Groom (eds.) (1990), *Frameworks for international cooperation*, London: Pinter

Tomasic, D.A. (1948), *Personality and culture in Eastern European Politics*, New York: G.W. Stewart

Tsakaloyannis, P. (1996), 'Greece', in C. Hill, *The Actors in Europe's Foreign Policy*, London: Routledge

Tsakaloyannis, P. (1996b), *Η πολιτική διάσταση της Ε.Ε* (the political dimension of the EU), Athens: Papazisis

Tsakaloyannis, P. and Bourantonis, D. (1997), 'The European Union's CFSP and the reform of the Security Council', *European Foreign Affairs Review*, Summer 1997, vol. 2, no. 2, pp.197-209

Tsoukalis, L. (1981), *The EC and its Mediterranean enlargement*, London: George Allen and Unwin

Tziotis, D. (1994), *Μακεδονία: Πολιτικές ευθύνες και δυσοίωνοι χρησμοί (Macedonia: Political responsibilities and fateful prophesies)*, Athens: Grigori

Urwin, D.W. (1995), 2nd ed., *The Community of Europe: a history of European Integration since 1945*, London: Longman

Valinakis, Y. (1987), 'Η Ελληνική συμμετοχή στην ΕΠΣ' (the Greek participation in EPC), in P. Kazakos and K. Stefanou (eds.), *Η Ελλάδα στην Ευρωπαϊκή Κοινότητα. Η πρώτη πενταετία* (Greece in the EC. The first five years), Athens: Sakkoulas

Valinakis, Y. (1991), *Η Ευρωπαϊκή Πολιτική και Αμυντική Συνεργασία* (The

European political and defence cooperation), Athens: Papazisis

Valinakis, Y. (1993), 'Η Ελλάδα στην ΕΠΣ: Τα πρώτα δέκα χρόνια' (Greece in the EPC: the first ten years), in L. Tsoukalis, *Η Ελλάδα στην Ευρωπαϊκή Κοινότητα: Η πρόκληση της προσαρμογής* (Greece in the EC: the challenge of adaptation), Athens: Papazisis

Valinakis, Y. (1994), 'Security policy', in Kazakos, P. and Ioakimidis, P.C., *Greece and EC Membership evaluated*, London: Pinter

Valinakis, Y. and Pitsarou, E. (1997), 'Greece's position on the revision of the CFSP', in P. Kazakos, P. Liargovas and E. Phocas (eds.), *What is the future of the European Union? The Maastricht Treaty Review*, Athens: Sideris

Veremis, Th. (1982), *Greek Security Considerations*, Athens: Papazisis

Veremis, Th. (1996), 'A Greek view of Balkan Developments', in K. Featherstone and K. Ifantis, *Greece in a changing Europe*, Manchester: Manchester University Press

Veremis, Th. and Couloumbis, Th. (1994), *Ελληνική Εξωτερική Πολιτική: Προοπτικές και Προβληματισμοί* (Greek foreign policy: perspectives and considetrations), Athens: Sideris

Von Goll, G. (1982), 'The Nine at the CSCE', in Allen, D., Rummel, R., and Wessels, W., *European Political Cooperation*, London: Butterworth

Waever, O. (1990), 'Three competing Europes: German, French, Russian', *International Affairs*, vol. 66, no. 3, pp. 153-70

Waite, R.G.L. (1998), *Kaiser and Fohrer: a comparative study of personality and politics*, Toronto: University of Toronto Press

Walden, S. (1994), *Μακεδονικό και Βαλκάνια (The Macedonian issue and the Balkans, 1991-1994)*, Athens: Themelio

Walker, R.B.J. (1987), 'Realism, change and International political theory', *International Studies Quarterly*, vol. 31, pp. 65-84

Walker, R.B.J. (1993), *Inside/Outside International Relations as Political Theory*, Cambridge: Cambridge University Press

Wallace, H. (1985), *Europe: the challenge of diversity*, London: Routledge

Wallace, H. (1985), 'Negotiation and coalition formation in the European Community', *Government and Opposition*, vol. 20, pp. 453-72

Wallace, H., Wallace, W. and Webb, C. (eds.) (1977), *Policy-Making in the EC*, London: John Wiley and Sons

Wallace, W. (1990), *The dynamics of European Integration*, London: Pinter

Wallace, W. and Paterson, W.E. (eds.) (1978), *Foreign policy-making in Western Europe: a comparative approach*, Farnborough: Saxon

Waltz, K. (1979), *Theory of International Politics*, Reading: Addison-Wesley

Warwick, D.P. (1975), *A theory of public bureacracy: politics, personality and organisation in the State department*, Cambridge, Mass: Harvard University Press

Weidenfeld, W. and Wessels, W. (eds.) (1986), *Ways towards the European Union: from treaty to the constitution?*, Bonn: Europa Union Verlag

Wessels, W. and Engel, C. (eds.) (1993), *The European Union in the 1990s: Ever closer and larger?*, Bonn: Europa Union

Whitman, R. and Manners, I. (2001), *The EU Member States' Foreign Policies*, Manchester: Manchester University Press

Winn, N. (1996), *European crisis management in the 1980s*, Aldershot: Dartmouth

Yañez-Barnuevo, J.A. and Viñas, A. (1992), 'Diez años de política exterior del gobierno socialista, 1982-1992', in A. Guerra and J.F. Tezanos (eds.), *La decada del Cambio*, Madrid: Sistema

Zacher, M.W. and Matthew, R.A. (1995), 'Liberal International Theory: common threads, divergent strands', in C.W. Kegley Jr (ed.), *Controversies in International Relations Theory*, London: Macmillan

Zaldivar, C.A. (1992), *España, fin de siglo*, Madrid: Alianza

Zaldivar, C.A. (1992), 'El año que se acabò un mundo. La política exterior de España en 1991', in *Anuario Internacional CIDOB 1991*, Barcelona: CIDOB

Zaldivar, C.A. and Ortega, A. (1992), 'The Gulf crisis and European Cooperation on security issues: Spanish reactions and the European framework', in N. Gnessoto and J. Roper (eds.), *Western Europe and the Gulf*, Paris: Institute for Security Studies

Zametica, J. (1992), 'The Yugoslav conflict', *Adelphi Paper 270*, London: Brassey's

Zetterholm, S. (ed.) (1994), *National Cultures and European Integration: exploratory essays on cultural diversity and common policies*, Oxford: Berg

Annex 1

Current Organograma of the Greek Ministry of Foreign Affairs

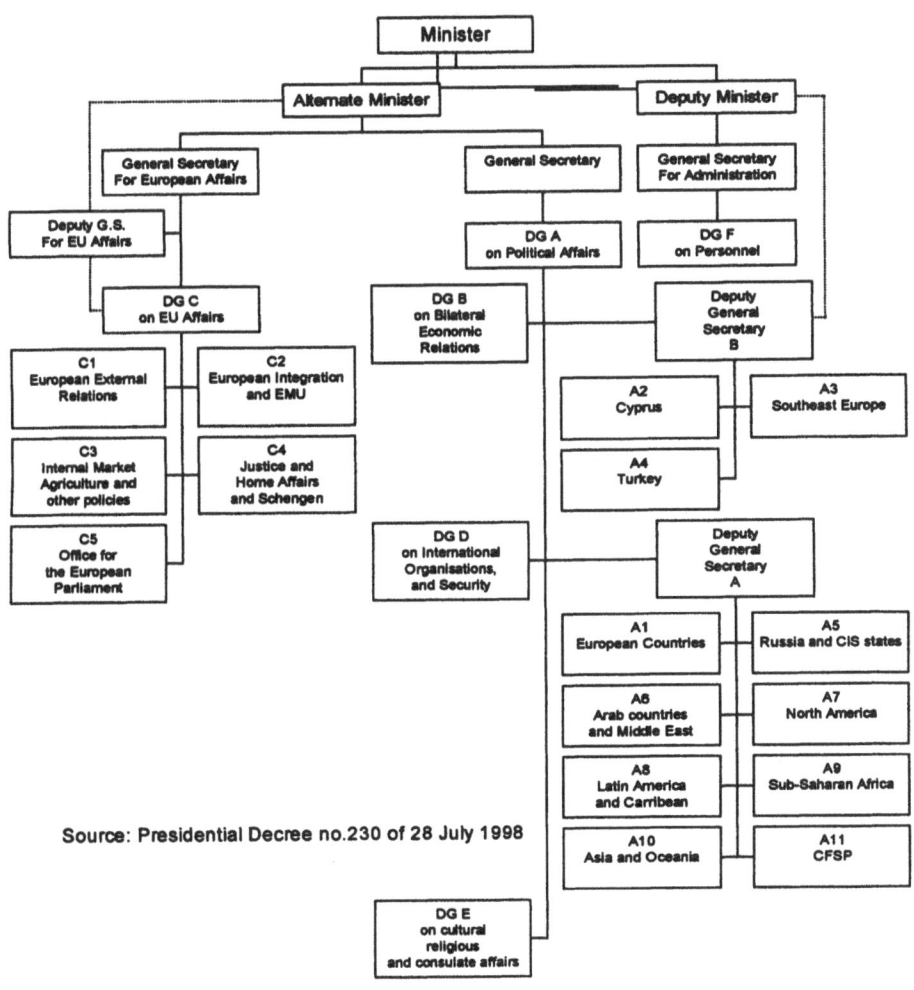

Source: Presidential Decree no.230 of 28 July 1998

221

Annex 2

Organograma of the Greek Foreign Ministry in 1975

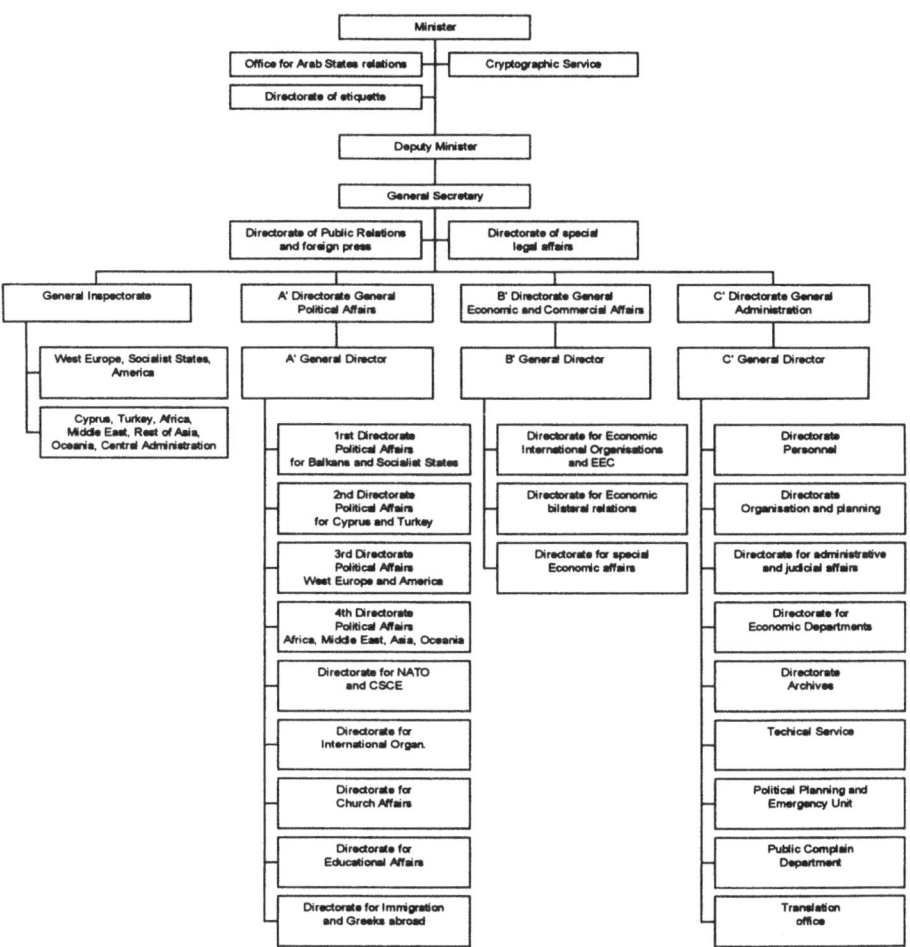

Source: Presidential Decree no.0115/7/AS207 of 20 June 1974 amended by
010/700/AS206 of 12 July 1975

Annex 3

Current Organograma of the Spanish Foreign Ministry

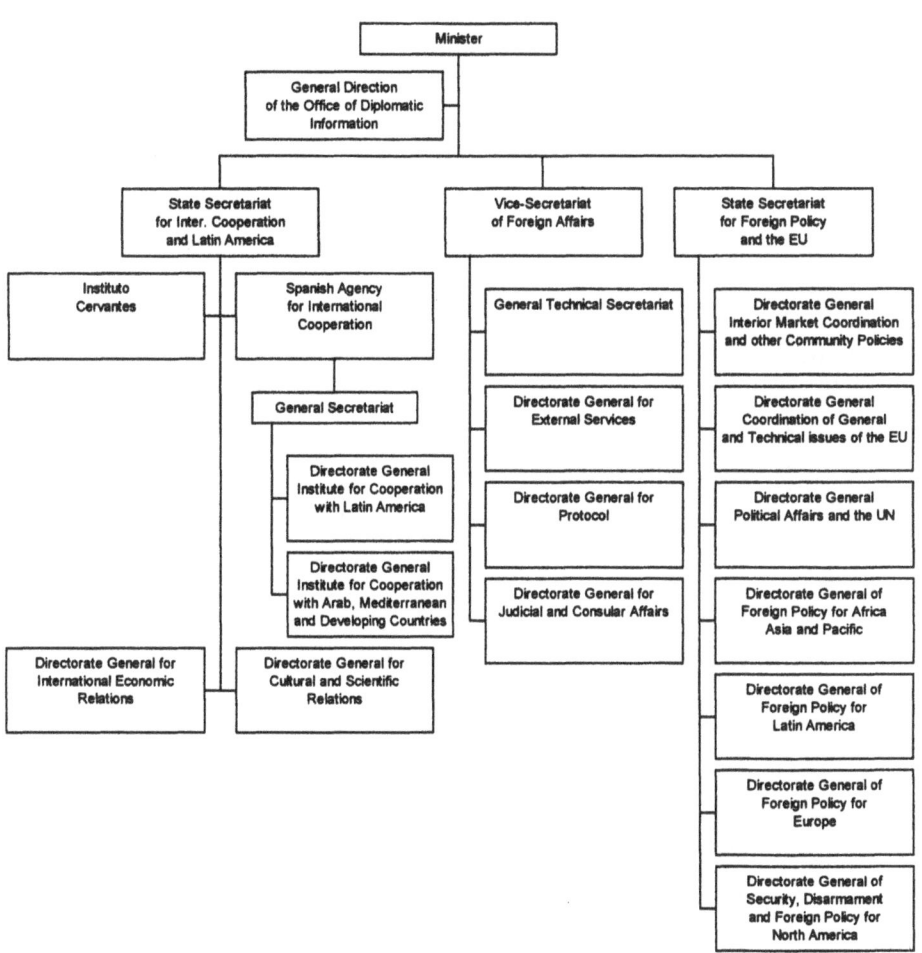

Source: Royal Decree no.2601 of 4 December 1998

225

Annex 4

Organograma of the Spanish Foreign Ministry in 1979

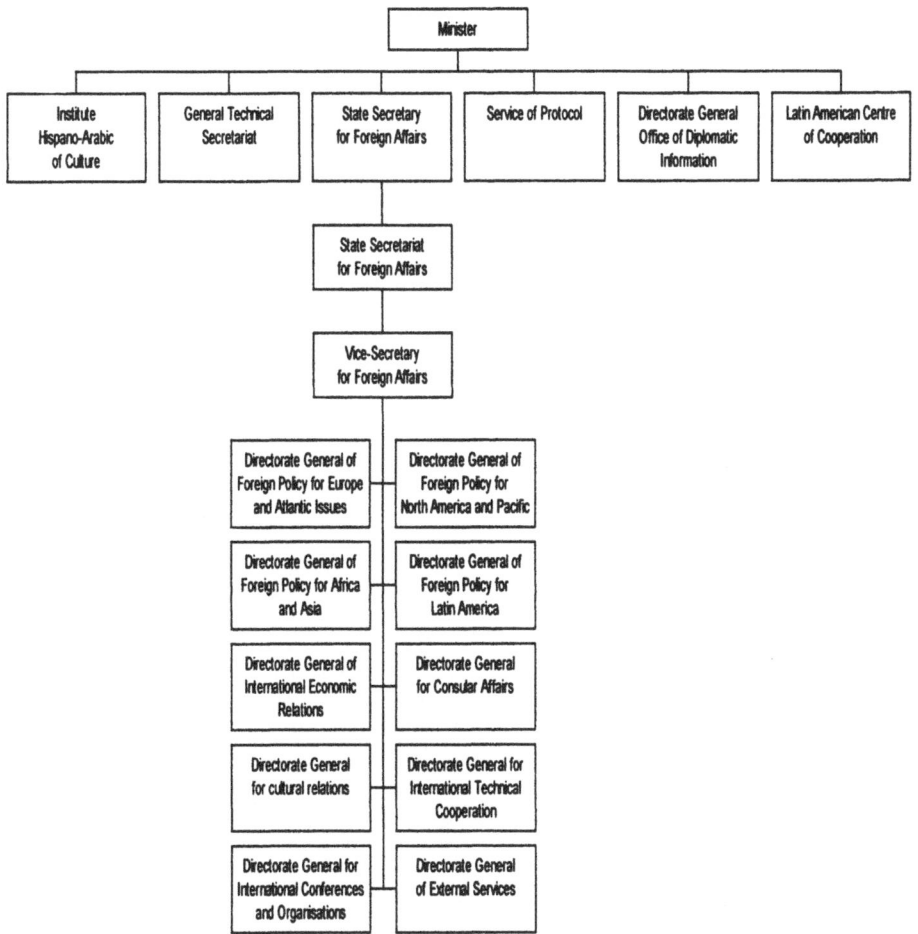

Source: Royal Decree no.984 of 27 April 1979

227